# ENTRUSTED
## *with a* CHILD'S HEART

## A BIBLICAL STUDY IN PARENTING
BY BETSY CORNING

ENTRUSTED MINISTRIES

# ENTRUSTED
## *with a* CHILD'S HEART

*To my children and their spouses, Emily & Adam, Luke & Elissa and Lee,*
*who allowed themselves to be the subjects of so many examples.*

*To my grandbabies, Anna, David, Johnny, Hudson, Hailey and David,*
*who keep my memory refreshed and remind me why this matters.*

*To my dear husband, David, my best friend on this earth, thank you for all your loving support.*

*With special thanks to Emily, for the design and production of this notebook*
*and to Nancy McDonaugh, Joan Wagner and Gina Cho for their faithful friendship*
*and loyal service in seeing this project through to completion.*

ENTRUSTED MINISTRIES
www.entrustedministries.com

This notebook is part of a complete ministry curriculum taught at Harvest Bible Chapel.
It includes a DVD series that makes it possible to transfer this teaching to other ministries.

# Every Day Counts!

Welcome to *Entrusted with a Child's Heart!* This Bible study is a compilation of many years of study blended with over thirty years of practical applications to everyday family life. I am here to tell you, God's ways work! This will be a landmark year for you and your family if you are determined to take to heart the principles of God's Word.

It seems that the former days of the "coffee klatch" are gone; those times when neighborhood women would gather as a part of their routine to discuss family and domestic issues of the day. In society today there is an alarming disconnect between women. We have become more isolated, more consumed with privacy and downtime away from people. We may live in urban, suburban or even rural settings, yet amidst the crowds and busyness, there is little meaningful connection between women. The times we do have with other women tend to be rushed or become exclusive to the ages of our children as we sit together at soccer practice or in the church nursery. There does not seem to be enough time to dedicate to deeper relationships or expanding circles of women.

Yet the Bible is so clear; the older women are to teach the younger women what they have learned and know to be true. I am so grateful for the faithful women in my life who have given me encouragement and direction, mostly during those early years of marriage. I watched them, asked loads of questions, and grew determined to follow the principles that they were living out before me. The examples of these godly women have especially inspired me to walk closely with the Lord and to treasure my roles as wife and mother. Their impact on my life continues today.

This guiding thought has prompted me to write this study so that mothers of all ages would gather and glean the principles of God's Word together. Through this study we will tap into God's resources as we seek His wisdom to finish the job He has called us to do. May you be greatly encouraged by His plan and the godly wisdom and fellowship of your small group. I hope that you will develop some wonderful and lasting friendships this year.

With much prayer this study is dedicated to each mother who trudges through these many pages with the heart to raise her family for the glory of God. Through the many years of raising and training your children, remember that the Lord has entrusted you with a child's heart. God bless you as we co-labor together!

# Table of Contents

# Table of Contents

# Lesson 1 Outline

## OUR FOUNDATION: FAITH IN JESUS
### A godly mother embraces Jesus as her Savior

I.    Is the Lord Building Your House?

II.   Checking Our Surroundings

III.  Setting the Foundation

IV.   Defining "Entrusted"

V.    The Motivation of Godly Parents

VI.   The Gospel Presentation

VII.  The Bridge Illustration
  A.  God's Creation
  B.  Man's Problem
  C.  God's Solution
  D.  Our Response
  E.  The Result
  F.  Three Options

VIII. Recapping the Salvation Message

## This week's Scripture memory verse:

**Psalm 127:1,** "Unless the LORD builds the house,
they labor in vain who build it; Unless the LORD guards the city,
the watchman keeps awake in vain."

# *Lesson 1*

## OUR FOUNDATION: FAITH IN JESUS
### A godly mother embraces Jesus as her Savior

## *I. Is the Lord Building Your House?*

When we seek to be godly, we are declaring our dependence upon God to help us do all the things that we do as mothers. How do we really know if the Lord is building our house (referring to our families)?
By the end of this lesson, you will personally know the answer to that question.

## *II. Checking Our Surroundings*

Have you ever been lost? The Bible says we are hopelessly, desperately lost without Jesus Christ.

📖 **Luke 4:18-19**
*THE SPIRIT OF THE LORD IS UPON ME, BECAUSE HE ANOINTED ME TO PREACH THE GOSPEL TO THE POOR. HE HAS SENT ME TO PROCLAIM RELEASE TO THE CAPTIVES, AND RECOVERY OF SIGHT TO THE BLIND, TO SET FREE THOSE WHO ARE OPPRESSED [DOWNTRODDEN]. TO PROCLAIM THE FAVORABLE YEAR OF THE LORD.*

📖 **These verses give four descriptions of What A "Lost Person" Looks Like:**

📖 _____, meaning bankrupt in spirit;

_____, meaning enslaved to sin;

_____, meaning unable to discern spiritual matters;

_____, meaning oppressed without hope of eternity.

Do any of these things describe where you are today? Do you have the certain hope of eternity in Christ? If we try to build our house without the hope of eternity, we are building our house in vain. In this lesson we are going to purposely and methodically study how to build a biblical home, starting with this foundation.

What is the Bible to me? Who is Jesus to me? These will be the foundation that we set.

The cornerstone of our faith is Jesus Christ. (**Isaiah 28:16**)

## III. Setting The Foundation

☐ The _____ foundational piece is our belief and confession of faith in _____.

☐ This piece of the foundation says we spend eternity with _____.

**Hebrews 13:14**
*For here we do not have a lasting city, but we are seeking the city which is to come.*

☐ We are not raising our children to just get through the _____, but rather with the

consideration of who they will be in twenty years and where they will be for _____.

☐ It all starts when they are just 6-8 months old and you can first observe that they have a _____

of their own.

☐ As their God-given authority, it is our responsibility to train them to submit to our _____

and, more importantly, to God's.

---

**Psalm 127:1,** "Unless the LORD builds the house,
they labor in vain who build it; Unless the LORD guards the city,
the watchman keeps awake in vain."

## N. Defining "Entrusted"

▢ Entrusting means "_____ _____ the trust, care, and protection of another".

God has _____ you with the care of each of your children.

▢ He is vitally concerned with how you care for them and _____ you train them. The reason is

because we care for them and train them on _____ _____.

▢ They are special creations and God has given them to you as a _____ that will last

_____. The gift of children is what He gives _____ to you.

God uniquely bestows them on us. It is not by accident or surprise that they are your children.

▢ **Psalm 104:30a**
*You send forth Your Spirit, they are created; "_____ of _____"*

▢ **Genesis 2:7**
*Then the LORD God formed man of dust from the ground, and breathed into his nostrils the _____ of _____; and man became a living being.*

Regardless of whether a baby was unplanned or unwanted, all babies are gifts of God, still blessings.

▢ **Psalm 104:29b**
*You take away their _____, they expire and return to their dust.*

People pervert God's way that children are to be born, and they sin against God to satisfy their own cravings and yet God still ordains that they should be created. They are still His gift, His sign of blessing. If there is any woman who has been in a desperate situation, still in her heart, she knows that her baby is a blessing, a gift.

☐ God specifically _____ you to be the parents of your children and He is entrusting you with their care to raise them to _____ Him alone.

☐ That is the _____ for which we were created. We have been given _____ to glorify God.

Not everybody glorifies God and yet He gives them the breath of life by His great mercy. If we think we can build anything apart from God, we are fooling ourselves, because we can't even take the very next breath without Him.

## V. The Motivation Of Godly Parents

☐ Eventually we turn our children back over to the care and protection of God because we know that they are really _____ and during the first twenty or so years we have been called to be good _____ of them.

☐ **3 John 4**
*I have no greater joy than this, to hear of my children walking in the truth.*

At the end of your life, this will mean everything to you. You are going to want to know that your children will be with you in heaven.

---

**Psalm 127:1,**"Unless the LORD builds the house,
they labor in vain who build it; Unless the LORD guards the city,
the watchman keeps awake in vain."

## VI. The Gospel Presentation

☐ This is where the _____ piece of the foundation is laid. All of mankind experiences the

miracle of the breath of life to his _____ body, but not all people glorify God.

☐ Why? Because the Bible speaks of a _____ birth in which God breathes the

breath of life into our _____. This spiritual birth does not happen when we are born

_____; it may not happen at all.

☐ It is up to each of us to respond and _____ or _____ this gift.

☐ It is _____ forced upon anyone. But, when it happens it is a _____ and it is because

we finally _____ that Jesus is the Son of God, as He said, and that He died for our sins

and was raised from the dead for our sakes.

☐ It is as if He takes our _____ and pays what we _____ God for our sins. He is the only

payment God will ever accept, because Jesus alone was the perfect and sinless _____.

☐ **John 14:6**
*Jesus said to him, "I am the way, and the truth, and the life; no one comes to the Father but through Me."*

☐ Have you witnessed the miracle of the breath of life to your _____? This breath

will never be taken away, it is _____. It is what the Bible refers to as being

"_____ _____."

☐ *In* **John 3:4-7,** *Jesus is speaking to a Jewish ruler named Nicodemus:*
*Nicodemus said to Him, "How can a man be born when he is old? He cannot enter a second time into his mother's womb and be born, can he?" Jesus answered, "Truly, truly, I say to you, unless one is born of water and the Spirit he cannot enter into the kingdom of God. That which is born of the flesh is flesh, and that which is born of the Spirit is spirit. Do not be amazed that I said to you, 'You must be born again.' "*

☐ To be _____ we _____ with God that we have not been able to live a completely

holy life free from any wrongdoing whatsoever.

## *VII. The Bridge Illustration*

**A.  God's Creation** – Man & Woman Created To Have A Relationship With Him

**Genesis 1:27**

*God created man in His own image, in the image of God He created him; male and female He created them.*

**B.  Man's Problem** – Separation Through Sin

**Isaiah 59:2**

*But your iniquities have made a separation between you and your God, And your sins have hidden His face from you so that He does not hear.*

**Romans 3:23**

*For all have sinned and fall short of the glory of God.*

**Romans 6:23**

*For the wages of sin is death, but the free gift of God is eternal life in Christ Jesus our Lord.*

**Hebrews 9:27**

*And inasmuch as it is appointed for men to die once and after this comes judgment.*

---

**Psalm 127:1,** "Unless the LORD builds the house,
they labor in vain who build it; Unless the LORD guards the city,
the watchman keeps awake in vain."

## C.  God's Solution – Gift of Eternal Life

▢  **John 5:24**

*Truly, truly, I say to you, he who hears My word, and believes Him who sent Me, has eternal life, and does not come into judgment, but has passed out of death into life.*

▢  **Ephesians 2:8-9**

*For by grace you have been saved through faith; and that not of yourselves, it is the gift of God; not as a result of works, so that no one may boast.*

▢  **2 Corinthians 7:10**

*For the sorrow that is according to the will of God produces a repentance without regret, leading to salvation, but the sorrow of the world produces death.*

## D.  Our Response – To Receive Jesus Christ As Our Lord & Savior

▢  **John 14:6**

*Jesus said to him, "I am the way, and the truth, and the life; no one comes to the Father but through Me."*

▢  **1 Peter 3:18**

*For Christ also died for sins once for all, the just for the unjust, so that He might bring us to God, having been put to death in the flesh, but made alive in the spirit.*

▢  **Romans 10:9-10**

*That if you confess with your mouth Jesus as Lord, and believe in your heart that God raised Him from the dead, you will be saved; for with the heart a person believes, resulting in righteousness, and with the mouth he confesses, resulting in salvation.*

## E.  The Result - A Restored Relationship With God

▢  **1 John 5:11-12**

*And the testimony is this, that God has given us eternal life, and this life is in His Son. He who has the Son has the life; he who does not have the Son of God does not have the life.*

▢  **Revelation 3:20**

*Behold, I stand at the door and knock; if anyone hears My voice and opens the door, I will come in to him and will dine with him, and he with Me.*

## F.  Three Options – Reject, Ignore, or Receive Jesus Christ

## VIII. Recapping the Salvation Message

▢ We acknowledge His provision of His Son Jesus as the _____ way back to God. We accept

His _____ to us by confessing with our _____ that Jesus is the Son of God and that we

believe that He was raised from the dead.

▢ When we do this, God removes the _____ we owe for our sin and gives us _____ life in

His Son.

▢ **Galatians 2:20**
*I have been crucified with Christ; and it is no longer I who live, but Christ lives in me; and the life which I now live in the flesh I live by faith in the Son of God, who loved me and gave [delivered] Himself up for me.*

▢ Because Jesus overcame the power of death when He rose from the dead, we are able to live with

Him for eternity if we have been spiritually _____.

▢ Without Jesus, we _____ glorify the One who _____ us. We start _____ when

God _____ His _____ Spirit into us.

▢ **2 Corinthians 5:17**
*Therefore if anyone is in Christ, he is a new creature; the old things passed away; behold, new things have come.*

▢ God is not so concerned with how you built your house _____ you knew Him. He is

_____ concerned with how you are building it now.

▢ The most important piece of the foundation is entrusting your own _____ to the one who made you.

▢ If we truly believe in Jesus, we _____ on our beliefs by building our homes in accordance with His

blueprint, the _____. Without this first piece of the foundation, the building will _____.

▢ **1 Corinthians 3:11**
*For no man can lay a foundation other than the one which is laid, which is Jesus Christ.*

---

**Psalm 127:1,**"Unless the LORD builds the house,
they labor in vain who build it; Unless the LORD guards the city,
the watchman keeps awake in vain."

# *Homefront Application*

## OUR FOUNDATION: FAITH IN JESUS
### A godly mother embraces Jesus as her Savior

1. Consider the teaching in this lesson. Are you assured that God has breathed life into your spirit so that you may be equipped through Him to build your family on biblical principles? If not, take time alone this week to pray over the key points of the lesson, acknowledging your predicament and God's gracious provision. Share your new decision with someone else— your husband, table leader, or close friend, and write the date on the inside of your Bible as a memorial.

   If this decision is not new, but you made it in the past, thank God for His lovingkindness in drawing you to Himself. Thank Him that He is working with you to build a strong biblical family.

2. Plan each week to learn your Scripture memory verse and be ready to recite it at your small group table. This is an ongoing weekly assignment. This week's verse was ***Psalm 127:1***.

   Now begin learning ***2 Timothy 3:14*** and hopefully this will become a weekly discipline. We will review all the Scripture memory verses together each week.

   *If your husband is not a believer you may wish to share the class illustration with him if he is open to it.

## I CHOOSE TO LIVE BY CONVICTIONS.

Signature: _____   Date: _____

# *Lesson 2 Outline*

## THE AUTHORITY OF GOD'S WORD
### A godly mother lives by biblical convictions

I.   The Authority of God's Word

II.  Biblical Convictions
  A.  Defining Biblical Convictions
  B.  Recognizing Counterfeits vs. the Original
  C.  Living at Crossed Purposes with God
  D.  Growing in Your Faith
  E.  Seven Majors of the Christian Faith
  F.  Choosing to be Godly Parents

III. Personal Convictions
  A.  Defining Personal Convictions
  B.  Designing Your Own "Family Plan"
  C.  Encouragement for the Single Parent

## *This week's Scripture memory verse:*

**2 Timothy 3:14,** "You, however, continue in the things you have learned and become convinced of, knowing from whom you have learned them."

# *Lesson 2*

## THE AUTHORITY OF GOD'S WORD
### A godly mother lives by biblical convictions

**First, we put in the most important foundational pieces:**

**1.** Confession of faith in Christ (Salvation)

**2.** Living under the authority of God's Word (Lordship)

## *I. The Authority of God's Word*

We cannot be saved and not believe the Bible because the Bible is the living and active Word of God and the authority for our lives. We cannot say, "We believe in You Jesus, but not what You say."

**John 1:1-5, 14**

**Colossians 1:15-17**

In Christ, there is no hopeless situation for you ever again. You are never at a point of being so desperate that God doesn't provide a way of truth for you, a way out.

Tolstoy once said, "Everyone thinks about changing the world, but no one thinks of changing himself."

## *II. Biblical Convictions*

### A. Defining Biblical Convictions

In the Bible, God has given us truths (absolutes) - _____ _____

that _____ no matter what.

Do you know that God's Word has spiritual laws in the same way that God has set up physical or mathematical laws?

**Romans 8:2**

*For the law of the Spirit of life in Christ Jesus has set you free from the law of sin and of death.*

There are spiritual laws and even if we don't believe them, they are absolute and true!

No matter how I _____ about it, no matter what I _____ about it, even no matter what I _____ about it. _____ _____ _____. They are _____ for all time and all cultures.

They are the commandments of God that we are to obey—no matter what! The Bible is the Truth. God cannot deny Himself. His Word does not deny itself or contradict itself. We lose sight of how precious a gift we have in God's Word. Do we think of the Word as precious and living? Do we really know what we have in the Bible? Do we use it? Does it guide our lives? Is it our life? One third of the people on earth don't even have access to a Bible. How much more should we recognize the importance and privilege of having and reading the Bible? Do you read it?

In the Bible, God shows us how to live through the example of the "father-son relationship". God is our authority; He is our Father. We place ourselves under His authority because He is a protective covering for us. We know that obedience to Him brings blessing to us. This is what we must teach our children. They come under our protective covering, under our authority, but they grow up knowing we all live under God's authority. Even as adults, we always live under the authority of God. God is teaching us what we are teaching our children.

## B. Recognizing Counterfeits vs. the Original

To recognize a counterfeit, you need to study and memorize the original. If something doesn't match the real thing, then you have a counterfeit. More information is not the answer. When we think we need more information, we are actually exposing ourselves to counterfeits.

**Romans 16:19b**

*…I want you to be wise in what is good and innocent in what is evil.*

The world holds the philosophy of, "Your children _____ to make an _____ choice.

They have a _____ to know, to be _____."

**Romans 6:23a**

*For the wages of sin is death…*

---

**2 Timothy 3:14**, "You, however, continue in the things you have learned and become convinced of, knowing from whom you have learned them."

Everything we have in Christ is a bonus that He's given to us—that He has bestowed on us by His free gift. Without Christ, we are bound by the law of sin and death.

### Matthew 7:13-14

*Enter through the narrow gate; for the gate is wide and the way is broad that leads to destruction, and there are many who enter through it. For the gate is small and the way is narrow that leads to life, and there are few who find it.*

### 1 John 5:19-20

*We know that we are of God, and that the whole world lies in the power of the evil one. And we know that the Son of God has come, and has given us understanding so that we may know Him who is true; and we are in Him who is true, in His Son Jesus Christ. This is the true God and eternal life.*

God is _____ evil to flourish in the world for a time. And He is _____ to see

whether you pick the counterfeit or the real thing; if you choose _____ or the _____ way.

### 1 Peter 2:16

*Act as free men, and do not use your freedom as a covering for _____, but use it as bondslaves of God.*

When we take our eyes off of the truth, we stumble. We get _____ about what is

truth and what isn't.

We need to be listening for the truth and aligning to the truth!

### Jeremiah 17:9

*The heart is more deceitful than all else and is desperately sick; who can understand it?*

We are not to follow our _____. We are to follow the Word of God, no matter what.

The Bible never tells us to make decisions based on how we _____.

### 1 John 2:15-16

*Do not love the world nor the things in the world. If anyone loves the world, the love of the Father is not in him. For all that is in the world, the lust of the flesh and the lust of the eyes and the boastful pride of life, is not from the Father, but is from the world.*

We are to separate ourselves from the world's value system, from the counterfeits of this world. People who refuse to do that are actually making trouble for themselves.

### 1 Peter 3:10

*For the one who desires life, to love and see good days, must keep his tongue from evil and his lips from speaking deceit.*

## C. Living at Crossed Purposes with God

Do you "live at crossed purposes with God"? If you do, you will struggle in life. But God is still a God of hope. He wants you to turn things around—He's trying to get your attention. People in this state live a life of deep regret because consequences start to pile up over time.

We are God's ambassadors to a lost world. When we say we are in Christ, we have to live like we are in Christ. We are to live with hope. God does not want us to deny His hope in our lives because it is so dishonoring to Him.

▢ When we don't _____; when we don't find ourselves _____ righteousness and

desiring to be Christlike, we have to wonder if we are even His children.

▢ God's own _____ themselves under His _____.

## D. Growing in Your Faith

▢ **Philippians 2:12-13**
*So then, my beloved, just as you have always obeyed, not as in my presence only, but now much more in my absence, work out your salvation with fear and trembling; for it is God who is at work in you, both to will and to work for His good pleasure.*

**John 17:17**
*Sanctify them in the truth; Your word is truth.*

▢ Because we _____ who God really is, we respect Him and live in _____ of Him.

And we are to live our lives in "healthy fear" of not _____ Him.

---

**2 Timothy 3:14,** "You, however, continue in the things you have learned and become convinced of, knowing from whom you have learned them."

**2.5**

▢ **Ephesians 4:14-15**

*As a result, we are no longer to be _____, tossed here and there by waves and carried about by every wind of doctrine, by the trickery of men, by craftiness in deceitful scheming; but speaking the truth in love, we are to _____ _____ in all aspects into _____ who is the head, even Christ.*

If you live your life with misapplied principles, at the end of it you are going to realize that it didn't work.

▢ **Psalm 19:7a**

*The law of the LORD is _____ , restoring the soul.*

We are to match our lives up to the perfect Word of God, not the counterfeits.

▢ When we are growing up in Him, we are growing in _____. We see the faithfulness, the trustworthiness of His promises to us and we become _____ that His way is _____.

▢ These are biblical _____. They are absolutely _____ in establishing a God-honoring family.

▢ Biblical convictions say, "Because _____ says it, I _____ it and I will _____ it, because I _____ Him," no matter what.

▢ We are so secure in His love for us that we can obey Him even when we don't know the outcome. This is faith.

▢ **Hebrews 11:1**

*Now faith is the assurance of things hoped for, the _____ of things not seen.*

Are you waiting for God to demonstrate His faithfulness to you?

▢ Obey His _____ and watch for Him to _____ you. Be _____ in Him, He is _____ your faith to see if you will _____ to obey Him even when things are very difficult.

▢ He wants to grow you up to be like _____.

**Hebrews 10:23**

*Let us hold fast the confession of our hope without _____, for He who promised is faithful.*

**Galatians 6:9**

*Let us not lose heart in doing good, for in due time we will _____ if we do not grow weary.*

Sometimes we want an instantaneous turnaround, but it will not be instantaneous if we've been "knitting" trouble for years.

The commandments of God are not _____.

They are not "when I feel like it", or "when I get around to it", or "if it happens to fit in my life". Instead, it's because God says it, I will do it, because obedience to Him promises a good result.

**Romans 12:2**

*And do not be conformed to this world, but be transformed by the renewing of your mind, so that you may prove what the will of God is, that which is good and acceptable and perfect.*

When we take God at His Word, we _____ convictions.

We develop a deeper understanding of His Truth. Every time you dig into the Word of God, you realize, "It's amazing!" The Lord will teach you new things all the time…more astounding Truth!

**All believers do not follow biblical truth because:**

1. They do not really know the Word (immaturity)

2. They are not convicted by the Word (desensitized)

---

**2 Timothy 3:14**, "You, however, continue in the things you have learned and become convinced of, knowing from whom you have learned them."

⬜ **John 14:21**

*He who has My commandments and keeps them, he is the one who _____ Me; and he who loves Me will be loved by My Father, and I will love him and will _____ Myself to him.*

⬜ He reveals more of _____ to us as we obey Him.

Do you believe that you can know God? Do you believe that you can have a personal relationship with Jesus Christ and that He can make a difference in your everyday life? The verse above is one of many that says, "Absolutely! Yes, you can." It's the message of the Gospel that Jesus restores our fellowship with our Heavenly Father. Before that, we were living under the law of sin and death, a rebellious, counterfeit life.

⬜ **Psalm 19:8b**

*The commandment of the LORD is pure, enlightening the eyes.*

As you study the Word, you become convinced (convicted) by it. You start to "get it" and "do it". You take a 180-degree turn and you follow God's Word. You are determined to make things right in your life. You begin to obey God wholeheartedly in a specific area. Then God discloses something new to you. Next, you begin to see the blessings of obedience in your life because it's being aligned with God. The principles of the Bible are true for all times, all believers, all cultures.

See APPENDIX 1– **Examples of Biblical Convictions**

The Bible is full of biblical convictions. They are the principles, the commandments of Scripture that we are to be convicted of, convinced of, and to obey, no matter what. All these biblical convictions can be simplified down to seven "majors" of the Christian faith.

### E. Seven Majors of the Christian Faith

**Ephesians 4:4-6**

*There is one body and one Spirit, just as also you were called in one hope of your calling; one Lord, one faith, one baptism, one God and Father of all who is over all and through all and in all.*

**These are the things that we do not compromise in our faith:**

1. One Body     The Church

2. One Spirit     The Holy Spirit

3. One Hope     The Return of Jesus

4. One Lord     Jesus, the Only Way to God

5. One Faith     Faith in the Truth of God's Word

6. One Baptism     Public Confession of Faith

7. One God     One True and Living God

### F. Choosing to be Godly Parents

You will be fighting a _____ if you choose to be godly parents and live by biblical _____.

You will be fighting the world of counterfeits. The world trains you in assertiveness and diversity; the Bible teaches submission to authority. The world emphasizes children's rights and freedoms and catering to their desires. Of course, we love our children and want what's best for them. God has given us good gifts that we are to enjoy, but we do not use our freedom to sin.

A life surrendered to God produces joy. The world says, "Live for yourself, not for the glory of God alone." We are not to be pleasure seekers. We are to be seeking God. We are fighting a battle and victory will not come to those who do not live according to biblical convictions.

---

**2 Timothy 3:14,** "You, however, continue in the things you have learned and become convinced of, knowing from whom you have learned them."

🖥 **Acts 17:11**

*Now these were more noble-minded than those in Thessalonica, for they received the word with great eagerness, _____ the Scriptures daily to see whether these things were _____.*

The Bereans heard and searched the Scriptures to see if what they heard was the truth. That is why there are so many Scriptures in these lessons, so you are not listening to one person's opinion but you are listening to the truth of God's Word.

## *III. Personal Convictions*

### A.  Defining Personal Convictions

🖥 In addition to biblical convictions, which are true for all of us, we also develop _____

convictions.

**Personal convictions**: As a result of what I have learned in the Scripture, my personal relationship with God, my life experiences, or my education, I have developed certain principles for my life that may not be directly written in the Word of God. They are not necessarily true for all times, for all cultures.

🖥 This is _____ my faith to what I know God would have me to do. It is never in

_____ ____ biblical convictions, but rather a further application of biblical convictions.

Personal convictions are not expressed explicitly in the Bible. You read the principles of God's Word, then you personalize these convictions to your family. This is where our convictions may differ. We don't have to have the same personal convictions, but we will all have the same biblical convictions. I can apply my personal convictions to my children and my family perhaps differently than you would apply them in your family.

All parents create rules and standards for their children. Some of them are not biblical but they are still necessary. There will come a clash of personal convictions where we won't all agree. Examples include: music, television, dropping your child off at the mall, etc.

We need rules for our families but we have to remember not to elevate personal convictions to the level of "Thus saith the Lord…" We do not want to be like the Pharisees who took the Word of God and added thousands of laws to it. Jesus hated their hypocrisy. They were forsaking the biblical standards for the laws they created, thereby neglecting the true spirit of the law.

**John 14:21**

*He who has My commandments and keeps them is the one who loves Me; and he who loves Me will be loved by My Father, and I will love him and will disclose Myself to him.*

The more we obey God's Word, the more He reveals Himself to us, the more He opens up and discloses His Truth to us. Do you want to know Him more deeply? Then obey Him. God's Word never changes but my understanding of it changes; therefore, I am always changing.

**Hebrews 13:8**
*Jesus Christ is the same yesterday and today and forever.*

## B. Designing Your Own "Family Plan"

- It is _____ to have family standards, to say, "This is the way the _____ family does it."

- Your children need to _____ that if another family does not have the same _____ convictions as you and your husband, that is _____.

- But, their job is still to _____ the God-given authority placed over them and we are to seek to _____ God as we raise them.

- This is where you will start to see the _____ of family _____ and you will hear the phrase, "But, Joe's mom lets him." And then you can say, "But that's not how we do it in the _____ family.

- Dad and I have talked about this and we are _____ that the standard we have _____ upon is best for _____ family."

- _____ seriously what your convictions are.

---

2 Timothy 3:14, "You, however, continue in the things you have learned and become convinced of, knowing from whom you have learned them."

Do you hold strong to biblical convictions, no matter what the stakes? Have you sat down with your husband and come to agreement on what your personal convictions for raising your family will be? If not, you've got a time-bomb ticking that will go off when your children hit their junior high years. They must *grow up* with the standards firmly in place.

▢ Your children will have the energy to challenge _____ convictions, especially if you and your husband do not present a _____ front.

▢ They know if you are not in _____.

They may try to play one parent against the other because they want their way! But if they hear these convictions consistently while they are growing up, that is security for them.

▢ Our children have to _____ _____ _____ the understanding of our family standards if they are going to _____ them.

If they grow up knowing your family standards from an early age, they will learn to trust God and they will learn to trust you, as looking out for their best interest.

▢ And when you say _____, they will not _____ you, but will be _____ for your guidance.

If they grow up with that understanding, you could still have a child challenge you here and there, but when you hold strong, they'll understand that this is security for them and that you are looking out for their best interest.

## C.  Encouragement for the Single Parent

If you are a single parent, you still must have solid standards and convictions for your kids. Lay them out there so they understand them. Your task will be more difficult, but it is certainly not impossible. With the Lord's help, you can do it!

In the last chapter of Joshua, Joshua was heavyhearted because they had just finished their 40 years in the wilderness but they did not completely conquer and take the Promised Land. He knew there were false gods still living in the land. God wanted them to purge all the counterfeits, but they didn't do it. Joshua gave the people this address before they went into the Promised Land:

**Joshua 24:14-15**

*Now, therefore, fear the LORD and serve Him in sincerity and truth; and put away the gods which your fathers served beyond the River and in Egypt, and serve the LORD. If it is disagreeable in your sight to serve the LORD, choose for yourselves today whom you will serve: whether the gods which your fathers served which were beyond the River, or the gods of the Amorites in whose land you are living; but as for me and my house, we will serve the LORD.*

Joshua was saying that no matter what they came across in this foreign land, he and his family were going to live by biblical convictions.

---

2 Timothy 3:14, "You, however, continue in the things you have learned and become convinced of, knowing from whom you have learned them."

# Homefront Application

## THE AUTHORITY OF GOD'S WORD
### A godly mother lives by biblical convictions

Get some time alone with your husband and:

1. Have a discussion regarding biblical convictions. What are they? Have you made a commitment together to live by biblical convictions? Are there any areas of life in which you are not living by biblical convictions? How is that affecting the family? In other words, do you see your family being hindered by lack of biblical conviction in any area?

2. Discuss personal convictions. How do they differ from biblical convictions? Do you agree on the personal convictions you have for your family?

What are your personal convictions or family standards for the following areas: dating, watching television, schools, music.

There are hundreds of possible areas to discuss. Pick any topic or area that you see as needing immediate attention.

P.S. Enjoy your time together. It may take some time to work through differences and come to agreements, but be determined to do it. Your family unity depends on it.

## I CHOOSE TO LIVE BY CONVICTIONS.

Signature: _____ Date: _____

# Lesson 3 Outline

## PERSONAL CONVICTIONS
### A godly mother establishes family convictions

I. Review of Biblical Convictions

II. Review of Personal Convictions

III. The Role of Conscience

IV. The Role of the Holy Spirit

V. The Role of Discernment

VI. Principles of Personal Liberty and Conscience

VII. Personal Preferences

VIII. The Role of God's Word

## This week's Scripture memory verse:

**Psalm 85:8**, "I will hear what God the LORD will say;
For He will speak peace to His people, to His godly ones; But let them not turn back to folly."

# Lesson 3

## PERSONAL CONVICTIONS
### A godly mother establishes family convictions

## I. Review of Biblical Convictions

Once you start to live by biblical convictions, decisions come so much more easily. Living by biblical convictions proves to God that we trust Him. This is the essence of faith. We follow the Word of God, first and foremost. Biblical convictions are those issues of absolute right and wrong. Biblical convictions are true for all times for all believers.

**Examples of Biblical Convictions:**

1. I will reap what I sow

2. Keep my promises

3. Be generous

4. Share the gospel

## II. Review of Personal Convictions

Personal convictions deal with those gray areas that are not addressed as a specific right or wrong in the Bible.

**They develop from a combination of two areas:**

1. An understanding of the Word of God and/or

2. Our life experience or expertise.

☐ **Examples of Personal Convictions:**

1. Dating guidelines

2. TV restrictions

3. Slumber party standards

4. School choices

**Example of "dating guidelines":**

You have to come up with these personal convictions much in advance! Otherwise, they will react and they will think you are reacting and that will cause a separation in your relationship.

☐ We have to know what we _____ and _____.

☐ All people live by personal convictions, even people who don't live by biblical convictions. They may even have _____ standards, but they lack the _____ of building their lives on the Word of God.

☐ **Psalm 127:1**
*Unless the LORD builds the house, they labor in vain who build it; Unless the LORD guards the city, the watchman keeps awake in vain.*

☐ **Matthew 7:26-27**
*Everyone who hears these words of Mine and does not act on them, will be like a foolish man who built his house on the sand. The rain fell, and the floods came, and the winds blew and slammed against that house; and it fell—and great was its fall.*

Everybody's house has storms but the house that stands is the one that is built on biblical convictions. God says, "You can start over today and I will help you build it." God is in the business of miracles and you can rebuild your house. Don't think it's too much work and fail to do it. If you continue to build that "beautiful house" on no foundation, it will collapse. So take the time to be building on the foundation of God's Word. It's very important. Say: "From this time on, I choose to live by biblical convictions."

---

**Psalm 85:8,** "I will hear what God the LORD will say;
For He will speak peace to His people, to His godly ones; But let them not turn back to folly."

3.3

☐ **2 Timothy 3:14–15**
*Continue in the things you have learned and become convinced of, knowing from whom you have learned them, and that from childhood you have known the sacred writings which are able to give you the wisdom that leads to salvation through faith which is in Christ Jesus.*

**Verse 16 and 17**
*All Scripture is inspired by God and profitable for teaching, for reproof, for correction, for training in righteousness; so that the man of God may be adequate, equipped for every good work.*

☐ We don't just have convictions for _____, but we _____ our

children to live by biblical convictions and how to begin to develop their own personal convictions.

Remember, your personal convictions have precedence over their personal convictions. And you can change your personal convictions. You will be constantly classifying and clarifying them.

## III. *The Role of Conscience*

☐ God has given every person a _____. Our conscience is the sense of

_____ goodness coupled with the internal obligation to do what is _____.

☐ It is the ability to know what is right and to have a sensitive regard for _____ and

_____.

☐ In other words, our conscience keeps us _____ of what is right.

☐ **Hebrews 13:18**
*Pray for us, for we are sure that we have a good conscience, desiring to conduct ourselves honorably in all things.*

☐ **Additional verses regarding the conscience:**

| | | | |
|---|---|---|---|
| **Acts 24:16** | **Romans 13:5** | **1 Corinthians 8:7** | **1 Peter 3:16** |
| **2 Corinthians 1:12** | **1 Timothy 3:9** | **1 Timothy 4:2** | |

☐ All people are _____ with an understanding of right and wrong, but people can _____

their conscience and _____ that what is right is right and what is wrong is wrong.

3.4

☐ **Isaiah 5:20**

*Woe to those who call evil good, and good evil; who substitute darkness for light and light for darkness; who substitute bitter for sweet and sweet for bitter!*

☐ If we _____ at these counterfeits too long and we are not strong in the Word, we

will be _____ by them and will eventually _____ and _____

_____.

☐ If we are strong in the Word and we keep looking at the counterfeits, we will likely get very

_____, even _____, and possibly fall into sin.

☐ Why? Because we may become tempted to _____ the _____ of God.

☐ **Malachi 2:17**

*You have wearied the LORD with your words. Yet you say, "How have we wearied Him?" In that you say, "Everyone who does evil is good in the sight of the Lord, and He delights in them," or "Where is the God of justice?"*

☐ God's justice is _____ and it cannot be thwarted. We are not to think, "Why does evil

prevail?" He will _____ and _____ every counterfeit.

☐ We are to live with the conviction that God's ways are _____ and His promises never

_____. Our minds are to _____ on the truth.

☐ **Philippians 4:8**

*Finally, brethren, whatever is true, whatever is honorable, whatever is right, whatever is pure, whatever is lovely, whatever is of good repute, if there is any excellence and if anything worthy of praise, dwell on these things.*

Living without biblical convictions is like telling God, "I know better than You. I can figure this out on my own."

---

**Psalm 85:8**, "I will hear what God the LORD will say;
For He will speak peace to His people, to His godly ones; But let them not turn back to folly."

## IV. The Role of the Holy Spirit

☐ When we become believers in Christ, God gives us a helper, the _____ _____,

who _____ our conscience.

☐ **John 14:16**
*I will ask the Father, and He will give you another Helper, that He may be with you forever.*

**Two primary roles of the Holy Spirit are:**

1. To convict us of sin and sharpen our awareness of good and evil

2. To conform us to God's Son (through our sanctification).

## V. The Role of Discernment

☐ Discernment, the ability to _____ between truth and counterfeits, comes with

_____ in Christ and a deepened _____ of Scripture.

And as we mature, we are to become more aware of the distinction between truth and counterfeits. The more we study the Word, the more obvious this becomes to us.

☐ **Hebrews 5:14**
*But solid food is for the mature, who because of practice have their senses trained to discern good and evil.*

## VI. Principles of Personal Liberty and Conscience

**Five principles of personal convictions from Romans 14:**

☐ 1. _____ issues do exist. There are some gray areas. **Verses 1-4**

☐ 2. We _____ need to develop personal convictions. **Verses 5 & 14**

☐ 3. Don't _____ the personal convictions of another. **Verses 1 & 10**

☐ 4. I must not let my personal convictions cause _____ among fellow believers. **Verses 19 & 21**

☐ 5. Biblical convictions take _____ over personal convictions. Christ is always
_____. **Verses 22 & 23**

**Romans 14**

*Now accept the one who is weak in faith, but not for the purpose of passing judgment on his opinions. 2 One person has faith that he may eat all things, but he who is weak eats vegetables only. 3 The one who eats is not to regard with contempt the one who does not eat, and the one who does not eat is not to judge the one who eats, for God has accepted him. 4 Who are you to judge the servant of another? To his own master he stands or falls; and he will stand, for the Lord is able to make him stand. 5 One person regards one day above another, another regards every day alike. Each person must be fully convinced in his own mind. 6 He who observes the day, observes it for the Lord, and he who eats, does so for the Lord, for he gives thanks to God; and he who eats not, for the Lord he does not eat, and gives thanks to God. 7 For not one of us lives for himself, and not one dies for himself; 8 for if we live, we live for the Lord, or if we die, we die for the Lord; therefore whether we live or die, we are the Lord's. 9 For to this end Christ died and lived again, that He might be Lord both of the dead and of the living. 10 But you, why do you judge your brother? Or you again, why do you regard your brother with contempt? For we will stand before the judgment seat of God. 11 For it is written, 'AS I LIVE, SAYS THE LORD, EVERY KNEE SHALL BOW TO ME, AND EVERY TONGUE SHALL GIVE PRAISE TO GOD.' 12 So then each one of us will give an account of himself to God. 13 Therefore, let us not judge one another anymore, but rather determine this—not to put an obstacle or a stumbling block in a brother's way. 14 I know and am convinced in the Lord Jesus that nothing is unclean in itself; but to him who thinks anything to be unclean, to him it is unclean. 15 For if because of food your brother is hurt, you are no longer walking according to love. Do not destroy with your food him for whom Christ died. 16 Therefore do not let what is for you a good thing be spoken of as evil; 17 for the kingdom of God is not eating and drinking, but righteousness and peace and joy in the Holy Spirit. 18 For he who in this way serves Christ is acceptable to God and approved by men. 19 So then let us pursue the things which make for peace and the building up of one another. 20 Do not tear down the work of God for the sake of food. All things are indeed clean, but they are evil for the man who eats and gives offense. 21 It is good not to eat meat or to drink wine, or to do anything by which your brother stumbles. 22 The faith which you have, have as your own conviction before God. Happy is he who does not condemn himself in what he approves. 23 But he who doubts is condemned if he eats, because his eating is not from faith; and whatever is not from faith is sin.*

Any conviction that you might think of for your family, pass it through these five principles. The bottom line is: do not cause another person to stumble. Be understanding of other people's personal convictions. Do not crusade your personal convictions, but do not go against your conscience. Life is really about Christ. We are to major on the majors and minor on the minors.

**Colossians 2:16-17**

*Therefore no one is to act as your judge in regard to food or drink or in respect to a festival or a new moon or a Sabbath day—things which are a mere shadow of what is to come; but the substance belongs to Christ.*

Always keep the substance belonging to Christ.

---

**Psalm 85:8**, "I will hear what God the LORD will say;
For He will speak peace to His people, to His godly ones; But let them not turn back to folly."

▢ The _____ of personal convictions is to unify _____ people in the body of Christ.

It's an amazing concept that God's Word applies today more than ever. This is the brilliance of personal convictions because God said you can think differently on these gray issues and still be unified the world over. In the United States, we have a tendency towards too much freedom. We really need to be striving for personal holiness.

What if my husband and I do not agree on the same personal convictions? Defer to the one who has the stronger, more sensitive conscience on the matter. The "Homefront Applications" at the end of each lesson are a great way to start digging into these issues together and have a meaningful time talking through them. You must present a united front for your children. Coming together in agreement on your personal convictions will help you and your husband become more united.

## VII. Personal Preferences

▢ Personal preferences are the areas we can _____ on if we think our children will act

_____.

We still have standards in these areas but if our children are taking an area of freedom to an extreme, we will know that it has become an issue of the heart. If something becomes overly controlling in a young person's life, we have to know how to deal with it as an attitude of the heart.

▢ As our children become teens we _____ _____ on the _____ we

exercise over them and begin to _____ them by _____.

▢ We allow them to make some _____ and _____ how they handle them.

Bad choices lead to more _____. Good choices lead to more _____.

If you exert too much authority on your teenager and treat them as a young child, you can exasperate them, and they will want to get out as fast as they can!

## VIII. The Role of God's Word

☐ Our lives are to be _____ with the Word of God.

☐ Every day brings new _____ to teach new truths or reinforce truths so that

God does His own work in them and they begin to develop their own convictions under your

_____.

☐ **Joshua 1:8**
*This book of the law shall not depart from your mouth, but you shall meditate on it day and night, so that you may be careful to do according to all that is written in it; for then you will make your way prosperous, and then you will have success.*

☐ **Psalm 119:9-11**
*How can a young man keep his way pure? By keeping it according to Your word. With all my heart I have sought You; Do not let me wander from Your commandments. Your word I have treasured in my heart, that I may not sin against You.*

☐ We are to look at life through the _____ of God's Word, not the other way around. We

are _____ to look at God's Word and make it fit into our _____. That is

creating a _____.

☐ Instead, we line our lives up to the _____ Word of God.

---

**Psalm 85:8,** "I will hear what God the LORD will say;
For He will speak peace to His people, to His godly ones; But let them not turn back to folly."

We must remove whatever is preventing us from seeing clearly and look to God's Word first. If we find ourselves thinking, "The Bible applies to me differently because of my life situation", then we are putting that filter before God's Word. This is a really important truth!

We all have some life biases, trials or tender spots and we have to be careful not to let these things become liabilities which cloud the Word of God in our lives. Instead, we want to be able to see truth. Looking through filters also causes us to settle for less. Why? Because we start to think and believe that God's best is not available to us. God can start afresh, but make sure that you look directly at the Word of God first.

**Example:** a Christian woman married to an unbelieving man

We start with what we have and we look at what the Word of God says. God says, "Submit out of obedience to Me. Exercise your faith in Me. I am using that challenge in your life to conform you to My Son. Do not let it be a hindrance. Let it be a sign of victory. Align your life with Me. Align your life with the Word of God." The word "align" comes from the word "ally". When you align yourself with God, He's your ally. What could possibly be better than that? But Satan wants us to keep looking through that filter and to keep things cloudy. He wants to make us ineffective. He wants us to think that there is that "something" in our life that is going to hold us back from having a fabulous, abundant life in Christ. But we can, so do not believe that lie.

Jesus understands our weaknesses. He Himself was tempted in all things and yet without sin. I am not necessarily talking about sinful issues, I am talking about anything in your life that is a "tender spot". Let God use that for His glory in your life, rather than seeing it as a hindrance. Remember **Psalm 85:8**, *I will hear what God the LORD will say; for He will speak peace to His people, to His godly ones; but let them not turn back to folly.*

God requires our obedience once we know what the right thing is. People think that _____

something wrong is sin, and it is (sin of commission). But sin is also _____ _____

what we know is the right thing to do (sin of omission).

**James 4:17**
*Therefore, to one who knows the right thing to do and does not do it, to him it is sin.*

**We have to remember to align ourselves according to:**

☐ **1.** Biblical Convictions

**2.** Personal Convictions

**3.** Personal Preferences

☐ Make the _____ to live by the principles found in God's Word. Learn to

_____ biblical convictions from personal convictions or preferences.

☐ Be _____ regarding your biblical convictions,

be _____ in regard to personal convictions, and

be _____ in regard to personal preferences.

We have the Word of God that is so valuable, so precious. God says, "You get to have it for every single day." This is amazing! Do we realize what a gift we have?

*Notes:*

---

**Psalm 85:8**, "I will hear what God the LORD will say;
For He will speak peace to His people, to His godly ones; But let them not turn back to folly."

# *Homefront Application*

## PERSONAL CONVICTIONS
### A godly mother establishes family convictions

1. Continue your discussions with your husband regarding personal convictions. Now that you are becoming accustomed to thinking about them, you will begin to consider new areas for which you will want to establish family standards.

2. Reread **Romans 14**, remembering the principles of personal convictions.

3. As you and your husband come to agreement on family standards, you will want to discuss them with your children. It isn't necessary that they know every individual conviction, but it will be so helpful to them to have an understanding of how Mom and Dad delineate boundaries. It will make them more likely to obey that which they clearly understand. Spend some time this week and share age-appropriate convictions with them.

(It would be great to do this with the whole family together and every so often have a "refresher" family meeting.)

## I CHOOSE TO LIVE BY CONVICTIONS.

Signature: _____  Date: _____

# Lesson 4 Outline

## GOD'S PLAN OF ORDER, PART ONE
### A godly mother lives by biblical priorities

I. God's Plan of Order

II. A Word to Single Mothers

III. Our First Priority: God

IV. Our Second Priority: Husband/Wife
    A. Establishing Guardrails for Your Family
    B. Examples of How to Grow in Marriage
    C. Living in Understanding and Agreement
    D. Know Your Role and Do it

V. Our Third Priority: Children

VI. Evaluating Our Homefront Priorities
    A. "Keeping My Thumb on the Pulse" of My Household
    B. Establishing Lifelong Non-negotiables

VII. Our Fourth Priority: Ministry

## This week's Scripture memory verse:

**Deuteronomy 6:6-7**, "These words, which I am commanding you today, shall be on your heart. You shall teach them diligently to your sons and shall talk of them when you sit in your house and when you walk by the way and when you lie down and when you rise up."

# Lesson 4

## GOD'S PLAN OF ORDER, PART ONE
### A godly mother lives by biblical priorities

## 1. God's Plan of Order

⬛ **1 Corinthians 11:3**
*But I want you to understand that Christ is the head of every man, and the man is the head of a woman, and God is the head of Christ.*

**Our biblical convictions / priorities should be:**

**1.** God

**2.** Husband

**3.** Children

**4.** Ministry

This lesson is about living an orderly life – a life of order. With every season of life that we go through (like a new birth in the family) we have to establish a "new normal". It will be this way your whole life. The first years of mothering are more physically exhausting. Then the season of parenting teenagers becomes more mentally and emotionally challenging. Do not wait for life to get "easier" before starting life disciplines because it will never happen. It is God's design that we start living out life priorities right where we are at.

⬛ God's plan of order is a _____ conviction.

Many people think this is a personal conviction and slip into cultural norms. Having an orderly life with biblical priorities is actually a biblical conviction. If we do not embrace this truth, God will destroy our ability to make our relationships work.

**Joel 2:25** (ESV)
*I will restore to you the years that the swarming locusts have eaten, the hopper, the destroyer, and the cutter, my great army which I sent among you.*

Do you sometimes feel like the locusts have eaten away at your life? This verse says that God sent the locusts. God will not allow things to work well in our lives when we go against His plan, so we want to understand God's plan of order.

❑ God has established a chain of command so that things run _____.

**Example:** The Roman Centurion (**Luke 7:6-9**)

❑ This man knew the _____ and the relevance of a chain of command and Jesus

marveled at his great _____ because he believed in God's line of authority.

## 11. A Word to Single Mothers

When I read the Bible, I am amazed at how many times God encourages us to look out for widows and orphans and single mothers.

❑ God is very mindful of the woman raising children on her own, especially if it is from no _____

of her own.

❑ The Bible is very clear regarding God's special protection for widows and orphans or

_____ mothers and children.

He gives many warnings to us that we are to be watching out and caring for women and children in these circumstances. We must not let them fall into mistreatment or need. If you know a single mom, look for a way to help meet a need for her.

❑ **Psalm 68:5-6**
*A father of the fatherless and a judge ("defender"–NKJV) for the widows is God in His holy habitation. God makes a home for the lonely; He leads out the prisoners into prosperity.*

What a difficult challenge it is to have to raise children without the counterbalance and protection of a husband and all the roles that he plays.

---

**Deuteronomy 6:6-7,** "These words, which I am commanding you today, shall be on your heart.
You shall teach them diligently to your sons and shall talk of them when you sit in your house
and when you walk by the way and when you lie down and when you rise up."

⌨ Women are able to raise godly children without a husband, but it will be more _____.

**Example:** Timothy who was raised by his mother and grandmother:

### 2 Timothy 1:5
*For I am mindful of the sincere faith within you, which first dwelt in your grandmother Lois and your mother Eunice, and I am sure that it is in you as well.*

### 2 Timothy 3:14-15
*You, however, continue in the things you have learned and become convinced of, knowing from whom you have learned them, and that from childhood you have known the sacred writings which are able to give you the wisdom that leads to salvation through faith which is in Christ Jesus.*

## III. Our First Priority: God

This is the context of today's memory verse, *These words which I am commanding you today* from **Deuteronomy 6:6-7**. What are "these words" referring to? It is actually referring to the verse previous:

### ⌨ Deuteronomy 6:5
*You shall love the L*ORD *your God with all your heart and with all your soul and with all your might.*

These are the words we are to be teaching our children in little moments throughout the day—to love the Lord our God. In the New Testament, Jesus repeats the same point:

### Matthew 22:37
*YOU SHALL LOVE THE L*ORD *YOUR GOD WITH ALL YOUR HEART, AND WITH ALL YOUR SOUL, AND WITH ALL YOUR MIND.*

Let's think about this priority of placing God first.

### ⌨ Revelation 2:2-4
*I know your deeds and your toil and perseverance, and that you cannot tolerate evil men, and you put to the test those who call themselves apostles, and they are not, and you found them to be false; and you have perseverance and you have endured for My name's sake, and have not grown weary. But I have this against you, that you have left your first love.*

Our love for Christ is to take _____ place and it is a big deal.

Christ is to be our first love, our first priority.

## IV. Our Second Priority: The Husband/Wife Relationship

☐ Next, we are to love our husband and give him his _____ place in our marriage. We

are to be _____ to our husband as to the Lord.

☐ **Ephesians 5:22-24**
*Wives, be subject to your own husbands, as to the Lord. For the husband is the head of the wife, as Christ also is the head of the church, He Himself being the Savior of the body. But as the church is subject to Christ, so also the wives ought to be to their husbands in everything.*

And so we _____ the leading of our husbands in all things, because he is _____

before God for us. The only exception is if he asks us to _____.

So we do not subject our children or ourselves to harm. That would be a sinful situation. The Bible says that you are not asked to live in fear or harm. We obey our husbands as if Christ Himself were asking us.

☐ The marriage relationship is to be our _____ human relationship.

**Example:** In your life, your husband is "it" and you are "it" for him. It is an exclusive relationship that lasts for life. Tell your husband tonight, "Honey, you are 'it'! You are all 'it'!"

Let your husband compliment you. It is hard for us sometimes to receive compliments, even from our husbands. It is not flattery. Accept his words for what they are. They come from his heart. Receive them; don't negate his feelings.

---

**Deuteronomy 6:6-7,** "These words, which I am commanding you today, shall be on your heart. You shall teach them diligently to your sons and shall talk of them when you sit in your house and when you walk by the way and when you lie down and when you rise up."

## A. Establishing Guardrails for Your Family

When establishing guardrails, you are protecting and preserving your marriage. You are building exclusivity into your relationship. We don't want to build just one guardrail. We want many guardrails to protect our marriages. If you know that evil is lurking around the corner to sneak into your relationship at any possible moment, you are going to say, "I want to establish some guardrails around our relationship."

### ▢ Romans 13:14

*But put on the Lord Jesus Christ, and make no provision for the flesh in regards to its lusts.*

This verse says, "Don't even give yourself an opportunity to slip up." Make sure you put up some guardrails because you could suddenly be at risk. What guardrails do you and your husband have in place?

### ▢ Numbers 32:23

*But if you will not do so, behold, you have sinned against the LORD, and be sure your sin will find you out.*

God says, "I will make sure your sin finds you out." Why? Because He wants to bring us back and restore us.

▢ Don't let yourself believe that your marriage and your relationship don't need to be heavily

_____.

Don't cause your husband to stumble because that would be sin for you also.

## B. Examples of How to Grow in Marriage:

1. _____

_____

2. _____

_____

3. _____

_____

4. _____

_____

## C. Living in Understanding and Agreement

We are also to live in _____ with our husbands. This is an area in need of constant attention.

**Amos 3:3**
*Do two men walk together unless they have made an appointment?*

**Amos 3:3** (NKJV)
*Can two walk together, unless they are agreed?*

It is so important to be in agreement. If you come to a point where you just cannot agree, and your husband is not asking you to sin, then you are to yield your will to his. You do not go against biblical conviction or your conscience. This is God's perfect design.

---

**Deuteronomy 6:6-7**, "These words, which I am commanding you today, shall be on your heart. You shall teach them diligently to your sons and shall talk of them when you sit in your house and when you walk by the way and when you lie down and when you rise up."

At times we are going to come to crossroads when we do not agree with our husbands. And the Lord is saying, "I want you to move forward. I do not want you to divide and go separate ways. I want you to be *one*, so one needs to yield. " This is God's perfect design because He wants us to move forward and not to come to "crossed purposes". When you are at crossed purposes, you will not move forward in your relationship.

To live in agreement, we must first live in _____.

**1 Peter 3:7**

*You husbands in the same way, live with your wives in an understanding way, as with someone weaker, since she is a woman; and show her honor as a fellow heir of the grace of life, so that your prayers will not be hindered.*

### WORKING TOWARD UNDERSTANDING AND AGREEMENT

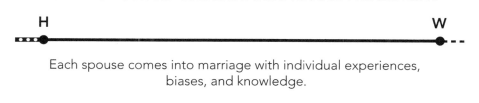

Each spouse comes into marriage with individual experiences, biases, and knowledge.

As couple learns to communicate and understand the other, they re-learn, re-think and evaluate their own thinking. Couple moves closer in understanding.

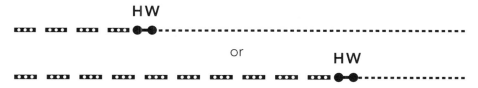

or

Couple comes to agreement on most issues as they move toward each other. Either spouse may move the greater distance toward new understanding.

### EXAMPLE OF FAILURE TO UNDERSTAND AND AGREE

Husband's dominating position over wife demands her submission to each and every decision.

## D. Know Your Role and Do it

☐ Before God we are all to be _____, husbands as well. And husbands are instructed to be especially _____ to a woman's needs and feelings.

He is required to love us as Christ loved the Church. The husband is responsible to make sure that his wife thrives and feels cherished.

☐ He is not in any way to be an _____ taskmaster or bully, but a joint heir to the kingdom of God.

We offer our submission. Our husbands are not to demand it. It is really a perfect design. It is the way that your marriage will thrive.

☐ We are not called to submit because we are in any way inferior to our husbands, because we are not.

☐ We _____ our submission out of _____ for the roles God has given him as _____, _____ and _____.

**Three roles God has given to husbands:**

☐ **1.** LEADER                 **Ephesians 5:22**

   **2.** PROVIDER              **1 Timothy 5:8**

   **3.** PROTECTOR            **1 Peter 3:7**

Most women look at their husbands when they marry them as a "knight in shining armor". They say, "Yes, I want somebody to lead me, provide for me and protect me." They jump on the back of the knight's horse and they ride off into the sunset. But as time goes on, they want to get off the horse. But we are to stay *on* the horse. Stay with your husband and do not come to crossed purposes and veer off. Your relationship can take the path that divides or you can build oneness. It's your choice. It takes more work to build oneness but it is so worth it!

---

**Deuteronomy 6:6-7**, "These words, which I am commanding you today, shall be on your heart. You shall teach them diligently to your sons and shall talk of them when you sit in your house and when you walk by the way and when you lie down and when you rise up."

**Ephesians 5:21**

*And be subject to one another in the fear of Christ.*

We are to have a "you before me" attitude, especially in the home.

Do not misunderstand submission. Single women are not required to submit to single men. Sometimes in dating relationships people attempt to imitate marital relationships. There is no biblical mandate for single men to have authority over single women. But when we place ourselves in a committed marital relationship, then we place ourselves under authority and we are called to submit.

Another example would be members in a church body. When you become a member, you submit yourself to the leadership, the elders. The leadership's responsibility is to keep the church biblically sound, not to run the everyday affairs of anyone's life. It is to guard biblical convictions, not personal convictions.

Society will try to make us believe that the _____ is the socially acceptable way to do things and that priorities for women have changed.

But from the Garden of Eden to this day, women have always attempted to reverse God's plan of priority. But this is the thing that actually keeps us from being truly fulfilled in our relationships. It puts us at crossed purposes.

In some cases, because of hardness of heart or stubborn pride, couples begin to withhold themselves under the pretense of submission and leadership. In other words, they think that they are keeping the biblical priorities but their hearts are not there. This will also place them at crossed purposes. It will create a breach in intimacy. Unless we offer our submission from the heart, it will cause a separation between us. Be on guard that you are not separated too much – spiritually, emotionally, physically, or in any way.

Respect your husband in the roles God has given him. Don't let yourself be pulled away and separate, or your oneness will shrivel up to the point that you don't feel like you even know each other anymore. You ask yourself, "Is this the person I married?" The commitments and the vows start to weaken. It seems easier to bail out, but God says that we are to stay committed. This submission will actually build oneness in your marriage. There is hope for every situation—always.

## COMMUNICATION DIAGRAM 1: GROWING IN ONENESS

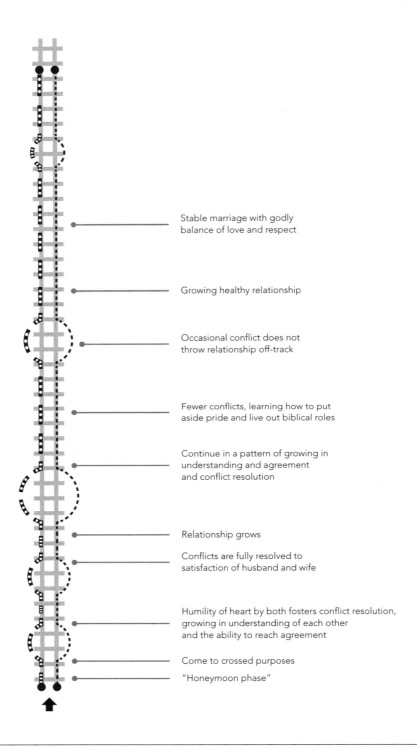

Stable marriage with godly balance of love and respect

Growing healthy relationship

Occasional conflict does not throw relationship off-track

Fewer conflicts, learning how to put aside pride and live out biblical roles

Continue in a pattern of growing in understanding and agreement and conflict resolution

Relationship grows

Conflicts are fully resolved to satisfaction of husband and wife

Humility of heart by both fosters conflict resolution, growing in understanding of each other and the ability to reach agreement

Come to crossed purposes

"Honeymoon phase"

**Deuteronomy 6:6-7,** "These words, which I am commanding you today, shall be on your heart. You shall teach them diligently to your sons and shall talk of them when you sit in your house and when you walk by the way and when you lie down and when you rise up."

## COMMUNICATION DIAGRAM 2: STAYING THE COURSE
### (when one spouse refuses to work on the marriage)

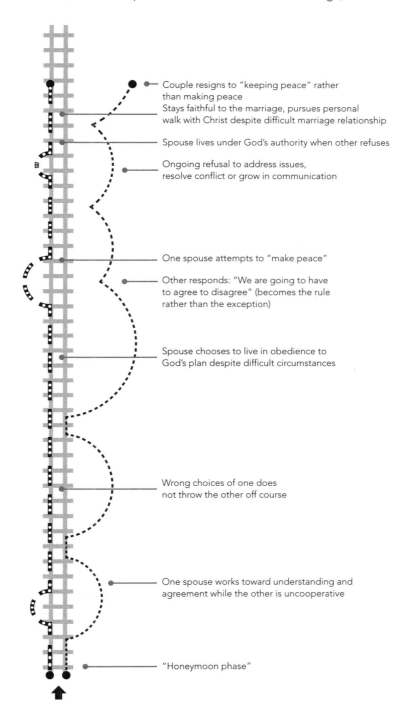

Couple resigns to "keeping peace" rather
than making peace
Stays faithful to the marriage, pursues personal
walk with Christ despite difficult marriage relationship

Spouse lives under God's authority when other refuses

Ongoing refusal to address issues,
resolve conflict or grow in communication

One spouse attempts to "make peace"

Other responds: "We are going to have
to agree to disagree" (becomes the rule
rather than the exception)

Spouse chooses to live in obedience to
God's plan despite difficult circumstances

Wrong choices of one does
not throw the other off course

One spouse works toward understanding and
agreement while the other is uncooperative

"Honeymoon phase"

COMMUNICATION DIAGRAM 3:
COMMUNICATION DISINTEGRATION

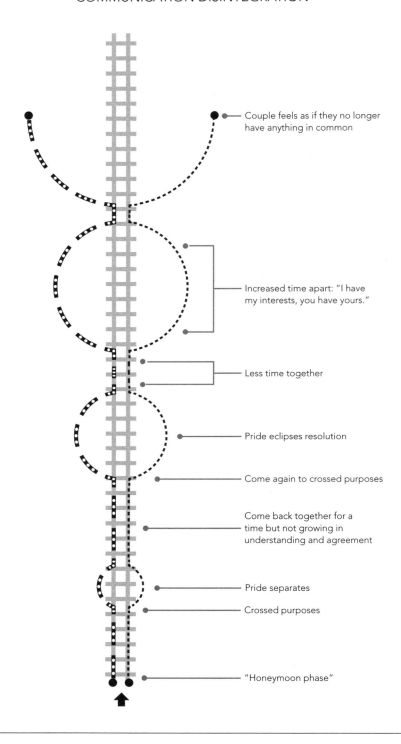

Couple feels as if they no longer have anything in common

Increased time apart: "I have my interests, you have yours."

Less time together

Pride eclipses resolution

Come again to crossed purposes

Come back together for a time but not growing in understanding and agreement

Pride separates

Crossed purposes

"Honeymoon phase"

**Deuteronomy 6:6-7**, "These words, which I am commanding you today, shall be on your heart. You shall teach them diligently to your sons and shall talk of them when you sit in your house and when you walk by the way and when you lie down and when you rise up."

**4.12**

As the previous charts illustrate, you may be walking along with your husband when suddenly, you come to crossed purposes and you decide to go separate ways. Then you make up and come back together. It is always pride that puffs us up and makes us separate for awhile until we humble ourselves and come back to each other. But if we get in the habit of separating over crossed purposes, the separations become greater and last longer before we come back. The oneness that we do have, ends up being these little, tiny pieces. Over time, they are less and less and you feel like you do not even know each other anymore. Do not let yourself be separated by pride. Submit to your husband and you will spend more time walking together.

We begin by placing ourselves under our husband's authority because we know we are really placing ourselves under God's authority. Since God is over our husbands, our husbands are accountable to God for the decisions that they make on our behalf. This is a huge responsibility! Men usually have the "big picture" of everything and women usually take on "all the details". That is why women are good nurturers and homemakers. God chose these roles for us because He knew we would be best suited for them, so embrace His plan. Can you say in your heart, "I'm good with it"? Submitting is not suffering, it is God's design for a great life.

Women will say, "I'm submitting but I'm hating it!" When your heart is not in it, stubborn pride puts you at crossed purposes. You can be submitting outwardly, but if it is not from your heart, your husband will not be fooled by your outward behavior and neither is God.

### 1 Samuel 16:7

*But the LORD said to Samuel, "Do not look at his appearance or at the height of his stature, because I have rejected him; for God sees not as a man sees, for man looks at the outward appearance, but God looks at the heart."*

If submitting is making us miserable, our misery is likely self-induced.

## God's Design for the Family

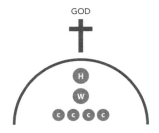

## Wife (and Children) Living Outside God's Design

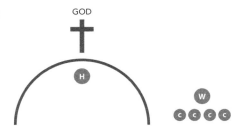

## Wife (and Children) Living Within God's Design even if Husband does not (1 Peter 3:1-6)

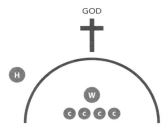

God has placed governing authorities and church leaders in authority over the husband. If a wife has a husband who is living outside of God's authority, and she feels she is in harm's way, then she appeals to the authorities of the church. If it needs to go further than that, she appeals to the governing authorities. (see **Romans 13**). God has designed a system of protection for us.

⬛ Work on being _____ to your husband. Keep him a _____.

_____ through everything with him until you come to a complete understanding.

---

**Deuteronomy 6:6-7**, "These words, which I am commanding you today, shall be on your heart. You shall teach them diligently to your sons and shall talk of them when you sit in your house and when you walk by the way and when you lie down and when you rise up."

**4.14**

▢ Then work on _____ the understanding towards agreement. _____ when your husband speaks without jumping in to make your thoughts known.

▢ Figure out _____ he thinks. Is there an error in his thinking or yours when matched up to biblical truth?

▢ Is there a difference in your thinking because you are just such _____ people, probably complete opposites?

▢ Still, we are to learn to live in _____ with our husbands. We are their helpmates. We know them better than anyone.

▢ If there is something in their lives that does not match up with the truth of God's Word, we can lovingly _____ them—and they are to do the same for us.

▢ Who better to help them than the one God created as their _____? This is not a green light to correct every little thing about them that may _____ you.

We can offer a challenge, but never with the motivation to change your husband. How would you feel if your husband's motivation was to change you? Women think this way a lot! This is the number one question I get. But husbands do not think that way. It is very difficult for us as women not to want to change our husbands. It is part of the curse of **Genesis 3**. Let the desire to change him go, because only then are you free from the bitterness that will build up when he does not change. He will sense it; he will resist it and it will work against oneness. Do not push your husband. Support and respect his leadership. Any motivation to change him will put you at crossed purposes. Don't stand in the way of God's work in his life.

This is what often happens: Women want their husbands to do something so they start pushing their husbands. The husband starts to back away from the wife. But when the wife backs off, then the husband starts to move towards the wife.

▢ The Bible clearly warns us not to be _____. It is _____ even about attempting to change them in any way.

▢ That is the work of the _____ _____ in them. It is only revealing in love an area of life in conflict with biblical truth and then _____ in the Lord.

☐ Your husband will respond to the Holy Spirit's _____ in his life without your pointing it out every time it surfaces.

☐ _____ the Lord to mold your husband, and trust your husband to be teachable.

_____ for your husband like no one else can.

☐ If you live in _____, he will value your thoughts and insights and ask for them.

He will want to know what you think about everything and you will grow closer.

Children are to see us as backing up Dad. This is a critical piece. If you are not in agreement, you submit to your husband's decision (with a few exceptions) because this is "living in agreement" before your children. You need to model before your children, "Hey, I'm with Dad. We're together." It will mean everything in the world to them as they grow up.

Do not let those little bursts of pride build up. The purpose is to move forward despite a stalemate. Move forward and stay together in oneness, despite the differences, and you will grow in intimacy. Do you want a normal, ordinary marriage or do you want an extraordinary, intimate marriage?

It is more important that you model living under your husband's authority than stubbornly refusing to follow his decisions just to make a silly point. Stepping out from his leadership will have greater long-term consequences. What we model may be visited on future generations. Children know if Mom and Dad are at crossed purposes.

## V. *Our Third Priority: Children*

☐ The parent-child relationship is not to be equal with the _____ -_____

relationship; our homes are not to be child-centered, but _____ -

_____.

We need to be Christ-centered and raise our children to focus on the Lord.

---

**Deuteronomy 6:6-7**, "These words, which I am commanding you today, shall be on your heart. You shall teach them diligently to your sons and shall talk of them when you sit in your house and when you walk by the way and when you lie down and when you rise up."

**4.16**

🖵 **Exodus 20:12**

*Honor your father and mother, that your days may be prolonged in the land which the LORD your God gives you.*

One of the reasons for the Babylonian exile was because the children did not honor their parents.

**Ezekiel 22:7a**

*In you they have made light of mother and father...*

## VI. Evaluating Our Homefront (Family) Priorities

### A. "Keeping My Thumb on the Pulse" of My Household

How do we make sure our children continue to live under our authority and still maintain their proper place of priority within the home? How do we keep ourselves aligned within God's plan and not do too much outside the home?

Here is a saying I have for myself: "that I keep my thumb on the pulse of my household". How do I know if I am meeting my objective? It is really very simple. I ask myself at any given moment, "How much milk is in the refrigerator right now?" This simple indicator tells me if I am in tune with my household. There are so many ways we do this as wives and mothers. Our lists could go on and on:

**Some other ways to "keep your thumb on the pulse" of your household might be:**

- knowing where to find the extra shoelaces

- knowing the size of everything that every family member wears

- sensing your child's emotional mindset at any given moment

- deciphering what it means when they shut the door a certain way

- remembering which jeans are their favorites

- being aware of what they are watching on TV

- tracking when they last practiced the piano and for how long

If we are not able to track with these things, then we have to ask ourselves if we are in tune enough with what is going on in our home. Something else may have slid in and is robbing you of the intimacy with your family. Families are to be a much greater priority than other things. Sometimes we rationalize that things are in order when they really are not.

**Psalm 85:8**

*I will hear what God the LORD will say; for He will speak peace to His people, and to His godly ones; but let them not turn back to folly.*

From time to time, certain things will happen in life that shake up the balance and you think, "I don't think I'm keeping my thumb on the pulse of my family." But we are determined to bring things back under God's plan of order by establishing those areas in which we will not compromise.

## B. Establishing Lifelong Non-negotiables

Because we know that we will reap what we sow, we want to be intentional about every season of life and how we are sowing into it. We do not want to look back in ten years and say, "That is how I always wanted to live, but I never followed through." We need to create a list of non-negotiables for every season of life that will help us hold to our priorities. This list represents the commitments that we are determined to keep, no matter what. By God's grace, living by these non-negotiables now will reap blessing in the future.

**You can make a list for yourself:**

1. _____

2. _____

3. _____

4. _____

5. _____

6. _____

7. _____

**Deuteronomy 6:6-7,** "These words, which I am commanding you today, shall be on your heart. You shall teach them diligently to your sons and shall talk of them when you sit in your house and when you walk by the way and when you lie down and when you rise up."

**Some of my examples of non-negotiables include:**

- As long as my children are in school, I will be home when they come home and I will be there before they leave in the morning.

- I will go to bed at the same time as my husband.

- I will have a plan to be in the Word of God every day.

## VII. Our Fourth Priority: Ministry

☐ The next priority is our ministry. Not only do we train our children so that ministry is a part of

_____, but we train them to order their priorities.

☐ In addition, we are to be involved in ministering to others _____ the home.

☐ **Galatians 6:7-10**, speaks about investing our lives in _____ things versus

_____ things.

**Galatians 6:7-10**
*Do not be deceived, God is not mocked; for whatever a man sows, this he will also reap. For the one who sows to his own flesh will from the flesh reap corruption,* (corruption here refers to things that undergo decay, they are destructible and have no eternal value), *but the one who sows to the Spirit will of the Spirit reap eternal life. Let us not lose heart in doing good, for in due time we will reap if we do not grow weary. So then, while we have opportunity, let us do good to all people, and especially to those who are of the household of the faith.*

☐ Here opportunity does not mean having the time to do it, it means _____ the time

to do it.

**Opportunity:** the convergence of seeing the need and the ability to meet it.

☐ We "lose heart" when our priorities slip and we forget _____ we do what we do. It is

losing our _____ love, like the church of Ephesus.

☐ **1 Corinthians 15:58**
*Therefore my beloved brethren, be steadfast, immovable, always abounding in the work of the Lord, knowing that your toil is not in vain in the Lord.*

**Proverbs 31:27**
*She looks well to the way of her household, and does not eat the bread of idleness.*

☐ If we hit a point of _____ and _____, and we know we can't keep our

thumb on the _____ of our family, we are _____ the point of ministry

where God would have us.

☐ This is the point of being _____, _____ and _____.

God does not want us to operate this way long term. We must take care not to let our priorities slip or we will find ourselves living from crisis to crisis. It is God's perfect design for us to live by biblical priorities.

---

**Deuteronomy 6:6-7**, "These words, which I am commanding you today, shall be on your heart. You shall teach them diligently to your sons and shall talk of them when you sit in your house and when you walk by the way and when you lie down and when you rise up."

# Homefront Application

## GOD'S PLAN OF ORDER, PART ONE
### A godly mother lives by biblical priorities

(Single mothers)

1. As a single mom you have the challenge to keep your home Christ-centered rather than child-centered without the assistance of a husband. This can be difficult enough for two parents. Remember that God will bless you as you put Him first in your home. Consider how you are living this out before your children. Would you say you have a Christ-centered home or a child-centered home? Why?

2. Look up these additional verses that may apply to you:

   *Psalm 146:9*

   *Proverbs 15:25*

   *Hosea 14:3*

   *Jeremiah 49:11*

   *Deuteronomy 10:18*

   *Psalm 10:14*

   *Isaiah 54:5-8*

   After reading these verses, has your understanding of God's concern for your family situation changed? How?

(Married women)

Complete the first two exercises on your own, then come together as a couple for the third step.

1. List the top 5 things that you believe are the most encouraging things that you can do for your husband or wife, as the case may be. Remember, these are things that he/she finds most encouraging.

2. Also, make a list of the top 5 things that your husband/wife can do for you that encourage you the most.

3. Compare your lists. How well do you understand each other? Discuss why you each chose what you did. Listen carefully to each other.

4. Be a student of your husband. Make it a regular practice to do the things that encourage him. Remember it is easy to do these things when you are happy with each other. Practice putting him first even when you don't feel like it.

## I CHOOSE TO LIVE BY CONVICTIONS.

Signature: _____    Date: _____

# Lesson 5 Outline

## GOD'S PLAN OF ORDER, PART TWO
### A godly mother is orderly

I. Review of Lesson 4: God's Plan of Order, Part One

II. Three Marital Relationship Categories
   A. Husband Leads & Wife Follows
   B. Husband Provides & Wife Supports
   C. Husband Protects & Wife Stays Close

III. "Waste of Life" and Other Lessons

IV. Review of Living in Understanding and Agreement
   A. Failure to Break Through to Meaningful Communication
   B. Breaking Through to Meaningful Communication

V. Review of Relational Priorities

VI. Proving our Commitments

VII. Evaluating our Priorities – Seeking God First

VIII. A Test of Abiding Love

IX. Applying Order to the Heart of the Matter
   A. Achieving Excellence vs. Perfection
   B. Spectrum of Order Diagram
   C. The Fruit of Excellence

## This week's Scripture memory verse:

**I Corinthians 14:33**, "For God is not a God of confusion but of peace, as in all the churches of the saints."

# Lesson 5

## GOD'S PLAN OF ORDER, PART TWO
### A godly mother is orderly

## I. Review of Lesson 4: God's Plan of Order, Part One

We discussed biblical priorities pertaining to the husband-wife dynamic for the home. The husband's roles are to lead, provide and protect his wife. The wife's role is to willingly offer her submission to these roles. Husbands put their wives before themselves and wives put their husbands before themselves in terms of priority. In terms of caring for one another, you are equal before God in every way but not the same. In the area of authority, however, God has put the man over the wife as a covering.

God has designed a system of leadership so that marriages and homes run in an orderly way. This plan is always under attack by Satan. Satan would have us believe that it diminishes women rather than being God's very best design for women. When Jesus talked about women being "joint heirs to the throne of life", it was a revolutionary concept for that time. Jesus radically changed the view of women in the culture then and also for our world today. It is so ironic that Satan would have us believe that this in any way puts women in an inferior position.

## II. Three Marital Relationship Categories

### A. Husband Leads & Wife Follows

**What does it mean to follow our husbands' leadership?**

If he is going to be the leader, then it is important for us to follow close. It is exasperating to try to lead somebody who you have to wonder if they are *with* you. I mean that in every sense of the word. Are we *with* our husbands? Are we *for* them? If the wife will not be *with* her husband, then her husband will start to pull away from her.

**When this happens, usually one of two consequences will eventually take place:**

1. The husband will let the wife carry more of the load. He will pull away and just say, "Okay, you do it. You're so good at this, you do it." This imbalance clearly precipitates new problems.

2. Or the opposite may happen when the husband responds by exerting more pressure on his wife and making her feel oppressed, controlled, and unduly uncomfortable.

5.2

Both of these consequences fall outside of God's design because they undermine the husband-wife relationship. (Neither example demonstrates living in understanding and agreement or in biblical submission.)

If we follow our husbands, which is God's design, our relationship will flourish. Though you and your husband are very different, if you are growing in Christ, you will be coming together. It is so important that your relationship not grow stagnant, that you not demand your own position, but that you are always moving toward "oneness".

A big part of this commitment is "living in understanding and agreement". The basis of how we learn to come under a husband's leadership, protection and provision is by coming to a place of understanding one another and learning to live in agreement. As you recall, if you come to a crossroads where you cannot quite agree, the wife submits to her husband's leadership. It is much more important to follow his leadership than to try to prove yourself right. Proving yourself to be right will always work against you in the long run.

"Not following" causes separation. The more this continues, the more the relationship starts to break down. Often, this break in the relationship will lead to ongoing conflict. There is an undercurrent of the unresolved conflict and an unwillingness to come back together as one. Over time, this continues to divide. Eventually, the two learn how to live with unresolved conflict.

Some people say, "Well, I never have any conflict in my marriage." It is okay to have conflict in your marriage! But work it out with understanding and agreement and come to a good conclusion.

If we learn how to simply cope with unresolved conflict, without talking things through, then we learn how to carry on this way. This way of functioning becomes seemingly normal but it causes division in the relationship. The wife especially starts to build resentment against her husband. She begins to feel like her thoughts and feelings are disregarded. When they continue at crossed purposes, she becomes more determined not to follow her husband's leadership because she feels, "What does it matter, anyway? It doesn't make a difference." Eventually she may decide, "I'm not going to cooperate." It is a further and deliberate shutting down of the oneness God intended.

I Corinthians 14:33, "For God is not a God of confusion but of peace, as in all the churches of the saints."

## B. Husband Provides & Wife Supports

How do we submit to our husbands' provision? We do so by being supportive helpers. We do not overspend. We look to the ways of our household as it says in **Proverbs 31:27**. We learn to be resourceful. Often, rather than thinking of ways to *earn* income, we can think of ways to *save* on expenses.

### Proverbs 31:11-12
*The heart of her husband trusts in her, and he will have no lack of gain. She does him good and not evil all the days of her life.*

We do not work against our husbands. We support the budget; we manage the homefront. It is a great idea to read **Proverbs 31** together.

## C. Husband Protects & Wife Stays Close

A husband is not being controlling or overbearing when he wants to know where his wife is and what she is doing. This is part of his role as protector. In fact, there should be no unaccounted for time in the day of either the husband or the wife. It does not mean that we constantly check up on each other, but that neither of us is going anywhere that is unknown or unapproved of by the spouse. The husband's protection is to be emotional as well as physical, and the wife is to stay close to her husband in both of these ways. If a husband or wife refuses to stay close, (emotionally or physically) it may lead to jealousy.

### James 3:16
*For where jealousy and selfish ambition exist, there is disorder and every evil thing.*

Jealousy and selfish ambition work against oneness. God's design is really simple and amazing! He has given the husband a mandate to love and understand his wife and the wife is commanded to submit to and respect her husband. Respect him "to his face and behind his back".

## III. "Waste of Life" and Other Lessons

We need to stay with God's plan, even when things get difficult! Do not waste precious time with your husband or your family because of stubborn pride. Do not rationalize your sin. The key is to humble yourself before the other person, regardless of who is to blame. Failure to do so will not build oneness; it will separate. Repent of the wrong and own it. The Bible says to *confess your sins to one another, and pray for one another so that you may be healed.* (**James 5:16**) If we humble ourselves, the other person will not likely try to take advantage of us.

Pride is the root cause of almost every marital problem. It has no place in your marriage. Do not fight the will of God in your life, in your marriage, and in the unity of your family!

**Philippians 2:13**
*For it is God who is at work in you...*

God is working on this with you. And it is a lot of work! Submit to God and submit to your husband. Left to our own devices, we will really go awry.

Once you choose your life mate, be determined to live by godly principles. Unless the other one commits grievous sin or abandonment, you have married the right person. Be committed to becoming the right person for your spouse.

If we cause our husbands to stumble, even by "not doing anything", or giving him "the silent treatment", we are accountable for that sin of withdrawing. It is wrong. If one of you has to win, you both lose. The hardest thing in life is learning the principle of "you before me".

When we realize we are going down the wrong path and we let pride sneak in, we need to humble ourselves and go before the one we have wronged. It is a conscious decision. These "breakthrough moments" vanquish the pride that has been building up, trying to create separation in your relationship.

Humility is the key to the engine of forgiveness and working towards oneness. Remember, it is not about trying to change that person, not making them become who you want them to become. It is working towards unity. It is God's job to change them.

We must be able to humble ourselves and initiate resolution. There is no moving forward without repentance. We need to own our part, regardless of the other person's part. This is one of the fruits of repentance—the absence of rationalization. No couple is "made for each other". We are *being* made for each other as we consistently apply God's design. Do not make the best of it; make it the best!

---

I Corinthians 14:33, "For God is not a God of confusion but of peace,
as in all the churches of the saints."

## IV. *Review of Living in Understanding and Agreement*

### A. Failure to Break Through to Meaningful Communication

**One–way Understanding:** "I understand myself and if you would just understand me everything would be fine."Inability to break through pride—living for one's own desires, needs, wants, demands, to be met.

### B. Breaking Through to Meaningful Communication

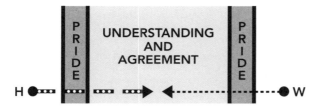

**Two–way Understanding:** "I understand myself and now I understand you." As a result, couple is able to come to agreement that takes both person's insights into consideration. Husband makes ultimate decisions regarding leading, providing, protecting. Each spouse looks out for the needs of the other over themselves.

## V. *Review of Relational Priorities*

**Our biblical convictions / priorities should be:**

**1.** God

**2.** Husband

**3.** Children

**4.** Ministry

### John 13:17
*If you know these things, you are blessed if you do them.*

When we alter God's plan, the family gets in trouble.

### 1 Corinthians 14:33
*For God is not a God of confusion but of peace, as in all the churches of the saints.*

### 1 Corinthians 14:40
*But all things must be done properly and in an orderly manner.*

### Colossians 2:5 (ESV)]
*For though I am absent in body, yet I am with you in spirit, rejoicing to see your good order among you and the firmness of your faith in Christ.*

### James 3:16
*For where jealousy and selfish ambition exist, there is disorder and every evil thing.*

God is not One who likes things to be disorderly and upset, He likes harmony. So how do we get an orderly life that pleases God?

**Think about this question: What do you do when your life seems out of control?**

• Do you take charge?

• Do you run and hide, bail out of commitments, stay home and isolate yourself?

• Or do you run to God immediately in prayer and to His Word?

The essence of today's lesson is, "Who am I in Christ? What is my first reaction?" The answers to these questions reveal what we truly believe about God's priority in our lives. The last lesson we left off in the area of "chaos" and we want to be working towards "order". God's plan for us is clear, but are we making choices and living our lives to make sure that this plan of order will happen?

---

**I Corinthians 14:33,** "For God is not a God of confusion but of peace, as in all the churches of the saints."

## VI. Proving our Commitments

☐ **Luke 6:46**

*Why do you call Me, "Lord, Lord," and do not do what I say?*

Genuine faith produces obedience.

☐ It is not enough to say that the Lord is first in our lives; we are to _____ it to Him.

☐ The way we prove it is to obey Him _____ all else, to give Him His rightful place in our

lives as _____.

So the next logical question would be, "What are you doing to prove your commitment of putting the Lord first"? Will you say, "I give You my attention first when things seem out of control, when there does not seem to be order in my life, or even when things are going well"? This is where faithfulness and the power of commitment come in—when things are very difficult.

☐ **Luke 9:62**

*But Jesus said to him, "No one, after putting his hand to the plow and looking back, is fit for the kingdom of God."*

☐ When things in life get very hectic, look at this time as a _____ of your faith and

_____ to your first love, not as an _____ obstacle. The Lord

tests our faith at times like these.

**Here are six practical ways we prove our love for Him:**

☐ **1.** Obey His Word and do not _____. Live by conviction.

**Matthew 6:33** (NKJV)
*Seek first the kingdom of God and His righteousness and all these things will be added unto you.*

_____ it to know it.

☐ **2.** Bring the whole _____ to Him.

Be absolutely committed to giving him your best – your firstfruits. Do not wait to see what is left over. This perspective will revolutionize your view of money. Even if it seems difficult to make this sacrifice, it is worth it and you will never regret it. The amount does not matter. What matters is the faithfulness. We cannot live apart from God's principles and then expect Him to bless it. Ask yourself, "Am I hindering the blessings of God in my life, simply because I am withholding from Him?"

☐ **Malachi 3:10**
*"Bring the whole tithe into the storehouse, so that there may be food in My house, and test Me now in this," says the LORD of hosts, "if I will not open for you the windows of heaven and pour out for you a blessing until it overflows."*

God has blessed us for a purpose. It is not for ourselves; it is to share with others.

Dedicate each day to the Lord. Ask yourself, "Am I putting the Lord first or am I doing other things that crowd Him out?" Making this a practice each morning causes you to think, "If this day is for the Lord, then what are the choices that I am going to make in the things that I do, the places that I go, and the things that I say, knowing that I just dedicated it to the Lord?"

☐ **3.** Keep the Sabbath.

God worked for six days and rested on the seventh day, not because He needed rest, but because He was setting an example of how we are to live. He set one day apart for us to rest in the Lord and to look back with gratitude and appreciation for all God has done for us that week. The world will try to make you always want to "get ahead", but the Sabbath allows us to rest from striving. What does God say about that?

**Psalm 127:2**
*It is vain for you to rise up early, to retire late, to eat the bread of painful labors; for He gives to His beloved even in his sleep.*

---

**I Corinthians 14:33**, "For God is not a God of confusion but of peace,
as in all the churches of the saints."

When we say, "Lord, I am going to take a day of the week that is different than any other day of the week. I am not going to strive to get ahead, but because You are first in my life, I prove it to You by pulling back and resting in You and thinking about You in gratitude." In return, He will give to you even while you sleep.

Keeping the Sabbath establishes a _____ _____ of trusting Him and not relying on ourselves.

Life will actually be more balanced if you pace yourself through your whole life rather than pushing, pushing, pushing.

### Exodus 34:21

*You shall work six days, but on the seventh day you shall rest; even during plowing time and harvest you shall rest.*

Jesus said that the Sabbath was made for man and not man for the Sabbath. The Sabbath is not about a list of things that you can or cannot do. It is about pulling away from the ordinary stresses of life and resting in the Lord in gratitude. I treasure the verses in **Hebrews 4:1-11** where God says the Sabbath is really a glimpse of heaven because when we get into heaven, we will be entering His rest.

4. _____ people

### Matthew 25:40

*Truly I say to you, to the extent that you did it to one of these brothers of Mine, even to the least of them, you did it for Me.*

One way we put God first in our lives is to serve people in need. I want to fully use up my life here on earth.

5. _____ the name of Christ.

### Romans 1:16

*For I am not ashamed of the gospel, for it is the power of God for salvation to everyone who believes, to the Jew first and also to the Greek.*

Remember the church from Ephesus? They were doing all these things we have talked about so far. But one thing got crowded out by the "busyness" of life: they lost their first love. They were operating in the external mode. We can do all these things in the external mode: study the Word, give our tithe, serve people, obey the Word, and observe the Sabbath. People can see that and think, "That person is really spiritual". But God says, "No, My first love is about what is going on inside of you." The church of Ephesus lost this. Never settle for simply "going through the motions".

6. Build a deep and _____ personal relationship with Him through prayer, devotion and communion that cannot be shaken.

**1 Thessalonians 5:16-18**

*Rejoice always; pray without ceasing; in everything give thanks; for this is God's will for you in Christ Jesus.*

What does this really mean? To me, it means that throughout the day, your mind meditates on the things of God, especially while doing mundane tasks.

"Practicing the Presence of God" (first coined by Brother Lawrence and modeled by my friend Larry Ebert of Navigators) is thinking about and being in His presence, having constant communion with Him. This is what it means to "pray without ceasing".

## VII. Evaluating our Priorities—Seeking God First

**Let's look further at these areas of proving our love to God and putting Him first.**

1. When your schedule gets hectic, is the first thing to go your Bible reading or quiet time or small group commitment?

2. Do you suppress the Holy Spirit's leading to help someone out?

3. Do you compromise a principle of God's Word when it does not suit your situation?

4. Do you hold back on giving because things are "tight" right now?

5. Do you treat every day the same just to get ahead?

6. Do you let yourself be drawn into listening, watching or thinking about meaningless garbage rather than practicing the presence of God?

7. When things go wrong, do you grumble first?

8. Do you fail to see God's hand in all things?

9. When things get really difficult, do you quit or abide?

10. Are you so busy that you are not available when a friend is in need?

---

I Corinthians 14:33, "For God is not a God of confusion but of peace, as in all the churches of the saints."

This is about putting our hearts in order, not just our outward behavior.

**Proverbs 4:23**
*Watch over your heart with all diligence, for from it flow the springs of life.*

When this is true, nothing can take you down.

## VIII. A Test of Abiding Love

**Psalm 112:6-8** (TLB)
*Such a man (woman) will not be overthrown by evil circumstances. God's constant care of him will make a deep impression on all who see it. He does not live in dread of what may happen. He has settled in his mind that Jehovah will take care of him. And that is why he is not afraid but can calmly face his foes.*

When we hold true to these things, God provides the _____ and order to stand

up under difficult circumstances, pressures of _____ life, and even extreme tragedy or

_____.

During a tragedy or crisis, God asks us, "Do you choose Me before all else, all other relationships?" He can give us an overflowing of His grace and a calm assurance that is inexplicable.

## IX. Applying Order to the Heart of the Matter

### A. Achieving Excellence vs. Perfection

When we get busy, we get disconnected from God, from our first love. We let our priorities slip and we start to load up on every single thing that seems so urgent in life. We build up on external order mostly—housekeeping, programs, tasks—without the internal order in place. In other words, we are trying to build order on our own strength. But this is all vanity in God's eyes. So we get frustrated and then we "try harder". If you are on a wrong course to start with, "trying harder" is not going to be the solution.

So then, as women, we try to do things perfectly. But we know we cannot do everything perfectly. We live in a fallen world. There is really nothing in and of ourselves to be perfect. The Bible says that to be perfect is to be complete and lacking in nothing. When we reach that glorified state, we will be perfect. But as long as we are on this earth, we will be dealing with imperfection. The Bible says in **James 1:4** that God is the One who completes us, so that we are lacking nothing. It is not anything we can do externally.

### Jeremiah 10:23

*I know, O Lord, that a man's way is not in himself, nor is it in a man who walks to direct his steps.*

This verse says we cannot take the next step apart from God because God directs it all. Sometimes we cannot figure out which way to go. The wisdom is just not in us. We need to tap into that internal order from God. We need the Lord desperately. Let's face it, without Him, we are clueless.

The "perfect mother" is the one who directs her child to be complete in Christ.

### Colossians 1:28 (NKJV)

*Him we preach, warning every man and teaching every man in all wisdom, that we may present every man perfect (complete) in Christ Jesus.*

It is Christ who completes us. He alone is the One who is able to perfect us. Godly perfection is given, not achieved, and available only through faith in Christ. Worldly perfection is rooted in the fear of man and a misunderstanding of the sanctification process.

"Striving for excellence is a virtue; striving for perfection is a sin." – Biblical Counseling Center

God's plan for us, His will for us, is to not be shaped by the outside world but to _____ our outer world through the _____ order we achieve by following His guidelines of _____. These are _____ - _____.

### Romans 12:2

*And do not be conformed to this world, but be transformed by the renewing of your mind, so that you may prove what the will of God is, that which is good and acceptable and perfect.*

The perfectionism of the world is _____ us to a limit God never intended for us.

But He does _____ us to excellence.

The difference is in the heart and motivation.

Instead of being _____ for _____ motivation and result; excellence is a _____, _____, Christ-centered motivation which leaves us feeling _____—not _____—because there is an _____ foundation of order.

I Corinthians 14:33, "For God is not a God of confusion but of peace,
as in all the churches of the saints."

**5.12**

When we understand the importance of building internal order into our hearts, we can properly begin to establish this order of priority. Then this will seep out into our external, public lives. We do not compromise our priorities. God has gifted different people with different temperaments, abilities, and tastes. Our goal is not to be like each other, but it is to be like Christ.

## B. Spectrum of Order Diagram

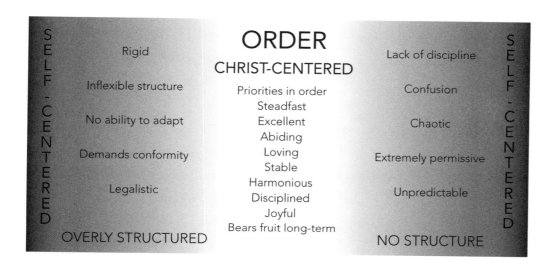

Sometimes people say, "Well, that is just the way that I am." But **Ephesians 4:14-15** says that we are to be growing in Christ, so we all need to be working towards Christlike order. God definitely wants us to be changing. Keep this diagram in mind when you think of all the different areas of family life and how you are working towards coming to this middle band.

The people on the "relaxed" right side are going to think the people on the "highly structured" left side need to "lighten up" and the people on the left think the people on the right need to "tighten up". Opposites usually marry each other so you both need to be working towards the middle.

## C. The Fruit of Excellence

☐ Excellence reaps _____ fruit. It brings _____ and stability to our families.

Remember the goal is not to be like each other, not cookie-cutter families, but it is to be like Christ.

☐ Do we have a plan to make this a reality in the lives of our children? Or are we

_____ in hot pursuit of goals that God never ordained?

☐ Children need to make _____ their number one priority if we are to establish

_____ order in their lives.

All of this trickles down from the parents to the children.

☐ Then they will know how to react and how to _____ _____ when crisis or tragedy hits.

---

**I Corinthians 14:33,** "For God is not a God of confusion but of peace,
as in all the churches of the saints."

# *Homefront Application*

## GOD'S PLAN OF ORDER, PART TWO
### A godly mother is orderly

1. Consider a way to make your life more orderly in each of the following areas:

   Putting God first

   Serving your husband

   Running the household

   Training your children

   Think about the areas presented in class. Choose any you like and customize them for your family or use them as a starting point in coming up with a suitable plan for your family. Remember that we are all working towards having Christ-centered, orderly homes. Don't let yourself feel overwhelmed. Start small so you will stay consistent. You will probably have to keep making adjustments and fine-tuning it to your family. But as you build strong habits you will reap strong fruit.

2. Discuss your ideas/plans with your husband so that you are both in agreement. Make any changes necessary so that you both will follow through in your child-training plans.

3. Think about implementing the chart found in Appendix 2 for training children in daily disciplines. It is a very effective tool for pre-schoolers through sixth grade. The "Tips Day" DVD gives further elaboration.

## I CHOOSE TO LIVE BY CONVICTIONS.

Signature: _____  Date: _____

# Lesson 6 Outline

## A MOTHER'S TOUCH
## AND THE NATURE OF A CHILD
A godly mother understands the significance of her role

## This week's Scripture memory verse:

**Proverbs 22:6**, "Train up a child in the way he should go,
Even when he is old he will not depart from it."

# Lesson 6

## A MOTHER'S TOUCH
## AND THE NATURE OF A CHILD
### A godly mother understands the significance of her role

### I. The Blessing of Children

▢ Remember the _____ time you held your child?

You never forget that, do you? There is nothing like it! You just love your baby so completely.

▢ There is an immediate and inexplicable _____ between you. Your child learns your face

and touch and sound and he/she _____ for those things.

▢ It is the _____ of a baby, of _____ baby.

**Psalm 127:3-5a**
*Behold, children are a gift of the LORD, The fruit of the womb is a reward. Like arrows in the hand of a warrior, So are the children of one's youth. How blessed is the man whose quiver is full of them.*

### II. The Significance of a Mother

How tragic it is that society would have us believe that a mother's touch and care are not a vital priority for every child. Mothers who try to "do it all"—to try and hold down a career and manage a household and nurture their children—find that the area most lacking is nurturing.

▢ The _____ thing to go in a home where Mom is trying to "do it all" is

_____ (Dr. Brenda Hunter, "The State of Childcare Today" CWA Convention).

She may be able to manage the finances and the household like a pro, but she will have little extra time for the tenderness and nurturing that her child desperately needs.

▢ She may have _____ order, but she will not be able to keep her thumb on the pulse of

her household, and more specifically on the pulse of her children's _____.

We have a higher calling. We want to nurture our children and we want to raise them up so that their hearts align with God.

▢ So _____ is the role of motherhood that the most important _____

role in a child's life is made to seem meaningless. Mothers who stay home with their children are

made to feel like they are _____ _____.

## III. *The State of Your Union*

Some of us have to work outside the home, but we must ask the hard question, "Am I away too much? Am I losing the pulse of my family?" That's a decision you and your husband must make and come to an "understanding and agreement". We can get entangled in so many things outside of the home. It can get easier to rely on extra income than it can be to rely on the Lord.

## IV. *Critical Choices*

Someday, what seemed so important to pull us out of the house really won't seem all that important. Are we showing our children that it is okay to be away from home? The bottom line is—to be apart divides. Too much separation separates. This sounds very obvious but the more you are apart from your children, the more distant you will be relationally.

▢ Children in Daycare Under the Age of One: In 1976–31% and in 1998–59%.

On October 24, 2000, I heard this quote on the evening news, "With all the accommodations now for working moms, there is no reason not to be working." No reason, except the number one reason, which is that we need to be there for our children. They went on to say that mothers are leaving home in record numbers. We feel the pressure of this, don't we?

The argument for working moms has always been that women had to work because of financial necessity, but that is not necessarily true. The Family and Work Institute stated that economic reasons are not the number one reason that women are leaving home. *Working Mother Magazine* (October, 2000) stated that the number one reason women are leaving home is "because they want to; they do not want to give up their careers."

---

**Proverbs 22:6**, "Train up a child in the way he should go,
Even when he is old he will not depart from it."

- To be made to think or feel that we are less important because we _____ our children over careers is a huge _____ of Satan.

- He is thrilled when women feel they need _____ than their children, husbands, and ministries to be _____.

Certainly we can do additional things, but are we doing those in place of being a significant person in our children's lives? I dedicate this lesson to all the mothers that need to be reminded of the significance that you have and the vital role you are playing in your children's lives. Just remember that it is a high privilege to be so intimately involved in the details of your child's life.

Sometimes we forget that our children are a miracle and that we are blessed by God to have them. Sometimes we forget that the rebirth of their spirits is a miracle and that we can actually love them with the love of Christ. We fall into the drudgery of the mundane. We get into a slump when we listen to what the world says that maybe we are not really necessary or maybe we really don't need to be at home. We start to believe a lie that we are not needed or valued in our child's life.

Sometimes when your children get older, they might make you feel that you are not valued. But you will see that your teenagers need you more than ever.

The unbelieving world proposes that children are better off in daycare than with their own mothers. I understand that daycare is a necessity for some mothers. But many are willing to put their children in daycare rather than just deal with the everyday details of a child's life. Remember the priority of "people over things" and "eternal over temporal".

I heard of a recent study concerning high school students from all over the country who excelled in a number of areas. They found just one factor that was common among them all. It was that they had dinner together as a family.

Dr. Brenda Hunter, psychologist and author of *Home by Choice: Raising Secure Children in an Insecure World*, says that the childcare crisis is really a crisis of the heart. What a child needs most to grow up is a healthy bond with his mother. She states that the child's hunger for his mother's presence is as strong as his physical hunger. We, as parents, know this is true.

## V. A Mother's Touch

Dr. Hunter says that warm bonds between child and mother are "societal gold". (Now don't think that I'm saying your child should never be apart from you because it is healthy for a child to be apart from his parents occasionally—for a few days or even a week at a time.)

Statistics show that children who are left with others (non-family) for several hours a week become highly independent, more interested in things than people, more interested in playing with toys than conversing with you, shun affection, avoid eye contact, and become more verbally aggressive.

Even when your children are older, they will still value your touch. Your physical touch is highly significant in your child's life. It is also the special things that you do for them in a certain way. Mom's ways represent comfort and security to them.

**1 Samuel 1-3:** A mother's touch in the story of Hannah & Samuel

- To think our children don't need our _____ from _____ to the time we _____ them is a tragedy.

- Don't let yourself believe that they have _____ the _____ for your hugs and kisses. Dr. Brenda Hunter says that we are raising a bumper crop of children growing up without _____ _____.

- She goes on to say that _____ comes from deep emotional deprivation and _____ of parental care, the very two things that society is telling us children can do without.

(Dr. Brenda Hunter, "The State of Childcare Today," CWA Convention, 1999)

Have you ever had a day when your baby was especially fussy and no matter what you did, it just didn't seem like the baby would settle down? You felt like you did not get anything accomplished! You may think that you wasted a day, but that was one of the most significant days in your baby's life! Because your baby needed you and you said, "I'm right here." And that night the baby slept great. And the next day they were back to their normal routine. Don't underestimate your presence. That day built security and comfort in your child.

---

**Proverbs 22:6**, "Train up a child in the way he should go,
Even when he is old he will not depart from it."

## VI. *The Tragedy of Abortion*

☐ _____ has devalued motherhood, but it has also devalued children. This is so evident

by the number of _____ performed in this country, _____ since

abortion was legalized in 1973. (In 2003, there were over 3,500 abortions per day, 146 per hour,

about one every 25 seconds.)

☐ Child abuse is up more than _____ since the legalization of abortion.

The following statistic from Focus on the Family states that an estimated 43% of American women will have at least one abortion by the age of 45. That is staggering!

This has got to be so devastating to the heart of a mother. If this has been a decision of your past, do not believe that it is the "unforgivable sin". You need to know that the Gospel is a message of hope and restoration. You do not have to live with that burden. You can give it over to Jesus and He will restore you. We must call it what it is before God and humble ourselves and confess it as sin, meaning "agreeing with God about what it was". We ask Him to restore us as we "turn away" from sinful choices—that is what repentance means. God promises to forgive you. There is a huge, heavy weight on women because of abortion and that weight can be lifted. It is *not* an "unforgivable sin".

☐ **Isaiah 5:20**
*Woe to those who call evil good, and good evil; who substitute darkness for light and light for darkness; who substitute bitter for sweet and sweet for bitter!*

## VII. *A Child's Best "Fifteen Minutes" of the Day*

Your child has a "prime 15-minutes a day" when they will really talk to you. It is different for each child—in the morning, after school, or before bedtime. It is those precious little moments when they are willing to talk to us that we want to be available and listen to them.

## VIII. Training Up a Child

We are not to coerce them into something that they are not, something that we choose them to be.

- [ ] We are to _____ them to place God _____ in their lives and watch how God

  _____ them to _____ _____ with their lives.

  Be ready because our choices are not necessarily God's choices. These things may not even be evident by the time they enter college.

- [ ] You will have trained them to _____ to God's authority in _____ circum-

  stances and to live by _____ _____ so that you can

  _____ in knowing God will place a special _____ on their lives.

- [ ] Still, we are their authority until we _____ them.

  It is really exciting and marvelous to watch what God will do in a child's life and who they will become. The world is trying to tell us that parents do not matter.

- [ ] But God says, "_____ do matter."

  We have been given something very, very significant to accomplish in the lives of our children. We are stewards of them.

## IX. The Nature of a Child

**Proverbs 22:6**
*Train up a child in the way he should go, Even when he is old he will not depart from it.*

The fact that children still exhibit individual traits is to be appreciated and enjoyed.

- [ ] We are created _____ from the rest of God's creation because we are created with a

  _____ and in His _____.

---

**Proverbs 22:6**, "Train up a child in the way he should go,
Even when he is old he will not depart from it."

**Genesis 1:27**

*God created man in His own image, in the image of God He created him, male and female He created them.*

▢ Our _____ in life is to _____ God and not ourselves. Life is

_____ about us, it is about _____. Our children's lives are _____ about them,

they are about _____.

▢ A child-centered home _____ with the goal of always _____ the child

_____. But this will create a child with an _____ and _____ view of

_____.

▢ **Galatians 6:3**

*For if anyone thinks he is something when he is nothing, he deceives himself.*

**Romans 7:18**

*For I know that nothing good dwells in me, that is, in my flesh; for the willing is present in me, but the doing of good is not.*

**Matthew 7:41**

*Keep watching and praying that you may not enter into temptation, the spirit is willing, but the flesh is weak.*

These verses show that we really have an intrinsic desire to worship God, to attribute worth to Him. This is what we need to be pointing our children to. We also need to remember that our children have a sin nature that needs to be controlled. When a child grows up with this understanding, they will not center the world around themselves, but they will place God on the throne of their lives.

▢ If we give our children too many _____, then we are really providing them with

_____ to be _____ – _____, especially in the early years.

▢ To continually _____ children to be thinking about what would _____

them to a tee at that very moment is _____ self-centeredness to make a _____

in your child's _____.

▢ Their hearts are to be _____ to God and to their parents' _____.

They will learn _____ loyalties if they are given a smorgasbord of

_____ every time a _____ is to be made.

☐ And they will grow up _____ _____ your authority because they will not see

you being _____ but rather always passing the choice on to them.

☐ In the moment, it seems like we are being _____. But the long view, the twenty-year view, is

that we will _____ a _____ - _____ young adult.

☐ The Bible tells us that we have all _____ a sinful nature through Adam.

☐ **Romans 5:12**
*Therefore, just as through one man sin entered into the world, and death through sin, and so death spread to all men, because all sinned.*

No one is innocent before God, even at birth.

☐ **Romans 3:10**
*There is none righteous, not even one...*

This sinful nature does not necessarily show itself immediately but it probably will by about six months.
You will learn that even though he does not necessarily use words, he can still be demanding and attempt to assert his will.

☐ Soon you will see that they want to do things _____ way.

☐ _____ defiance gets a spank.

☐ Simple _____ brings the event of discipline _____ _____ so that the child

understands what they did that was _____ and what the _____ behavior is.

☐ They are also _____ that you love them. And now they know that you have set a little

_____ for them not to _____.

---

**Proverbs 22:6**, "Train up a child in the way he should go,
Even when he is old he will not depart from it."

▢ And when the situation comes up again, you will handle it _____ the same

way, because they will _____ that you are _____ and they must

_____.

For little ones, we will start out with just one or two things that we can see that they need to be trained in.

▢ As our children grow older, we are _____ that they have a _____

_____.

▢ It helps to remind us of the importance of _____ discipline; that discipline has a

distinct _____ of _____ that sin nature.

We are not sinners because we sin; we sin because we are sinners.

▢ **Additional verses about:**

| **MAN'S SIN NATURE:** | **THE "GOODNESS" OF MAN:** |
| --- | --- |
| **Isaiah 6:5** | **Luke 18:19** |
| **Jeremiah 2:35** | **Romans 7:18** |
| **Jeremiah 11:8** | **Romans 3:12** |
| **Romans 3:23** | |

▢ When they _____ the Lord Jesus, they become partakers in His _____

_____, but there are still those years and years of _____ to teach them

to _____ _____ their fleshly nature and to _____ _____ the divine

nature modeled by Christ.

▢ **2 Peter 1:3-4**
*Seeing that His divine power has granted to us everything pertaining to life and godliness, through the true knowledge of Him who called us by His own glory and excellence. For by these He has granted to us His precious and magnificent promises, so that by them you may become partakers of the divine nature, having escaped the corruption that is in the world by lust.*

Notes:

---

**Proverbs 22:6**, "Train up a child in the way he should go,
Even when he is old he will not depart from it."

# *Homefront Application*

## A MOTHER'S TOUCH
## AND THE NATURE OF A CHILD
A godly mother understands the significance of her role

1. Think about each of your children. Can you identify their "15 most important minutes of the day," that time when they are most likely to open up and share their thoughts? For some kids it may be the same time everyday, for others it may "jump around," and for some it may be 60 minutes! If you can't think of it, you could be missing it. If you can identify it, make a special effort to be available at those key times. These are special teaching and bonding moments.

2. Reread *2 Peter 1:3-4* and meditate on what it means to be partakers of His divine nature.

3. Be encouraged this week as you quietly notice how your family values your "touch."

## I CHOOSE TO LIVE BY CONVICTIONS.

Signature: _____    Date: _____

# Lesson 7 Outline

## ESTABLISHING AUTHORITY, PART ONE
## THE FEAR OF GOD

A godly mother establishes authority in her child's life

I. Effective Training Requires a System

II. Establishing Parental Authority

    A. A Condition of the Heart

    B. Setting the Foundation Early

    C. When Parental Authority Ends

III. Releasing Children from Parental Authority

    A. Signs of Readiness

    B. "Parents for Life"

IV. Starting Point: The Fear of the Lord

    A. Stepping Under or Stepping Out

    B. God's Authority

V. Training Children to Fear God

    A. Eradicating the Weed of Rebellion

    B. The Importance of the Father's Role

    C. Moving from Authority to Guidance

    D. Conclusion

VI. The Lord's Provision for Those Who Fear Him

## This week's Scripture memory verse:

**Hebrews 12:11**, "All discipline for the moment seems not to be joyful, but sorrowful;
yet to those who have been trained by it, afterwards it yields the peaceful fruit of righteousness."

**Philippians 2:14**, "Do all things without grumbling or disputing."

# *Lesson 7*

## ESTABLISHING AUTHORITY, PART ONE
## THE FEAR OF GOD
### A godly mother establishes authority in her child's life

## 1. *Effective Training Requires a System*

Training is a necessary part of life. It is necessary that we train our children and it is necessary that we have a system to do it. Even if we do nothing, we are still training our children, but they will probably be trained in ways we do *not* want them to be trained.

We want to have a proper system to train them in God's ways, because the bottom line is we want to raise our children not merely to be Christians, but to be effective "Kingdom Workers" for God. We can train them to sleep through the night, or we can train them not to sleep through the night. We can train them to obey us the very first time or we can train them to wait until the tenth time. We can train them to ask for twenty things before they go to bed. We can train them to rule the house. Obviously, we want to train them in God's ways.

*All discipline for the moment seems not to be joyful, but sorrowful.* That will go through your head, many, many times through the years. Your children will not necessarily grasp everything you train them in when they are young. You will still be working on things when they are teenagers. You will think, "This is still not joyful".

We are looking for that "peaceful fruit of righteousness" that we will eventually obtain when we have effectively trained our children.

**Three dangers to watch out for in training a child:**

☐ **1.** Starting too early when they are not developmentally ready.

☐ **2.** Starting too late so that you have to undo poor habits or training.

☐ **3.** Inconsistency in training so that the child isn't really learning what you are trying to teach them.

Along with consistency, we will need persistence. Sometimes we say, "I do not think that what I am doing is working." That is because effective training requires a lot of time *and* repetition!

## II. Establishing Parental Authority

### A. A Condition of the Heart

☐ Just as in the area of child training, the understanding of and respect for authority is not

_____.

☐ If we do not carefully train them in this area, it will not just _____ as they grow up.

Certain developmental changes will automatically happen, but respecting authority is not one of them. That is why it is key that in the first years of life we train them in that. You can get older and still not respect authority.

☐ Society says that if we just "love them enough" _____ everything will all work out.

☐ But submission to authority and selfishness are not a matter of _____, but rather

conditions of the _____.

☐ Selfish, defiant children are struggling to define life _____ from God when the very

thing they need to learn to do is _____ on God.

### B. Setting the Foundation Early

☐ The _____ this all begins the better, which is just the _____ of the way

society would have us think.

**Ecclesiates 11:9**
_Rejoice, young man, during your childhood, and let your heart be pleasant during the days of young manhood. And follow the impulses of your heart and the desires of your eyes. Yet know that God will bring you to judgment for all these things._

---

**Hebrews 12:11**, "All discipline for the moment seems not to be joyful, but sorrowful; yet to those who have been trained by it, afterwards it yields the peaceful fruit of righteousness."

**Philippians 2:14**, "Do all things without grumbling or disputing."

Youth is the time of life when we are more carefree and we get to enjoy things more. But if taken too far, we will be judged for our foolish choices, and will suffer consequences for them.

⌨ It is our _____ to be in authority over them, knowing that God is in authority _____

us. That part never _____. But our authority over our children _____.

## C.  When Parental Authority Ends

When does our authority over our children end? Does it end at age eighteen, which is when our American culture and governing authorities tell us that they are "legal adults"? Do we allow them to grow up thinking that at age eighteen they can do whatever they want?

We must guard against this mindset because none of us ever get to do whatever we want. We all live under God's authority. We do not want our children to begin to emotionally separate themselves as teenagers from our family. Then by their eighteenth birthday, they cannot wait to get out of the house and get away from you. There is no unity in that.

One way parental authority ends would be when your children get married.

⌨ **Genesis 2:24**

*For this reason a man shall leave his father and his mother, and be joined to his wife; and they shall become one flesh.*

One of the things we want our children to be is "morally mature" before we release them.

How about a young adult that is older than eighteen and unmarried?

⌨ They live under our authority as parents until the father _____ them.

⌨ **Galatians 4:1-2**

*Now I say, as long as the heir is a child, he does not differ at all from a slave although he is owner of everything, but he is under guardians and managers until the date set by the father.*

## III. Releasing Children from Parental Authority

### A. Signs of Readiness

☐ As parents we _____ for certain signs that demonstrate that they are

_____ to be released:

☐ 1. Strong biblical _____ — they will _____ true to the things of God

whether you are _____ or_____.

☐ 2. _____ moral, emotional, intellectual, social, and physical maturity so that they

can manage life _____ of your household.

Do not throw your young adult into an impossible situation. Work with them so they learn to be responsible. Many of these skills are learned while they are still at home. Let them learn from their mistakes under your guidance.

☐ 3. Demonstrate the ability to _____ support themselves.

They cannot be financially dependent on Mom and Dad and expect to be released. They are still under your authority as long as you are financing them.

☐ Don't _____ a child who is _____ to be released.

If you realize there are ways in which your child is not yet ready to be released, work on them but do not teach them to be dependent on you. At the same time, do not exasperate a young adult who is "ready" to be living on their own.

---

**Hebrews 12:11,** "All discipline for the moment seems not to be joyful, but sorrowful; yet to those who have been trained by it, afterwards it yields the peaceful fruit of righteousness."

**Philippians 2:14,** "Do all things without grumbling or disputing."

## B.  "Parents for Life"

Our American culture tends to fund the reckless living of teens from the ages of about thirteen to eighteen or twenty. There is no cultural or biblical precedent for this situation. Throughout history, children in their early teens worked for their parents or learned to support themselves. They were much more responsible than some of the kids in our culture.

Although the government has established eighteen years as the legal age of independence, for family and relational purposes, we want to continue to develop closeness with our children, even after they have moved away.

Tragically, too many kids get the philosophy from the culture that says, "Hey, I am going to do whatever I want when I am eighteen!" This is a travesty against the family. It starts to divide and separate.

In this class, we generally use the age of about twenty years old when we release our children because they are typically around twenty-two or so when they finish college. Most kids, because of the high expense of college in the United States, cannot afford to be financially independent from their parents before then.

Some of their desires to be more independent and self-sufficient are founded and legitimate because they are growing up and maturing, so help them in those things. We are not talking about controlling their lives. We are working towards releasing them from our authority so that they will stand on their own. But we are their parents for life and that is a sweet dynamic because we always want them to come back.

⬚  Once we have the ability to understand, we are _____ for what we believe.

## IV.  Starting Point: The Fear of the Lord

⬚  **Numbers 14:26-29, 31**
*The Lord spoke to Moses and Aaron, saying, "How long shall I bear with this evil congregation who are grumbling against Me? I have heard the complaints of the sons of Israel, which they are making against Me. Say to them, 'As I live,' says the Lord, 'just as you have spoken in My hearing, so I will surely do to you; your corpses will fall in this wilderness, even all your numbered men (soldiers), according to your complete number from twenty years old and upward, who have grumbled against Me. Your children, however, whom you said would become a prey—I will bring them in, and they will know the land which you have rejected.'"*

God judged the people over twenty years old because He knew that they could judge between good and evil.

☐ The Lord was demonstrating to this new _____ what He desired from them, that

they _____ without _____, in essence that they learn the _____

of God.

☐ Our fear of God requires, first of all, that we _____ who He is, that He can do whatever He

pleases, and that He is _____ in authority over us.

## A. Stepping Under or Stepping Out

☐ It is actually a _____ thing to step outside of that authority because as we grow we learn

that the relationship of authority affords security and protection.

☐ Since we know that God is loving and _____ we trust His authority over us as

_____.

This says that part of fearing God is not having to live in fear of other things. Are you fearful of something in your life? That fear is pushing aside your fear of God. The fear of God dispels all other fears.

**Hebrews 10:26-31**

*For if we go on sinning willfully after receiving the knowledge of the truth, there no longer remains a sacrifice for sins, but a terrifying expectation of judgment and THE FURY OF A FIRE WHICH WILL CONSUME THE ADVERSARIES. Anyone who has set aside the Law of Moses dies without mercy on the testimony of two or three witnesses. How much severer punishment do you think he will deserve who has trampled under foot the Son of God, and has regarded as unclean the blood of the covenant by which he was sanctified, and has insulted the Spirit of grace? For we know Him who said, "VENGEANCE IS MINE, I WILL REPAY." And again, "THE LORD WILL JUDGE HIS PEOPLE." It is a terrifying thing to fall into the hands of the living God.*

---

**Hebrews 12:11**, "All discipline for the moment seems not to be joyful, but sorrowful; yet to those who have been trained by it, afterwards it yields the peaceful fruit of righteousness."

**Philippians 2:14**, "Do all things without grumbling or disputing."

▢ This passage refers to the _____, the person who has blatantly rejected the _____, though they have heard the _____.

▢ As a result, there is _____ other way for them to be _____.

They may even seem to have been on the verge of accepting Christ, yet they deliberately reject Him and choose habitual sin with no regard for God's ultimate authority over them.

▢ They _____ salvation. They have no fear of God, though they should be "_____".

## B. God's Authority

▢ The word authority comes from the word _____, meaning, "one who _____ or gives _____".

▢ He is the _____ of our existence, and His _____ position is one of authority.

### Isaiah 45:9-10

*Woe to the one who quarrels with his Maker—An earthenware vessel among the vessels of the earth! Will the clay say to the potter, 'What are you doing?' Or the thing you are making say, 'He has no hands'? Woe to him who says to a father, 'What are you begetting?' Or to a woman, 'To what are you giving birth?'*

**Example of Job**: When we question God, we are questioning His authority over us. He is God and does as He pleases. We just need to trust Him in every situation.

Is there anything in our lives that we are not trusting God with, that we are fearful of and holding onto, that we will not let Him have His way with in our lives? Do we question Him, shake our fists at Him and ask, "How dare you do that in my life?"

▢ This is the Old Testament version of a child saying, "What do you _____ you're doing?" or "You can't _____ me what to do."

## V. *Training Children to Fear God*

### A. Respecting Parental Authority

☐ This kind of _____ is an _____ to God and should also be an

_____ to us as parents.

☐ We are to have _____ tolerance for _____, _____ speech. It is to

be addressed _____ time and not overlooked.

☐ It is a _____ that must be pulled from day one. If this weed is allowed to grow at

all, it will _____ become an _____ weed patch that will take great

_____ to dig out.

### B. The Importance of the Father's Role

☐ _____ especially need to address this very strongly with children, so that they know

without a _____, one _____ or _____ word has their dad's

(parent's) _____ attention.

This is absolutely out of bounds and an affront to your authority. It is okay for your kids to be afraid of crossing the line of your authority. It is healthy. It is protective. It is security.

"We love you, but we mean business"

### C. Moving from Authority to Guidance

☐ When children are born they have _____ authority and we control _____ in

their lives. We have _____ authority.

---

**Hebrews 12:11,** "All discipline for the moment seems not to be joyful, but sorrowful;
yet to those who have been trained by it, afterwards it yields the peaceful fruit of righteousness."

**Philippians 2:14,** "Do all things without grumbling or disputing."

▢ As infants, they are _____ to do anything for themselves. As they grow older and we

train them as they are developmentally able in certain areas, we step back and _____ their

_____.

▢ At these times we use more _____ and less authority.

▢ The _____ comes when parents let up on authority too _____ or if they hold

on tight to authority too _____.

▢ In the first instance, they will begin giving _____ when the child is far too young.

**Ezekiel 2:8b**
*Open your mouth and eat what I am giving you.*

▢ Authority needs to remain close to 90-100% until the age of _____.

▢ We want to establish a solid _____ and we want them to thoroughly respect the

_____ authorities that they will be encountering like school teachers, coaches, instructors,

and officials.

If we let up on authority too young, they will treat all authorities like they are learning to treat us—disrespectfully or too casually. If they do not respect our authority, they are not learning to respect other authorities, even if they outwardly display the right behavior. Inwardly, if they have not learned to respect authority, it is not going to hold. We can force them (within reason) to do anything physically, but we want to be working on their hearts. We want their hearts to be surrendered to us and ultimately to the Lord.

If they get too comfortable and start to see authorities as peers, they are going to think, "They are here to meet my demands." Have you ever known a person (child or adult) that thought that? They view themselves as being above authority. As they grow older, they will have little regard for rules or boundaries.

▢ _____ also have to have a high regard and respect for authority. If we don't, we can't

_____ our children to do so.

### D. Conclusion

⬜ **Proverbs 9:10**

*The fear of the Lord is the beginning of wisdom, and the knowledge of the Holy One is understanding.*

⬜ So our _____ point is the fear of God.

Many parents would like to skip this part. They do not want to instill hard boundaries with their children when they are young. That just seems so "mean" or authoritarian. But that is failing to build the foundation when they are so receptive and ready to learn. We need to do this or they are not going to learn a healthy fear of stepping over the line of their parents' authority, let alone God's. It all must start very young.

⬜ And since our children learn about who their Heavenly Father is through our _____, we are placed as their authority to teach them what it means to fear God.

⬜ Part of this comes from fearing and _____ us as parents.

In the spiritual sense, sometimes we have to "dive-tackle" our kids. It is so much easier to set this in place when they are young. You have to intervene on their behalf to rescue them from danger, from a course of certain tragedy, and place them on the proper course. That is what discipline is—setting up authority and the fear of God in a child's life. We do not want them to grow up thinking they can keep edging closer to the guardrail. This is what they will do if we do not get this principle firmly in place. It is a response of rescuing, redirecting and loving a child.

If a child learns that Mom and Dad just try to reason and rationalize with them in everything that they do, they have no frame of reference as to the outward limits of any particular behavior. If Mom and Dad never come down hard on anything, they will have no fear of testing limits, or inching to the edge of the cliff.

If the fear of God and his parents' discipline does not become a secure part of a child's foundation, you will end up with a child that not only tests the limits, but is determined to "run in front of a truck" or stand on the brink of calamity. How many times have we seen parents "standing at the edge of the street" watching their teen heading for sure tragedy and they feel completely powerless to do anything? Rescue your child, even as a teenager! If this training has not happened yet, you have to start now. Intervene strongly while there is hope.

⬜ **Exodus 20:20**

*Moses said to the people, "Do not be afraid; for God has come in order to test you, and in order that the fear of Him may remain with you, so that you may not sin."*

---

**Hebrews 12:11**, "All discipline for the moment seems not to be joyful, but sorrowful; yet to those who have been trained by it, afterwards it yields the peaceful fruit of righteousness."

**Philippians 2:14**, "Do all things without grumbling or disputing."

⬜ Here the fear of God protects us from _____.

⬜ It is this fundamental understanding of who God is and His _____ in our lives that

will have a major impact on the _____ our children's lives go.

They have to understand that their sin and disobedience is actually an offense against a holy God, for which they will reap the consequences.

⬜ **2 Corinthians 5:10**
*For we must all appear before the judgment seat of Christ, so that each one may be recompensed for his deeds in the body, according to what he has done, whether good or bad.*

**Ecclesiastes 12:13**
*The conclusion, when all has been heard, is: fear God and keep His commandments, because this applies to every person.*

## VI. The Lord's Provision for Those Who Fear Him

You may wonder, "Does God see me, the average person, and bless me for my belief in Him? I'm in a really hard situation; I'm the only believer in my family. Does God really bless me? I don't feel blessed. Does it really make a difference?" This part of the lesson is for anyone in a difficult situation, that you would take to heart this last section.

Even if you are the only person who believes in your entire household, God says, "I see you." It matters to Him that you fear God and He wants to bless your household because of it. I hope this truth changes your life forever.

⬜ **1 Corinthians 7:13-14** (NKJV)
*And a woman who has a husband who does not believe, if he is willing to live with her, let her not divorce him. For the unbelieving husband is sanctified by the wife, and the unbelieving wife is sanctified by the husband; otherwise your children would be unclean, but now they are holy.*

God protects your household and your family in certain ways. Some of those "secret things that belong to God" (**Deuteronomy 29:29**), He does for you, even if you are the only believer in your family. God pours out a blessing on the believer and His grace to you actually spills over to the rest of the family and keeps them from undue spiritual harm. Only when we get to heaven will we really know what this entails. God extends special protection over the family on behalf of the believer. So God says, "Don't leave the household, even though it is difficult (unless there is a potentially harmful and dangerous situation by which you have to leave)."

**7.12**

Look up the following verses in your small group and write down some of the specific blessings that God has for those who truly fear Him:

1.  Deuteronomy 10:20-21

    _____

    _____

2.  Psalm 15:1-4; Proverbs 16:6; 2 Corinthians 7:1

    _____

    _____

3.  Psalm 25:12

    _____

4.  Psalm 25:13

    _____

5.  Psalm 25:14

    _____

6.  Psalm 31:19

    _____

7.  Psalm 34:7

    _____

8.  Psalm 67:7

    _____

9.  Psalm 103:11-13, 17

    _____

    _____

    _____

**Hebrews 12:11**, "All discipline for the moment seems not to be joyful, but sorrowful; yet to those who have been trained by it, afterwards it yields the peaceful fruit of righteousness."

**Philippians 2:14**, "Do all things without grumbling or disputing."

10. Psalm 111:5

_____

11. Psalm 112:1-2

_____

12. Psalm 112:5-8

_____

_____

13. Psalm 115:11

_____

14. Psalm 128:1-4

_____

_____

15. Psalm 145:19

_____

16. Psalm 147:11

_____

17. Proverbs 3:7-8

_____

18. Proverbs 9:10

_____

19. Proverbs 14:26

_____

20. Proverbs 15:16; Proverbs 19:23

_____

21. Isaiah 33:6

_____

22. Jeremiah 32:39

_____

23. Acts 10:35

_____

24. 2 Corinthians 5:11

_____

_____

**Hebrews 12:11**, "All discipline for the moment seems not to be joyful, but sorrowful;
yet to those who have been trained by it, afterwards it yields the peaceful fruit of righteousness."

**Philippians 2:14**, "Do all things without grumbling or disputing."

# Homefront Application

## ESTABLISHING AUTHORITY, PART ONE
## THE FEAR OF GOD

A godly mother establishes authority in her child's life

1. Have a chat with your husband and consider each of your children. Do they have respect for authority? For the God-given authorities in their lives and for God Himself? (This question applies to older children.)

2. Beyond just standards, do your children have a healthy fear of crossing certain boundaries or do they often "push the envelope" of your limits? Do they see sin as an offense against a holy God, not merely something their parents don't want them to do? Do you set strong limits or do you need to reestablish some boundaries? Don't believe that they are too old to have the boundaries tightened if you know it is what your family really needs. Remember, you are rescuing them from testing the limits to the edge of the cliff. Now is the time.

3. In regards to the three dangers in training, can you identify an area of training that is a struggle with your young children? Can you identify why the training is ineffective?

## I CHOOSE TO LIVE BY CONVICTIONS.

Signature: _____  Date: _____

# *Lesson 8 Outline*

## ESTABLISHING AUTHORITY, PART TWO:
## THE REIGN OF CHRIST IN THE HEART OF MAN

A godly mother trains her children to see God as their lifelong authority

I.     Resisting God's Authority: The Arrogance of the World

II.    Submitting to God's Authority

III.   When it's Hard for Parents to Let Go

IV.    Justice and Mercy

V.     God's Blessings to Those Who Fear Him

VI.    Consequences of Living Outside of God's Authority

VII.   Parental Responsibilities

## *This week's Scripture memory verse:*

**Psalm 147:10-11,** "He does not delight in the strength of the horse;
He does not take pleasure in the legs of a man. The LORD favors those who fear Him,
those who wait for His lovingkindness."

**Lamentations 3:27,** "It is good for a man that he should bear the yoke in his youth."

# Lesson 8

## ESTABLISHING AUTHORITY, PART TWO:
## THE REIGN OF CHRIST IN THE HEART OF MAN
### A godly mother trains her children to see God as their lifelong authority

### 1. Resisting God's Authority: The Arrogance of the World

There is only one Giver and Creator of life, one Lord—it is Jesus Christ. No matter what scientific advances man may make, this is still true. When an athiest claims to *know* that "there is no god", what he is really saying is, "I know *everything*, therefore I know that there is no god." God is not threatened in the least by these claims; they are arrogance before God and foolishness to Him.

Every _____ and _____ thought lifted up by man ultimately stems

from the _____ that man worships that which is _____ over the Creator.

He places himself equal with God.

**Romans 1:25**
*For they exchanged the truth of God for a lie, and worshiped and served the creature rather than the Creator, who is blessed forever. Amen.*

This lesson is about fearing God, rather than creatures. Satan is also a creature. People may think that there is God and there is Satan; that there is good and there is evil and that they are equal in some way. There is no equality between God and Satan. God is infinitely more powerful and omniscient. Satan is merely a created being.

God is not _____ by what we think we can do. Even our _____ ideas are

insignificant before Him. He is not interested in our accomplishments or _____.

What _____ Him is a proper perspective of _____ _____ _____;

that we _____ Him.

**Psalm 147:10-11**
*He does not delight in the strength of the horse; He does not take pleasure in the legs of a man. The LORD favors those who fear Him, those who wait for His lovingkindness.*

Now when you think about that, you can think about all the wonderful ways God gifts us and the wonderful things we do in this life. But what really delights the heart of God is that you recognize Him for who He is.

God instructs us not to be _____ in our thinking.

**2 Corinthians 10:5**
*We are destroying speculations and every lofty thing raised up against the knowledge of God, and we are taking every thought captive to the obedience of Christ.*

Do you have some thoughts that "run away"? We can take every thought captive to the obedience of Christ.

People who are "_____ _____," who philosophize _____ the realm of

the knowledge of God, are actually _____ to every counterfeit devised.

Even though they see themselves as "free", nothing could be further from the truth. They are captive and enslaved to every counterfeit.

Living a life of victory is really living a life of surrender. Can you say, "The thing that is happening in my life, it is okay with me because I know that you are sovereignly in control over it."

## II. Submitting to God's Authority

Without the _____ of God in our lives we cannot possibly _____ God,

and He will not _____ us.

This is a major theme of the Bible. We do our children a grave injustice if we do not teach them this when they are very young, that they need to live under authority. Christ reigns forever. We are never past the point of being under His authority. We need to hold onto this as a good thing and not fight against it!

The child who quickly learns this _____ of God will _____ a life of blessing.

---

**Psalm 147:10-11,** "He does not delight in the strength of the horse;
He does not take pleasure in the legs of a man. The LORD favors those who fear Him,
those who wait for His lovingkindness."

**Lamentations 3:27,** "It is good for a man that he should bear the yoke in his youth."

**Colossians 1:15-19**

*He is the image of the invisible God, the firstborn of all creation. For by Him all things were created, both in the heavens and on earth, visible and invisible, whether thrones or dominions or rulers or authorities—all things have been created through Him and for Him. He is before all things, and in Him all things hold together. He is also head of the body, the church; and He is the beginning, the firstborn from the dead, so that He Himself will come to have first place in everything. For it was the Father's good pleasure for all the fullness to dwell in Him.*

## III. When it's Hard for Parents to Let Go

**Lamentations 3:27**

*It is good for a man that he should bear the yoke in his youth.*

There is a great sense of accomplishment and satisfaction in hard work. It is good for us to have that and for our children to learn how to work physically hard. Children must learn this if they are going to experience the blessing that it brings..

Our husbands know when our sons need to "bear the yoke". Sometimes as moms, we want to coddle our kids. We have to be able to step back and let our husbands teach our sons to be men. To be strong men, they must learn to "bear the yoke" when they are young. Both boys and girls need hard lessons to mature.

We _____ our children from years of _____ if they _____ this yoke in their youth. God says that this is "_____" and as it should be.

Children who _____ learn to submit to their parents also learn to submit to teachers, employers, and other authorities.

The person who does _____ learn this, but _____ him/herself and continually _____ authority will have a life of grief that will _____ all those around them.

Thank goodness for husbands who train our sons to become men. They provide the balance for our tender side. Both sides are necessary and that is why we must work together.

Sometimes our children will have to go through heavy trials, either by their choice or God's choice. God chooses trials for our children in order to grow them up. They have to learn to bear the yoke.

## IV. Justice and Mercy

Here is an important principle to remember in this area of establishing authority: The person who understands authority looks for justice to be done. They are not looking for a way out of the consequences they earned. "Justice" is receiving the correct and exact reward or punishment that I earned. But "mercy" is *not* receiving the punishment that I earned. If somebody gives me mercy but I do not understand what I am receiving mercy from, then I will never truly understand mercy. I will never truly understand that I am being delivered from a punishment that I have earned.

When a mother decides not to discipline a child because it is "more loving" to show mercy, she is actually doing the child a disservice. If authority is not truly established, he will grow up not expecting justice, consequences, discipline or any type of punishment. Instead, he will always expect to be "let off".

On the other hand, when they have learned that what they have done is a sin against God and their parents, they will expect justice. When they have come to that point, then we can give mercy. The key is that we see our sin as God sees it and then accept the just consequence. This is the essence of humbling our hearts before God and establishing authority.

### 2 Chronicles 16:9
*For the eyes of the LORD run to and fro throughout the whole earth, to give strong support to those whose heart is blameless toward Him.*

To have a blameless heart means to be in "right standing with God", to be "not guilty" before Him.

## V. God's Blessings to Those Who Fear Him

God is _____ and _____ to those who fear Him, but those who do

not are _____ to every sort of _____ because they walk away from His

_____.

---

Psalm 147:10-11, "He does not delight in the strength of the horse;
He does not take pleasure in the legs of a man. The LORD favors those who fear Him,
those who wait for His lovingkindness."

Lamentations 3:27, "It is good for a man that he should bear the yoke in his youth."

**8.5**

We have a relationship with our Heavenly Father. It is one in which we are to abide or remain with Him. When we choose to walk away from our Heavenly Father, He is still our Father, even though we put "a break" in the fellowship. We all will go through tragedies and crises in our lifetimes. But walking with God through them makes the difference.

**His _____ to those who fear Him:**

1.  **Deuteronomy 10:20-21**
    *You shall fear the LORD your God; you shall serve Him and cling to Him, and you shall swear by His name. He is your praise and He is your God, who has done these great and awesome things for you which your eyes have seen.*

    They see God do _____ things in their lives and the _____ and

    _____ go to Him.

2.  **Psalm 15:1-4**
    *O LORD, who may abide in Your tent? Who may dwell on Your holy hill? He who walks with integrity, and works righteousness, and speaks truth in his heart. He does not slander with his tongue, nor does evil to his neighbor, nor takes up a reproach against his friend; in whose eyes a reprobate is despised, but who honors those who fear the LORD. . .*

    **Proverbs 16:6**
    *By lovingkindness and truth iniquity is atoned for, and by the fear of the LORD one keeps away from evil.*

    **2 Corinthians 7:1**
    *Therefore, having these promises, beloved, let us cleanse ourselves from all defilement of flesh and spirit, perfecting holiness in the fear of God.*

    They _____ with God, resulting in righteous living that keeps them from evil.

3.  **Psalm 25:12**
    *Who is the man who fears the LORD? He will instruct him in the way he should choose.*

    They experience God's guidance in making wise _____.

4.  **Psalm 25:13**
    *His soul will abide in prosperity, and his descendants will inherit the land.*

    They experience the _____ life in Christ and are rich in the things of God.

5. **Psalm 25:14**

   *The secret of the LORD is for those who fear Him, and He will make them know His covenant.*

   They are able to have true _____ with Him.

6. **Psalm 31:19**

   *How great is Your goodness, which You have stored up for those who fear You, which You have wrought for those who take refuge in You, before the sons of men!*

   They receive God's _____, which He actually _____ up for them.

7. **Psalm 34:7**

   *The angel of the LORD encamps around those who fear Him, and rescues them.*

   They are _____ by Him and receive His assurance that He is always

   _____.

8. **Psalm 67:7**

   *God blesses us, that all the ends of the earth may fear Him.*

   They are blessed for the purpose of becoming His _____ to the world.

9. **Psalm 103:11-13, 17**

   *For as high as the heavens are above the earth, so great is His lovingkindness toward those who fear Him. As far as the east is from the west, so far has He removed our transgressions from us. Just as a father has compassion on his children, so the LORD has compassion on those who fear Him . . . But the lovingkindness of the LORD is from everlasting to everlasting on those who fear Him, and His righteousness to children's children.*

   They receive His _____ for their sins and His _____ extends

   even to their children's children.

10. **Psalm 111:5**

    *He has given food to those who fear Him; He will remember His covenant forever.*

    They receive the promise of God that He will _____ provide for their

    _____.

---

Psalm 147:10-11, "He does not delight in the strength of the horse;
He does not take pleasure in the legs of a man. The LORD favors those who fear Him,
those who wait for His lovingkindness."

Lamentations 3:27, "It is good for a man that he should bear the yoke in his youth."

**11. Psalm 112:1-2**

*Praise the LORD! How blessed is the man who fears the LORD, who greatly delights in His commandments. His descendants will be mighty on earth; the generation of the upright will be blessed.*

They receive the multiplied blessing of their obedience to _____ generations.

**12. Psalm 112:5-8**

*It is well with the man who is gracious and lends; he will maintain his cause in judgment. For he will never be shaken; the righteous will be remembered forever. He will not fear evil tidings; his heart is steadfast, trusting in the LORD. His heart is upheld, he will not fear, until he looks with satisfaction on his adversaries.*

They are _____ from all other _____ through their obedience to God.

**13. Psalm 115:11**

*You who fear the LORD, trust in the LORD; He is their help and their shield.*

They receive intervention and _____ from God.

**14. Psalm 128:1-4**

*How blessed is everyone who fears the LORD, who walks in His ways. When you shall eat of the fruit of your hands, You will be happy and it will be well with you. Your wife shall be like a fruitful vine within your house, Your children like olive plants around your table. Behold, for thus shall the man be blessed who fears the LORD.*

They truly _____ their families, and the Lord blesses their _____.

**15. Psalm 145:19**

*He will fulfill the desire of those who fear Him; He will also hear their cry and will save them.*

They _____ out to God and He _____ their prayers.

**16. Psalm 147:11**

*The LORD favors those who fear Him, those who wait for His lovingkindness.*

They are _____ by God for their patience and hope in Him.

### 17. Proverbs 3:7-8

*Do not be wise in your own eyes; fear the LORD and turn away from evil. It will be healing to your body and refreshment to your bones.*

They have their _____ preserved as they keep away from evil.

### 18. Proverbs 9:10

*The fear of the LORD is the beginning of wisdom; and the knowledge of the Holy One is understanding.*

They receive _____ and understanding from God Himself.

### 19. Proverbs 14:26

*In the fear of the LORD there is strong confidence, and his children will have refuge.*

They are _____ and secure in Him.

### 20. Proverbs 15:16

*Better is a little with the fear of the LORD than great treasure and turmoil with it.*

### Proverbs 19:23

*The fear of the LORD leads to life, so that one may sleep satisfied, untouched by evil.*

They experience satisfaction, _____ and peace from knowing that God is sovereign.

### 21. Isaiah 33:6

*And He will be the stability of your times, a wealth of salvation, wisdom and knowledge; the fear of the LORD is his treasure.*

They experience stability, _____ and purpose in _____ through knowing Him.

### 22. Jeremiah 32:39

*. . . and I will give them one heart and one way, that they may fear Me always, for their own good and for the good of their children after them.*

They are unified as _____ and assured that He watches out for their good.

---

**Psalm 147:10-11,** "He does not delight in the strength of the horse;
He does not take pleasure in the legs of a man. The LORD favors those who fear Him,
those who wait for His lovingkindness."

**Lamentations 3:27,** "It is good for a man that he should bear the yoke in his youth."

### 23. Acts 10:35

*But in every nation the man who fears Him and does what is right is welcome to Him.*

They humble themselves before God and are unified in the body of Christ, the _____,

the world over.

### 24. 2 Corinthians 5:11

*Therefore, knowing the fear of the Lord, we persuade men, but we are made manifest to God; and I hope that we are made manifest also in your consciences.*

They live life with an _____ perspective and a compassion for the lost.

This is just a list of 24 blessings and we can add and add and add to it! Be sure to review this list from time to time and think, "These are the things that God gives to me". Do I really even see them? They are amazing! They are amazing blessings here on earth that we have right now.

### Psalm 68:19 (NKJV)

*Blessed be the Lord, Who daily loads us with benefits, the God of our salvation!*

We put Him _____ and He _____ loads us with benefits, first and foremost

being salvation.

So great are His benefits to those who fear Him. But what about those who don't fear Him?

### Proverbs 3:5-6

*Trust in the LORD with all your heart and do not lean on your own understanding. In all your ways acknowledge Him and He will make your paths straight.*

We do our best, but ultimately we must learn to put our trust in the Lord. Otherwise, we feel the pressure to figure out every detail on our own. That is a heavy burden. The fact that God helps us and gives us peace as we make major life decisions is a huge blessing.

## VI. Consequences of Living Outside of God's Authority

1. **Proverbs 14:2**

   *He who walks in his uprightness fears the LORD, but he who is devious in his ways despises Him.*

   Those who do not fear God _____ His commandments and despise Him by

   _____ to follow His guidelines.

2. **Jeremiah 2:19**

   *. . . Know therefore and see that it is evil and bitter for you to forsake the LORD your God, and the dread of Me is not in you, declares the LORD GOD of hosts.*

   Those who do not fear God forsake Him and they will _____ harm for

   _____ away from Him.

3. **Jeremiah 10:23**

   *I know, O LORD, that a man's way is not in himself, Nor is it in a man who walks to direct his steps.*

   Those who do not fear God do not acknowledge that they are _____ capable of guiding

   their lives properly _____ from Him.

4. **Jeremiah 22:21**

   *I spoke to you in your prosperity; but you said, 'I will not listen!' This has been your practice from your youth, that you have not obeyed My voice.*

   Those who do not fear God do not recognize that _____ they have is _____ Him.

5. **Jeremiah 22:21**

   Those who do not fear God refuse to _____ to the things of God.

6. **Jeremiah 22:21**

   Those who do not fear God have not learned to _____ to authority as a child and now

   disobedience is a _____ _____ _____.

---

**Psalm 147:10-11,** "He does not delight in the strength of the horse;
He does not take pleasure in the legs of a man. The LORD favors those who fear Him,
those who wait for His lovingkindness."

**Lamentations 3:27,** "It is good for a man that he should bear the yoke in his youth."

**7. Isaiah 8:12-13**

*You are not to say, 'It is a conspiracy!' In regard to all that this people call a conspiracy, and you are not to fear what they fear or be in dread of it. It is the LORD of hosts whom you should regard as holy. And He shall be your fear, and He shall be your dread.*

Those who do not fear God live in _____ amidst the circumstances of this life

because they _____ confidence in God. Instead they place their trust in _____

and in their _____ understanding. They _____ their fear from the One

who understands and _____ all men.

**8. Daniel 4:37** (NKJV)

*. . . And those who walk in pride He is able to put down.*

Those who do not fear God _____ themselves and do not realize God will bring

them _____.

## VII. *Parental Responsibilities*

### A.  To Manage our Families

**1 Timothy 3:4**

*He must be one who manages his own household well, keeping his children under _____ with all _____*

**1 Timothy 3:12**

*Deacons must be husbands of only one wife, and good _____ of their _____ and their own households.*

We are called to manage and control our households, and specifically our children. Not having these

characteristics is what _____ us from leadership in _____.

God wants us to emulate His biblical _____-_____ before men. If we do not live in

submission before God, we will not be able to _____ others to that place and especially

not our _____ children.

## B. To Be Faithful

Another reason why this is so important is _____. God's _____ protect us.

Sometimes your children have been protected from harm because of your _____.

At times your _____ have _____ them in ways you will not realize

in this lifetime.

## C. To Teach our Children to Face Challenges and Consequences

We encounter _____ every day that get our attention, that make us _____

on Christ; events that make Him real in our _____ existence.

All of these events, all of the things that _____ in our lives and in the lives of our chil-

dren, big or small, are _____ by God so that we will maintain our perspective of Him

and our _____ upon Him.

All too often, parents (especially mothers) will do anything to keep their children from _____

such events head on by _____ them consequences.

It begins with _____ things but escalates to more _____ situations.

**Examples:** making excuses for them, handling a difficult situation for them, getting them out of serving a
detention, not holding them accountable for their actions, getting them off the hook when they are in trouble,
teaching them how to talk their way out of situations, smiling and laughing when they get out of a consequence,
bailing them out of serious situations.

If Mom or Dad _____ in every time, they will not respect authority. It is because there is no

_____ of consequences.

---

Psalm 147:10-11, "He does not delight in the strength of the horse;
He does not take pleasure in the legs of a man. The LORD favors those who fear Him,
those who wait for His lovingkindness."

Lamentations 3:27, "It is good for a man that he should bear the yoke in his youth."

## D.  To Teach Appropriate Submission to Other Authorities

If these lessons are not learned when they are _____, God will continue to

_____ them and teach them _____ people and authorities _____

than their parents.

Even _____ who did not bear this yoke in their youth may continue to

_____ with this in adulthood. That is why we have church _____.

If we haven't learned to submit to authority thus far, God _____ a system to

reach the person who _____ the leadership of a church and the authority of God's

_____ in their life.

This system has two main _____: to lovingly _____ the individual so that

they can _____ their lives to God's plan and to _____ the _____

of believers by holding people _____ if they stray too far.

Too many people live _____ lives. Fathers, especially, are the _____ of

the family. (Remember **Psalm 127:1**)

It is _____ to teach authority to a 2-year-old when you compare it to teaching a 13-year-

old who looks at you eyeball to eyeball or a 16-year-old who _____ over you.

In the past, people would say, "I would never do that—my parents would kill me!" because there was a fear of their parents' authority. They knew their parents would not literally "kill them" but it meant, "I know a definite line that my parents have set up for me and if I step over that line, I'm in big, big trouble and I will be held accountable." You just do not hear that much anymore. You do not hear of kids being afraid of severe consequences.

Living in understanding builds a trust in authority. When the kids know that there is a line that they cannot cross, they are more secure. Because they know their parents are protecting them from going too far in any direction. It is in their best interest.

As our children _____ and they see their parents, especially their father, as a

_____ leader, they will learn to make _____ choices while living within

God's _____ of protection for them.

They must learn to be _____ - _____ as youths.

A headstrong, stubborn adult will be almost impossible to deal with because they will not want to answer to anyone and will refuse to admit when they are wrong. Teaching children to admit when they are wrong is a very important aspect of parenting.

### Proverbs 17:10
*A rebuke goes deeper into one who has understanding than a hundred blows into a fool.*

Be determined, as their mom, to build this protection around them.

---

**Psalm 147:10-11,** "He does not delight in the strength of the horse;
He does not take pleasure in the legs of a man. The LORD favors those who fear Him,
those who wait for His lovingkindness."

**Lamentations 3:27,** "It is good for a man that he should bear the yoke in his youth."

# Homefront Application

## ESTABLISHING AUTHORITY, PART TWO:
## THE REIGN OF CHRIST IN THE HEART OF MAN
### A godly mother trains her children to see God as their lifelong authority

1. Consider the authority of God in your own life and how you demonstrate your submission to and respect for authority. Knowing that your children and others can detect your attitudes or actions in this area, are you properly modeling this foundational principle? Do examples come to mind where you feel you "blew it"? Instead of just trying to change ourselves, we need to confess to God our shortcomings and seek to reestablish a proper perspective of authority and the fear of God. Only then will we be able to truly live it before our children.

2. This week when you pray, thank God for the "daily load of benefits" He gives to you and your family. Watch for the benefits as they come pouring out to you. Recognize them and be thankful. Read the list of blessings to those who fear God (from your class notebooks). You may even want to read them at the dinner table or to your children at bedtime. We want our children to learn that God cares for us individually and specifically in our everyday lives.

3. Carefully consider each of your children. Have you established yourselves (you and your husband) and the Lord as authorities in their lives? Discuss this concept with your husband if you feel they are headed off track. Agree on a plan to reestablish this principle in their lives. It will, of course, depend upon their age, but the younger they are, the easier it will be.

## I CHOOSE TO LIVE BY CONVICTIONS.

Signature: _____  Date: _____

# Lesson 9 Outline

## MANAGING A CHILD
### A godly mother manages her children well

I. **The Biblical Mandate**
   A. The Three Levels of Motivation
   B. Internal Versus External

II. **Honoring Parents**

III. **Full-Circle Discipline**

IV. **Peacemakers or Peacekeepers**

V. **Practicing the Presence of God**

VI. **Modeling Submission to Authority**
   A. To Your Husband
   B. To Your Parents
   C. Genuine Conflicts

VII. **Exasperating Behaviors**
   *16 Things that Provoke Children to Anger or Exasperate Them*

## This week's Scripture memory verse:

**Ephesians 6:1-4,** "Children, obey your parents in the Lord, for this is right.
HONOR YOUR FATHER AND MOTHER (which is the first commandment with a promise),
SO THAT IT MAY BE WELL WITH YOU, AND THAT YOU MAY LIVE LONG ON THE EARTH.
Fathers, do not provoke your children to anger,
but bring them up in the discipline and instruction of the Lord."

# Lesson 9

## MANAGING A CHILD
### A godly mother manages her children well

## 1. The Biblical Mandate

If we are allowing our children to control the household, then we are going to have chaos and disorder in the home. If your everyday decisions (what your family does, what they are involved in) hinge on whether they really want to do it or not, then they are controlling the household and you are building a *child-centered home*. To be a *disciplined, self-controlled* person means learning how to do some of the things you do not really want to do.

☐ **1 Timothy 3:4**

*He must be one who manages his own household well, keeping his children under control with all dignity.*

If the "norm" is a meltdown and a tantrum, then we are not good managers of our own children. The Bible instructs us to be good managers and not to let our children be unmanageable.

☐ **1 Samuel 3:13**

*For I have told him that I am about to judge his house forever for the iniquity which he knew, because his sons brought a curse on themselves and he did not rebuke them.*

☐ The New King James version uses the word "_____" in place of the word "rebuke."

God gave Samuel a vision regarding Eli (the priest) and his household.

☐ He said that because Eli did not _____ his sons, they were now _____ _____

_____ and the priesthood would be taken from Eli's familial line forever.

This prophecy was fulfilled during the reign of King Solomon (**1 Kings 2:26-27**).

☐ God _____ us to be in control of our children, so He also shows us how it is possible.

We are to take His plan absolutely seriously because it is a _____ conviction.

**Psalm 85:8**

*I will hear what God the LORD will say; for He will speak peace to His people, to His godly ones; but let them not turn back to folly.*

As our children are growing up, they are learning to be self-controlled — in essence, to manage themselves. Our jobs are to teach them how to manage themselves, but not to be their constant manager.

## A. The Three Levels of Motivation

**There are three reasons a child will obey:**

**1.** because there is something in it for them. The goal is to please _____.

**2.** because they want to please someone or meet their expectations. The goal is to please

_____.

**3.** because they know it glorifies God. The goal is to please _____.

To live to please self is the _____ form of motivation. This form of motivation offers

_____.

The deeper issue is that we don't naturally gravitate to do good but we do gravitate towards

_____ ourselves, so training children to do what glorifies God must start very early.

---

**Ephesians 6:1-4**, "Children, obey your parents in the Lord, for this is right.
HONOR YOUR FATHER AND MOTHER (which is the first commandment with a promise),
SO THAT IT MAY BE WELL WITH YOU, AND THAT YOU MAY LIVE LONG ON THE EARTH.
Fathers, do not provoke your children to anger,
but bring them up in the discipline and instruction of the Lord."

## B. Internal Versus External

We don't want to reinforce self-centeredness or sibling rivalry. We want to teach them that it is about the internal heart and pleasing God rather than the external thing at the moment.

⬛ Discipline must address the attitude of the _____, so that the child may bring his or her actions

in line with what would glorify God.

⬛ Even though they learn that they are to obey you, their ultimate _____ is to glorify

God. As children they glorify God by being obedient to their parents.

## II. Honoring Parents

⬛ **Ephesians 6:1-4**

*Children, obey your parents in the Lord, for this is right.* HONOR YOUR FATHER AND MOTHER *(which is the first commandment with a promise),* SO THAT IT MAY BE WELL WITH YOU, AND THAT YOU MAY LIVE LONG ON THE EARTH. *Fathers, do not provoke your children to anger, but bring them up in the discipline and instruction of the Lord.*

God wants us to model this verse with our lives to our children. Honor is both an outward demonstration *AND* an internal condition of the heart. We want to honor our parents with our hearts, not just by what we say. The promise in this verse is that when you learn the secret of an obedient life, then God will bless your life.

### III. Full-Circle Discipline

☐ Discipline must go _____ _____.

☐ **What you must help them understand (full–circle discipline):**

**1.** _____ the problem happened

**2.** What behavior needs to _____ (what was the wrong behavior)

**3.** What right behavior needs to _____ it

**4.** What response or attitude would _____ God

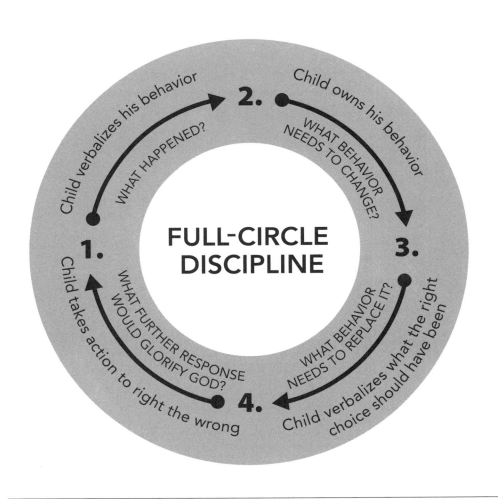

---

**Ephesians 6:1-4,** "Children, obey your parents in the Lord, for this is right.
HONOR YOUR FATHER AND MOTHER (which is the first commandment with a promise),
SO THAT IT MAY BE WELL WITH YOU, AND THAT YOU MAY LIVE LONG ON THE EARTH.
Fathers, do not provoke your children to anger,
but bring them up in the discipline and instruction of the Lord."

▢ These steps bring the event full circle. These steps are what God _____ us if we wish to train our children in the ways of God and not provoke them to anger.

▢ Inconsistency will provoke your children to anger because they are looking to you to _____ train them.

If you are inconsistent, capricious, or unpredictable, trying to obey you will be very frustrating.

▢ But if you make your intervention an _____, you will find that your children learn quickly and you will see them developing a motivation to live for God and _____ themselves.

## IV. *Peacemakers or Peacekeepers*

▢ Help children understand what God wants to teach them.

"God knew this could happen when children play together, because He understands how you think."
We want to be "peacemakers", not "peacekeepers".

**Matthew 5:9**
*Blessed are the peacemakers.*

## V. *Practicing the Presence of God*

▢ Make God real and ever _____ at the earliest possible age. They will _____ on the attitude of their hearts and lose focus on the toy.

▢ They will learn to be consoled by God and live to please Him even when you are not with them.
Help them to _____ on Christ when you are not there to take them through a situation.

▢ A child whose motivation is not to please God, but remains at the lowest form, which is to please self, will _____ against your best efforts because they will not understand the purpose for their obedience and they will be exasperated or frustrated in trying to live a life that God will not bless.

▢ They are to learn to honor us as their parents for their whole lives, but their _____ must consistently remain to honor God.

## VI. *Modeling Submission to Authority*

### A. To Your Husband

☐ **1 Peter 3:1-2**
*In the same way, you wives, be submissive to your own husbands so that even if any of them are disobedient to the word, they may be won without a word by the behavior of their wives, as they observe your chaste and respectful behavior.*

☐ _____ your husband even if he is not a believer in the Lord Jesus because it is a godly example to your children.

☐ Simply the way you _____ him may be the very thing that makes him become interested in the Lord.

☐ Your children know if you _____ submit to or follow your husband. They know if you are disrespectful or dishonoring to him.

☐ If you are, very likely, your children will say the _____ things to you, no matter how much you love them. And if your _____ is not with your husband, how can you expect more from your children?

☐ Likewise, if you are dishonoring or disrespectful to your _____, even though you are no longer under their authority, how can you possibly expect your children to respect or honor you?

---

Ephesians 6:1-4, "Children, obey your parents in the Lord, for this is right.
HONOR YOUR FATHER AND MOTHER (which is the first commandment with a promise),
SO THAT IT MAY BE WELL WITH YOU, AND THAT YOU MAY LIVE LONG ON THE EARTH.
Fathers, do not provoke your children to anger,
but bring them up in the discipline and instruction of the Lord."

## B. To Your Parents

▢ **There are four main reasons why we honor our parents:**

    **1.** God commands it.

    **2.** God blesses us if we do it.

▢   **3.** At some point, you will regret not doing it.

    **4.** Your children will follow your example.

**Providence:** How God works and orchestrates the events of history and man towards a desired end

## C. Genuine Conflicts

▢ **Luke 12:51-53**

Honor your family because they are your constant on this earth. Make peace with them.

▢ By nature we want to give respect or honor only to people who we feel are _____ of it.

▢ But if we do, then we are caving in to our fleshly nature where God would have us rise _____ the

circumstances and respect the person with the high motivation of pleasing God.

God, of course, desires that we live lives deserving of our children's respect. But we are to honor our parents, regardless of whether or not they deserve it.

▢ **1 Peter 2:18-23**
*Servants, be submissive to your masters with all respect, not only to those who are good and gentle, but also to those who are unreasonable. For this finds favor, if for the sake of conscience toward God a person bears up under sorrows when suffering unjustly. For what credit is there if, when you sin and are harshly treated, you endure it with patience? But if when you do what is right and suffer for it you patiently endure it, this finds favor with God. For you have been called for this purpose, since Christ also suffered for you, leaving you an example for you to follow in His steps, WHO COMMITTED NO SIN, NOR WAS ANY DECEIT FOUND IN HIS MOUTH; and while being reviled, He did not revile in return; while suffering He uttered no threats, but kept entrusting Himself to Him who judges righteously.*

- This passage of Scripture tells us to do what _____ God regardless of what people _____ to us. He sees it _____ and He judges righteously.

- If your children have learned to be consoled by the _____ and sovereignty of God, they will handle such things more easily.

- **Philippians 2:14-16**
  *Do all things without grumbling or disputing; so that you will prove yourselves to be blameless and innocent, children of God above reproach in the midst of a crooked and perverse generation, among whom you appear as lights in the world, holding fast the word of life, so that in the day of Christ I will have reason to glory because I did not run in vain nor toil in vain.*

- If we receive "a detention" or any treatment in life that we deem overly _____, God says that if we receive that consequence due to sin, then we _____ the difficulty as a _____ return for the behavior. And so we have no reason or excuse to complain.

- If we are _____ and are treated harshly but keep a pure attitude and do what is _____, we still have no business complaining. Why?

- Because as soon as we complain, we are no longer _____ God in the situation.

- But if we can _____ the attitude that I will do what those in authority over me ask me to do, then God takes special notice of that. It is _____ to Him.

- This is the attitude that Jesus had and that He wants us to follow. Our children have to _____ this.

---

**Ephesians 6:1-4**, "Children, obey your parents in the Lord, for this is right.
HONOR YOUR FATHER AND MOTHER (which is the first commandment with a promise),
SO THAT IT MAY BE WELL WITH YOU, AND THAT YOU MAY LIVE LONG ON THE EARTH.
Fathers, do not provoke your children to anger,
but bring them up in the discipline and instruction of the Lord."

**9.8**

## VII. Exasperating Behaviors

▢ Children who don't grow up in the discipline and instruction of the Lord have a higher likelihood of

becoming _____ or frustrated teenagers.

▢ The number one reason teenagers receive _____ is for problems in dealing

with anger.

▢ **Colossians 3:20-21**
*Children, be obedient to your parents in all things, for this is well-pleasing to the Lord. Fathers, do not exasperate your children, so that they will not lose heart.*

▢ **Exasperation**: To incite or inflame the anger of; to enrage; to cause irritation or annoyance to the point of injudicious action (to inflict UNDUE hurt).

**Warning:** Do not take this to mean that if your child gets mad at you or upset that you are necessarily exasperating them.

▢ They may simply be angry because they cannot have their _____ way. They may be fighting

against God's way in their life. This is not provocation, but rather _____.

## 16 Things that Provoke Children to Anger or Exasperate Them:

☐ 1. UNREALISTIC EXPECTATIONS

**1 Corinthians 13:11**
*When I was a child, I used to speak like a child, think like a child, reason like a child; when I became a man, I did away with childish things.*

☐ Remember, they are _____.

☐ 2. BEING TOO STRICT OR EXCESSIVELY INVOLVED

**James 3:17**
*But the wisdom from above is first pure, then peaceable, gentle, reasonable, full of mercy and good fruits, unwavering, without hypocrisy.*

☐ Remember to be _____.

☐ 3. COMPARING THEM TO OTHERS

**2 Corinthians 10:12**
*For we are not bold to class or compare ourselves with some of those who commend themselves; but when they measure themselves by themselves and compare themselves with themselves, they are without understanding.*

**Proverbs 15:4**
*A soothing ("wholesome"—NKJV) tongue is a tree of life, but perversion in it crushes the spirit.*

☐ Remember, it is _____ to make comparisons; what matters is what Christ thinks of us.

---

Ephesians 6:1-4, "Children, obey your parents in the Lord, for this is right.
HONOR YOUR FATHER AND MOTHER (which is the first commandment with a promise),
SO THAT IT MAY BE WELL WITH YOU, AND THAT YOU MAY LIVE LONG ON THE EARTH.
Fathers, do not provoke your children to anger,
but bring them up in the discipline and instruction of the Lord."

4. **NEGLECT OR LACK OF ATTENTION**

   **Proverbs 3:27**
   *Do not withhold good from those to whom it is due, when it is in your power to do it.*

   Remember, they are a _____ from God to you and they are worth your _____.


5. **OVERLY HARSH IN DISCIPLINE OR CONSEQUENCES**

   **Proverbs 14:17**
   *A quick-tempered man acts foolishly, and a man of evil devices is hated.*

   **Proverbs 10:19**
   *Where there are many words, transgression is unavoidable, but he who restrains his lips is wise.*

   Remember, do not discipline in _____.


6. **DISCIPLINING WITHOUT ADMONITION OR EXPLANATION**

   **Admonish** means to warn or express disapproval in a gentle, earnest way; to counsel, teach, give instruction

   **Colossians 1:28**
   *We proclaim Him, admonishing every man with all wisdom, so that we may present every man complete in Christ.*

   Remember, admonishing our children helps make them _____ in Christ.

☐ **7. UNPREDICTABILITY OF HOME LIFE**

When a child doesn't know what to expect, his life will be out of order (may include role reversal).

**1 Corinthians 14:40**
*But all things must be done properly and in an orderly manner.*

☐ Remember, God's ways are _____ and stable.

☐ **8. LACK OF AFFECTION**

**1 Thessalonians 2:7-8**
*But we proved to be gentle among you, as a nursing mother tenderly cares for her own children. Having so fond an affection for you, we were well-pleased to impart to you not only the gospel of God but also our own lives, because you had become very dear to us.*

☐ Remember, a mother's _____ is important in a child's life.

☐ **9. LACK OF BOUNDARIES OR GIVING THEM TOO MUCH FREEDOM**

**Proverbs 19:19-20**
*A man of great anger will bear the penalty, for if you rescue him, you will only have to do it again. Listen to counsel and accept discipline, that you may be wise the rest of your days.*

**Proverbs 25:28**
*Like a city that is broken into and without walls is a man who has no control over his spirit.*

☐ Remember the _____ in setting boundaries.

---

Ephesians 6:1-4, "Children, obey your parents in the Lord, for this is right.
HONOR YOUR FATHER AND MOTHER (which is the first commandment with a promise),
SO THAT IT MAY BE WELL WITH YOU, AND THAT YOU MAY LIVE LONG ON THE EARTH.
Fathers, do not provoke your children to anger,
but bring them up in the discipline and instruction of the Lord."

**9.12**

10. **MODELING ANGER**

How can we expect them to not show anger if it is what they learn at home?

**Proverbs 22:24-25**

*Do not associate with a man given to anger; or go with a hot-tempered man, or you will learn his ways and find a snare for yourself.*

**Remember, children can learn our _____ habits.**

11. **DISCORD BETWEEN PARENTS**

God's plan of order becomes confusing when the child's own parents are not modeling it.

**Malachi 2:13-14**

*This is another thing you do: you cover the altar of the LORD with tears, with weeping and with groaning, because He no longer regards the offering or accepts it with favor from your hand. Yet you say, 'For what reason?' Because the LORD has been a witness between you and the wife of your youth, against whom you have dealt treacherously, though she is your companion and your wife by covenant.*

**Remember, God wants families of _____.**

12. **NOT ADMITTING WHEN YOU ARE WRONG**

**Hebrews 12:15**

*See to it that no one comes short of the grace of God; that no root of bitterness springing up causes trouble, and by it many be defiled.*

**Remember, don't let bitterness _____ up in your family. Admit when you are**

**_____ and ask forgiveness.**

13. **DOUBLE STANDARDS OR HYPOCRISY**

**Matthew 23:27-28**
*Woe to you, scribes and Pharisees, hypocrites! For you are like whitewashed tombs which on the outside appear beautiful, but inside they are full of dead man's bones and all uncleanness. So you, too, outwardly appear righteous to men, but inwardly you are full of hypocrisy and lawlessness.*

Remember to live a pure and righteous life before your children; they _____ the real you.

14. **PHYSICAL OR VERBAL ABUSE**

**Colossians 3:8-9**
*But now you also, put them all aside: anger, wrath, malice, slander, and abusive speech from your mouth. Do not lie to one another, since you laid aside the old self with its evil practices.*

Remember, hostility toward your children is _____.

15. **NOT LISTENING TO THEM OR GIVING THEM AN OPPORTUNITY TO EXPLAIN THEMSELVES**

**Proverbs 18:13, 17**
*He who gives an answer before he hears, it is folly and shame to him. 17 The first to plead his case seems right, until another comes and examines him.*

Remember to live in _____ with your children.

16. **NOT DOING WHAT YOU SAID YOU WOULD**

**Proverbs 13:1**
*Hope deferred makes the heart sick, but desire fulfilled is a tree of life.*

**Matthew 5:37**
*But let your statement be 'Yes, yes' or 'No, no'; anything beyond these is of evil.*

Remember, _____ what you say you will _____.

---

**Ephesians 6:1-4,** "Children, obey your parents in the Lord, for this is right.
HONOR YOUR FATHER AND MOTHER (which is the first commandment with a promise),
SO THAT IT MAY BE WELL WITH YOU, AND THAT YOU MAY LIVE LONG ON THE EARTH.
Fathers, do not provoke your children to anger,
but bring them up in the discipline and instruction of the Lord."

**9.14**

# Homefront Application

## MANAGING A CHILD
### A godly mother manages her children well

1. Consider what types of motivation you use most in your home.

   Do any adjustments need to be made?

   Are they achieving obedience out of the child's love to do what is right or for selfish reasons?

   Some "rewards" are helpful and fun even for older children and teens, so don't think you have to ban them; just consider the whole picture in regards to training them to be obedient.

2. Talk over the list of ways we can exasperate our children.

   Think about the areas that may be stumbling blocks in your own parenting.

   Meditate on the verses that are specific to that area.

   Next week we will expand on each of these areas to learn how to replace those things that exasperate our children with things that encourage them to love, honor, and obey their parents.

   The first step is recognizing if we have developed harmful patterns that will exasperate our children. It is so important for husbands and wives to be in agreement in these areas.

## I CHOOSE TO LIVE BY CONVICTIONS.

Signature: _____

Date: _____

# *Lesson 10 Outline*

## PUTTING OFF AND PUTTING ON: LEARNING GODLY HABITS

A godly mother does not exasperate her children

*I.*   *Introduction*

*II.*   *The Process of Growth*

*III.*   *Quiz*

| *Exasperating Behaviors:* | | *Replace with:* |
|---|---|---|
| _____ | 1. Unrealistic expectations | UNDERSTANDING |
| _____ | 2. Being too strict or excessively involved | GRACE |
| _____ | 3. Comparing them to others | ACCEPTANCE |
| _____ | 4. Neglect or lack of attention | PROPER PRIORITIES |
| _____ | 5. Overly harsh in discipline or consequences | SELF-CONTROL |
| _____ | 6. Disciplining without explanation | ADMONISHMENT |
| _____ | 7. Unpredictability of home life | ORDERLINESS |
| _____ | 8. Lack of affection | TENDERNESS |
| _____ | 9. Lack of boundaries | SOUND JUDGMENT |
| _____ | 10. Modeling anger | FORBEARANCE |
| _____ | 11. Discord between parents | HARMONY |
| _____ | 12. Not admitting when you are wrong | SEEKING FORGIVENESS |
| _____ | 13. Double standards or hypocrisy | LIVING BY CONVICTION |
| _____ | 14. Physical or verbal abuse | LOVE |
| _____ | 15. Not giving them an opportunity to explain | LISTENING |
| _____ | 16. Not doing what you said you would | INTEGRITY |

*IV.*   *Quiz Score Sheet*

*V.*   *Quiz Results*

## *This week's Scripture memory verse:*

**Matthew 5:37**, "But let your statement be 'Yes, yes' or 'No, no';
anything beyond these is of evil."

# *Lesson 10*

## PUTTING OFF AND PUTTING ON: LEARNING GODLY HABITS
### A godly mother does not exasperate her children

## *1.  Introduction*

This whole class is about being entrusted with your child's heart, which means holding onto your child's heart through all the ups and downs of life. The idea is that your child would know that you are WITH them, that you are FOR them.

How, through all the storms of life, do you keep your child's heart with you, not just their external behavior? When our children are young, we know when their heart is with us, but as they get older, their heart might defect. You want to make sure that as you are disciplining them, you keep their heart with you.

**Help them understand the full circle:**

1. **Why** the problem happened

2. What behavior needs to **change**

3. What right behavior needs to **replace** it

4. What response or attitude would **glorify God**

   *(repentance, confession, restitution, forgiveness, humility . . .)*

## II. The Process of Growth

☐ If your child is out of control, it is a sure bet that you don't have their _____. If this is your situation, then setting this child back on track is a huge _____ for you right now.

☐ In fact, the only two things more important are your walk with the _____ and your relationship with your _____ (understanding and agreement) because you will need to be strong in these two areas to reestablish biblical family dynamics.

Everything else in life could be set on the back burner for awhile until you can concentrate and focus on your child. It will be so important and so worth it! I'm talking about the things that we may be doing in our lives that exasperate them, that give them a feeling of hopelessness, that they can't ever please us. We don't want to cause our child's heart to stray.

☐ It is not enough that we recognize a wrong approach or method, we must _____ it with a proper biblical method.

**Luke 11:24-26**
*When the unclean spirit goes out of a man, it passes through waterless places seeking rest, and not finding any, it says, 'I will return to my house from which I came.' And when it comes, it finds it swept and put in order. Then it goes and takes along seven other spirits more wicked than itself, and they go in and live there; and the last state of that man becomes worse than the first.*

☐ This passage is referring to a _____ surrender to change. The person is ridding himself of a wrong behavior but cannot _____ it from returning because he has not protected himself by replacing it with a new right behavior.

Notice that the wicked behavior came back sevenfold. This is the person who says, "I yell at my kids. I know it's wrong, but I just can't help it and it's getting worse." Maybe the kids are even starting to yell back. We don't want to grow in wicked behavior; we want to replace it with right behavior.

☐ Replace the wrong behavior with a new pattern so that there is _____ _____ for the old behavior to return.

☐ Without a buffer (guardrails) we fall back into sin when _____ and opportunity meet.

---

**Matthew 5:37**, "But let your statement be 'Yes, yes' or 'No, no';
anything beyond these is of evil."

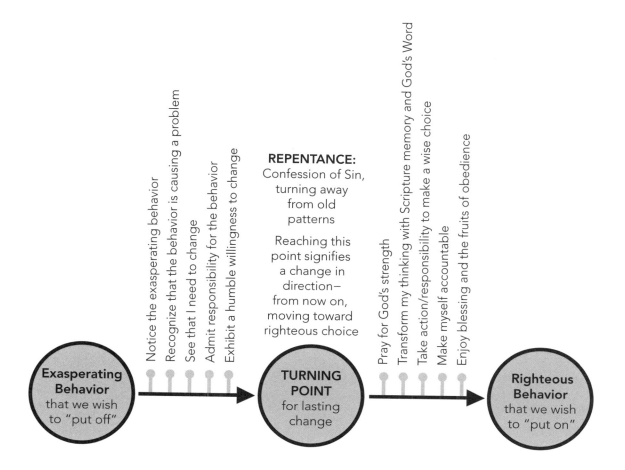

**Some of the specific behaviors we are to put off and put on are:**

### Colossians 3:8

*But now you also, put them all aside: anger, wrath, malice, slander, and abusive speech from your mouth.*

### Colossians 3:12-14

*So, as those who have been chosen of God, holy and beloved, put on a heart of compassion, kindness, humility, gentleness and patience; bearing with one another, and forgiving each other, whoever has a complaint against anyone; just as the Lord forgave you, so also should you. Beyond all these things put on love, which is the perfect bond of unity.*

These are not referring to little one-time events. These are talking about the persistent patterns or blindspots that we recognize.

The general principle here is put on **G**_____.

We all need more grace in our lives.

## III. Quiz

Rate yourself from 1 to 10 in each of the following 16 areas based on the frequency of these behaviors in your home. Keep track of your score on the sheet provided at the end of this lesson (p.10.19).

| | | |
|---|---|---|
| **0 - 1** | Rarely or Almost Never | *This is not a struggle in our family or we have learned to successfully build a buffer from the wrong behavior.* |
| **2 - 3** | Seldom | *When this occurs, we work it out to a good result.* |
| **4 - 5** | Occasionally | *I am aware that this happens more than it should.* |
| **6 – 7** | Often | *I am aware that this is a problem in our family.* |
| **8 - 10** | Very Often | *I am aware that this is one of the key issues for our family to resolve. This area is in crisis in our family.* |

---

**Matthew 5:37,** "But let your statement be 'Yes, yes' or 'No, no';
anything beyond these is of evil."

## 1.  UNREALISTIC EXPECTATIONS

Making demands upon a child that they are not developmentally able to meet or perhaps they will never have the ability to meet; or just simply making too many demands.

**1 Corinthians 13:11**
*When I was a child, I used to speak like a child, think like a child, reason like a child; when I became a man, I did away with childish things.*

## Remember, they are children.

**Further Insights:**

- Watch for developmental signs that indicate they are able to learn what you are teaching.

- Regularly discuss with your husband how your children are doing.

- Do you share the same goals for your child?

- If your child is having difficulty, do you see the problem the same as your husband (or even as your child)?

- Do you both agree on the amount of time your child is spending away from the family pursuing other things?

- Are you in agreement regarding the child's activities, household duties, homework expectations, etc.?

- Does your child's life have a spiritual, social, physical, and academic balance?

- Are the activities they are involved in building into their character?

- Are your expectations age-appropriate?

- Are you living according to your established family convictions and standards?

- What conviction do you have about your expectations?

**Warning:** When you and your husband agree on your family standards and convictions, don't waver. Let the child grow into them without demanding immediate and complete compliance (if the expectation is a matter of maturity). Always hold the standard high so that they know that is what they are working for, that is your ultimate goal for them.

**Warning:** Children may challenge your standards or expectations, but that doesn't necessarily mean your expectations are unrealistic; they just don't want to become disciplined. This is why you and your husband regularly reevaluate your training procedures and make adjustments or encourage each other to hang tough because that is what is needed. Then stick together on your agreement. Your job is to follow through as your child matures.

- Do they fail to meet your expectations because of simple lack of _____?

- Kids will do some immature things, sometimes even when they should know better.

- Teach them to be _____ to seek forgiveness and then be quick to forgive.

- In cases where we blow it, when they come to us with a repentant heart and we respond with judgment, anger, wrath, or unforgiveness, their hearts will harden because the response is _____.

- The proper response to misunderstandings or accidents is _____, not anger or disapproval. But be _____.

  Treat a child how you would want to be treated in that situation.

- **The behavior to put on is U_____.**

## 2. BEING TOO STRICT OR EXCESSIVELY INVOLVED

- **James 3:17**
  *But the wisdom from above is first pure, then peaceable, gentle, reasonable, full of mercy and good fruits, unwavering, without hypocrisy.*

  **Remember to be reasonable.**

---

**Matthew 5:37,** "But let your statement be 'Yes, yes' or 'No, no'; anything beyond these is of evil."

Give them privacy and areas of privilege and responsibility. Help them understand how privilege and responsibility are related (lack of responsibility = loss of privilege). Allow them to make mistakes so that they can learn from them. Be gracious in explaining lessons you are teaching.

▢ We are to be _____ and easily _____. The key here is _____ we respond to them.

▢ **We are to put on G_____.**

## 3. COMPARING THEM TO OTHERS

▢ **2 Corinthians 10:12**
*For we are not bold to class or compare ourselves with some of those who commend themselves; but when they measure themselves by themselves and compare themselves with themselves, they are without understanding.*

**Remember, it is unwise to make comparisons; what matters is what Christ thinks of us.**

Don't compare siblings or families. Don't compare physical appearance, abilities, spirituality, etc. It's okay to make factual statements or evaluations, but not comparisons.

▢ **The behavior to put on is A_____.**

## 4. NEGLECT OR LACK OF ATTENTION

▢ **Proverbs 3:27**
*Do not withhold good from those to whom it is due, when it is in your power to do it.*

**Remember, they are a blessing from God to you and they are worth your time.**

**Further Insights:**

- Are you spending too much time away from them?

- Do you enjoy being with your children or would you rather someone else took them off your hands? And for how long?

- Do you excuse your time apart because you see the activity as worthwhile?

- Do you rationalize an activity as worthwhile because you want to pursue something for yourself?

- Do you rely on others to teach them things that you should be teaching them?

## Remember your family standards and personal convictions.
If you neglect these things, they will pick them up from someone else and most likely they won't be the same as what you would have for them.

- This area may also include _____, wrongly teaching them that things are

  more valuable than relationships.

- **The behavior to put on is the proper place of P_____.**

## 5. OVERLY HARSH IN DISCIPLINE OR CONSEQUENCES

**Proverbs 14:17**
*A quick-tempered man acts foolishly, and a man of evil devices is hated.*

**Proverbs 10:19**
*Where there are many words, transgression is unavoidable, but he who restrains his lips is wise.*

**Ephesians 4:26-27**
*Be angry, and yet do not sin; do not let the sun go down on your anger, and do not give the devil an opportunity.*

God does not condone selfish anger stemming from lack of self-control. This verse speaks of anger against immorality, injustice and other sins.

---

**Matthew 5:37,** "But let your statement be 'Yes, yes' or 'No, no';
anything beyond these is of evil."

**Righteous anger** (from the Biblical Counseling Center): A considered, thoughtful response to sin, when it is rightly aroused and rightly directed and in defense of the character of God.

**It is:**

1. motivated by a desire to accomplish God's purposes,

2. modeled after His example, and

3. manifested according to His Word.

Still, don't let even righteous anger make you a _____ person.

Be able to say at the end of each day, "I leave it with the Lord." Otherwise, Satan will use the opportunity to make us resentful and useless for ministry. Usually, anger is lack of control, patience, or gentleness.

**James 1:20**
*The anger of man does not achieve the righteousness of God.*

**Remember, do not discipline in anger.**

**Further Insights:**

- Rather, be in control of yourself when you discipline a child or have an "event."

- Think about how you relate to people. Do you get angry easily?

- If you tend to show anger towards your children, do you show that anger with other people also, or are you using your children to release your frustrations? Don't let yourself continue in this damaging behavior. Talk with your children and explain to them that you are working on controlling your temper and ask their forgiveness for specific times when you have been overly harsh.

- The godly way to deal with anger is by replacing the impulse with a pure behavior.

- Society for some reason believes that this is a behavior that we cannot control, that we have to vent it or somehow let it out; that giving it to God just won't do it. That is a counterfeit.

**Proverbs 15:1**
*A gentle answer turns away wrath, but a harsh word stirs up anger.*

A child who has been disciplined too harshly may not show anger on the outside, but inside he will be churning with resentment that will build and build until it explodes.

☐ Anger will teach your child the fear of _____ and not the fear of God.

It may make them obey you, but it is not righteous behavior before God. Agree with your husband on discipline. Be consistent, but not overbearing. If the correction centers on your anger, it will be punitive and ineffective, and it won't be over until you've completely vented. Our discipline is to be corrective, not punitive.

☐ **The behavior we are to put on is S_____ – C_____.**

## 6. DISCIPLINING WITHOUT ADMONITION OR EXPLANATION

☐ **Admonish** means to warn or express disapproval in a gentle, earnest way; to counsel, teach, give instruction.

**Colossians 1:28**
*We proclaim Him, admonishing every man with all wisdom, so that we may present every man complete in Christ.*

☐ **Remember, admonishing our children helps make them complete in Christ.**

☐ Again, we are using all four steps of discipline by _____ the path that brought

the child to the point of discipline, helping him understand where he veered off, what was the

condition of his heart, and how he can make it right.

☐ Rather than exasperating him because he is in the _____ on the purpose of your discipline,

he will completely understand your purpose and will even begin to internalize this method of

rewalking the course and eventually will hold himself accountable before God.

Neglecting this process will not grow our children up in wisdom. Rather, they will shrug off warnings and limits and do their own thing.

☐ This is otherwise known as growing in _____ .

---

**Matthew 5:37,** "But let your statement be 'Yes, yes' or 'No, no';
anything beyond these is of evil."

**Proverbs 18:2**

*A fool does not delight in understanding, but only in revealing his own mind.*

⌨ **The behavior we are to put on is A_____.**


## 7.   UNPREDICTABILITY OF HOME LIFE

⌨ When a child doesn't know what to expect, his life will be out of order.

**1 Corinthians 14:40**

*But all things must be done properly and in an orderly manner.*

**Remember, God's ways are orderly and stable.**

**Further Insights:**

- Consider your home life. Does it follow God's plan of priorities and order? Do any changes need to be made?

- Order gives children security. It makes home for them the best place to be.

- Does your home have a consistent routine that allows harmony between family members? We are all different, but we are all to be orderly.

⌨ **The behavior we are to put on is O_____.**


## 8.   LACK OF AFFECTION

⌨ **1 Thessalonians 2:7-8**

*But we proved to be gentle among you, as a nursing mother tenderly cares for her own children. Having so fond an affection for you, we were well-pleased to impart to you not only the gospel of God but also our own lives, because you had become very dear to us.*

**Remember, a mother's touch is important in a child's life.**

**Further Insights:**

Do you show affection to them every day (even several times a day)? And do they do the same to you? This is so important. If you have gotten out of the habit or let the hugs fall by the wayside, start back up. It is almost impossible for a child's heart to stray from you if you show each other physical affection every day.

**10.11**

☐ Show them how much you _____ a simple hug and kiss. Teach them that kindness,

thoughtfulness, and tenderness are highly valued and a source of great _____

to you (and others).

☐ Teach your children to hug each other and tell each other that they love them. This simple training

will go a long way in cutting off _____ rivalry.

☐ **The behavior we are to put on is T_____.**

## 9. LACK OF BOUNDARIES OR GIVING TOO MUCH FREEDOM

☐ **Proverbs 19:19-20**
*A man of great anger will bear the penalty, for if you rescue him, you will only have to do it again. Listen to counsel and accept discipline, that you may be wise the rest of your days.*

**Proverbs 25:28**
*Like a city that is broken into and without walls is a man who has no control over his spirit.*

**Remember the purpose in setting boundaries.**

**Further Insights:**
Agree with your husband on the limits you set for your children and stick to them. When you have agreed on them, present them to your children, remembering not to bowl them over with too many rules. Be concise.

☐ This is especially important if your children are not used to boundaries and they have not been

_____ introduced to them through the years. Train them to think wisely and to

think about the consequences of their actions _____ they engage in an activity.

---

**Matthew 5:37,** "But let your statement be 'Yes, yes' or 'No, no';
anything beyond these is of evil."

**10.12**

**General Rule:** Would this activity have my mom's:

**1.** full permission and

**2.** approval and

**3.** could anybody get hurt?

⬜ We are to be sound in our thinking and doctrine. Beyond that, we must be _____with our children about the _____ we place and the convictions we have regarding the activities or behaviors in their lives.

⬜ **We are to put on S_____ J_____.**


## 10. MODELING ANGER

⬜ **Proverbs 22:24-25**
*Do not associate with a man given to anger; or go with a hot-tempered man, or you will learn his ways and find a snare for yourself.*

**Remember, children can learn our sinful habits.**

⬜ If you struggle with anger, it is very hard to _____.

Chances are, your entire family and maybe even those outside the family know it. Don't be fooled into thinking this is not a serious problem, because the effects of angry behavior are very far-reaching.

⬜ So don't let it _____ your children.

Husbands and wives need to be accountable to each other in this. But if the problem is serious, biblical counseling and accountability with others may also be necessary.

⬜ **We are to put on F_____.**

### 11. DISCORD BETWEEN PARENTS

▢ God's plan of order becomes confusing when the child's own parents are not modeling it.

#### Malachi 2:13-14

*This is another thing you do: you cover the altar of the LORD with tears, with weeping and with groaning, because He no longer regards the offering or accepts it with favor from your hand. Yet you say, "For what reason?" Because the LORD has been a witness between you and the wife of your youth, against whom you have dealt treacherously, though she is your companion and your wife by covenant.*

**Remember, God wants families of unity.**

#### Further Insights:

In cases of blatant, unrepentant sin that divides a family, He would have us seek a support structure of relatives, friends, and people within the church.

▢ **We are to put on H_____.**

### 12. NOT ADMITTING WHEN YOU ARE WRONG

▢ **Hebrews 12:15**
*See to it that no one comes short of the grace of God; that no root of bitterness springing up causes trouble, and by it many be defiled.*

**Remember, don't let bitterness build up in your family.**

▢ _____ when you are wrong and ask forgiveness. Remember that children know if they have been wronged. If we admit that to them, they will _____ see us as weak or unworthy of their respect. Remember, they already know.

They will be very forgiving and gracious. And isn't that what we want to cultivate in them?

▢ If we cannot admit when we are wrong to them, they will learn that behavior from us and their

_____ relationships will struggle.

---

**Matthew 5:37**, "But let your statement be 'Yes, yes' or 'No, no';
anything beyond these is of evil."

◻ If we keep "short accounts" with each other, we will remain close because we are not allowing a

_____ of unforgiveness to build up.

There are no enduring relationships without forgiveness. We need to be quick to seek forgiveness and quick to forgive.

◻ **We are to put on F_____.**

## 13. DOUBLE STANDARDS OR HYPOCRISY

◻ **Matthew 23:27-28**
*Woe to you, scribes and Pharisees, hypocrites! For you are like whitewashed tombs which on the outside appear beautiful, but inside they are full of dead man's bones and all uncleanness. So you, too, outwardly appear righteous to men, but inwardly you are full of hypocrisy and lawlessness.*

**Remember to live a pure and righteous life before your children.**

Your children know the "real" you.

**Further Insights:**
Live out your biblical and personal convictions before your children. Help them understand the purposes of your convictions and how they were developed.

◻ _____ strong character to your children.

◻ **We are to put on L_____ B____ C_____.**

## 14. PHYSICAL OR VERBAL ABUSE

⬜ **Colossians 3:8-9**

*But now you also, put them all aside: anger, wrath, malice, slander, and abusive speech from your mouth. Do not lie to one another, since you laid aside the old self with its evil practices.*

**Remember, do not be hostile to your children.**

⬜ Replace old patterns of sinful speech with _____ speech.

⬜ **We are to put on L_____.**
(Love is an action, not a mere feeling. Love cannot coexist with hostility.)

## 15. NOT LISTENING TO THEM OR GIVING THEM AN OPPORTUNITY TO EXPLAIN THEMSELVES

⬜ **Proverbs 18:13, 17**

*He who gives an answer before he hears, it is folly and shame to him. The first to plead his case seems right, until another comes and examines him.*

**Remember to live in understanding with your children.**

⬜ Do we cut them off without _____ what they have to say because we don't want to deal with the situation or we are just too tired to take it _____ _____?

⬜ **We are to put on the behavior of careful L_____.**

---

**Matthew 5:37,** "But let your statement be 'Yes, yes' or 'No, no'; anything beyond these is of evil."

## 16.  NOT DOING WHAT YOU SAID YOU WOULD

▢ **Proverbs 13:12**

*Hope deferred makes the heart sick, but desire fulfilled is a tree of life.*

**Further Insights:**

Do you make promises to your children that you don't keep? They take to heart what you say, so make sure they don't perceive something as a promise that you don't mean as a promise.

▢ **Matthew 5:37**

*But let your statement be 'Yes, yes' or 'No, no'; anything beyond these is of evil.*

**A.**  Do what you say you will do.

**B.**  Do not make flippant oaths that you have no authority to make. It also means don't add words or use words that don't convey what you really mean.

**Examples:** exaggerating, teasing

**C.**  When you say yes, mean it and stick to it. And when you say no, mean it and stick to it. Follow through so that they learn that yes really means yes, and no really means no. You don't have to give a justification for your answer that suits them.

There are only two exceptions to giving a definitive answer on the spot: if they have new information to add or if the decision cannot be made right then. Tell them when you will give them your decision. And then make sure to tell them by then and earlier if possible.

▢ **Remember, they are counting on you to be true with your words and actions.**

▢ **We are to put on I_____.**

▢ **IN ALL THESE THINGS WE ARE PUTTING ON C_____.**

It is having the mind and heart of Christ that will cause a child's heart to remain with us.

▢ Pray that you would have Christ's heart toward your children. They will be _____ to that; it is

a place that they will _____ to be.

*Notes:*

---

**Matthew 5:37**, "But let your statement be 'Yes, yes' or 'No, no';
anything beyond these is of evil."

## IV. Quiz Score Sheet

| Exasperating Behaviors: | Replace with: |
|---|---|

_____ 1.   Unrealistic expectations                    UNDERSTANDING

_____ 2.   Being too strict or excessively involved     GRACE

_____ 3.   Comparing them to others                    ACCEPTANCE

_____ 4.   Neglect or lack of attention                 PROPER PRIORITIES

_____ 5.   Overly harsh in discipline or consequences   SELF-CONTROL

_____ 6.   Disciplining without explanation             ADMONISHMENT

_____ 7.   Unpredictability of home life                ORDERLINESS

_____ 8.   Lack of affection                            TENDERNESS

_____ 9.   Lack of boundaries                           SOUND JUDGMENT

_____ 10.  Modeling anger                               FORBEARANCE

_____ 11.  Discord between parents                      HARMONY

_____ 12.  Not admitting when you are wrong             SEEKING FORGIVENESS

_____ 13.  Double standards or hypocrisy                LIVING BY CONVICTION

_____ 14.  Physical or verbal abuse                     LOVE

_____ 15.  Not giving them an opportunity to explain    LISTENING

_____ 16.  Not doing what you said you would            INTEGRITY

## V. Quiz Results

Pray for God's wisdom and guidance; self-willed change won't be enough. Scores even as low as a 2 need some adjusting.

**Scores 2-4:** Spend time with your husband discussing what changes are needed. Agree over them together with a plan of action. Pray together about them. Be accountable with each other on how you are doing. Determine if you need to ask forgiveness of your children and do it. Explain your new course of action so they understand.

**Scores 5-7:** Same as above with stronger accountability; may need to be accountable to small group leader in addition to each other.

**Scores 8-10:** This is an area of serious need. You are in danger of building bitterness and resentment in your child, which you probably already see. It is imperative that you and your husband come to agreement on these issues. If this is difficult for you, you will need intervention and accountability from godly friends or your small group leader. Apply the principles from this class.

**Psalm 85:8**
*I will hear what God the Lord will say; For He will speak peace to His people, to His godly ones; But let them not turn back to folly.*

---

Matthew 5:37, "But let your statement be 'Yes, yes' or 'No, no';
anything beyond these is of evil."

# Homefront Application

## PUTTING OFF AND PUTTING ON:
## LEARNING GODLY HABITS

### A godly mother does not exasperate her children

1. This was an intense lesson. Take some time this week to review your notes and your quiz.

2. Discuss the quiz with your husband. You are two different and unique people and as such may need to address completely different areas.

3. Is this lesson spotlighting an area God wants you to address? Gently discuss these issues together. Be sensitive and encouraging. Help each other make progress as parents. Keep these conversations private between the two of you but be willing to be teachable. It will glorify God and your family will benefit tremendously.

## I CHOOSE TO LIVE BY CONVICTIONS.

Signature: _____  Date: _____

# Lesson 11 Outline

## COMMITTED TO DISCIPLINE
### A godly mother is committed to discipline

I.  The Foundation of Commitment

II. Following Through on Our Commitment
   A. Our Mind / Intellect
   B. Our Will / Volition
   C. Our Emotion / Affection
   D. The Importance of Balancing All Three: Mind, Will & Emotion
   E. Applying the Proper Method of Training

III. Focusing on Discipline - Committed to Training: The Will

IV. Popular Misconceptions (What Spanking is Not)

V. Anatomy of a Spanking Event (What Spanking Is)

VI. Conventional Objections to Spanking

VII. Reproof as Discipline (Older Children)

# This week's Scripture memory verse:

**Proverbs 13:24**, "He who withholds his rod hates his son,
but he who loves him disciplines him diligently."

**Proverbs 29:15**, "The rod and reproof give wisdom,
but a child who gets his own way brings shame to his mother."

# Lesson 11

## COMMITTED TO DISCIPLINE
### A godly mother is committed to discipline

## I. The Foundation of Commitment

If we want a child that's going to grow up and "not bring shame to us", we must be commited to discipline.

**Our discipline will emphasize:**

1. "The rod" – for younger children

2. "Reproof" – for older children

We all have distinctly different children. God has ONE set of principles for us to raise and discipline them.

God's principles are clear and unwavering and apply to each and every child. No child is

_exempt_ .

**Psalm 85:8**
*I will hear what God the LORD will say; for He will speak peace to His people, to His godly ones; but let them not turn back to folly.*

## II. Following Through on Our Commitment

When we _apply_ biblical truth (convictions) to raising each child, God will bring forth the

fruit. Our job is to be undauntingly _committed_ to carrying out His instruction.

*The Power of Commitment Jerry White*

*The following principles are from The Power of Commitment by Jerry White, 1985, Navpress:*

**When the Bible refers to "the heart", it's really talking about three areas in combination:**

- MIND / Intellect *~~Titus 2:6  Phil 4:8~~* *information*

- WILL / Volition

- EMOTION / Affection

## A.  Our Mind / Intellect

Our MINDS are to be committed to the TRUTH of God's Word so that we are able to make

_____Sound_____ judgments (discernment).

"The MIND is the seat of INTELLECT and KNOWLEDGE resulting in theology." (Jerry White, p. 26)

## B.  Our Will / Volition

Next, the WILL refers to carrying out __decisions__ and living in obedience. It is the place

where we _____ to act on what we think and believe.

We can choose to do things God's way or our own way. It is a matter of our __will__.

"The WILL is the seat of DECISION and OBEDIENCE resulting in a holy life." (Jerry White, p. 26)

---

**Proverbs 13:24,** "He who withholds his rod hates his son,
but he who loves him disciplines him diligently."

**Proverbs 29:15,** "The rod and reproof give wisdom,
but a child who gets his own way brings shame to his mother."

## C. Our Emotion / Affection

▢ Next is the HEART (emotion)—the area of belief and __affection__. It is the place of our emotions that we are to keep balanced by the first two areas.

▢ "The HEART is the seat of BELIEF and AFFECTION resulting in a desire for God." (Jerry White, p. 26)

## D. The Importance of Balancing All Three: Mind, Will & Emotion

### 1. Problems When We Focus on Only One Area

▢ If we focus on the MIND only we become dogmatic and intellectualized in our theology with no __joy__; always growing in truth but not __applying__ the truth and seeing God change us. Knowing we are growing in Christ is what gives us joy! Knowing we are not the same gives us hope!

▢ If we focus on the WILL only we become legalistic without a growing knowledge of truth and __obey__ out of compulsion rather than out of love for Christ.

▢ If we focus on the HEART (EMOTION) only we become __unstable__, living by how we feel without obedience to God's Word or understanding of it.

### 2. Problems When We Focus on Only Two Areas

( MIND + WILL ) only = lack of joy, mechanical worship, not motivated out of love

( MIND + EMOTION ) only = lack of follow-through on commitments/discipline

( EMOTION + WILL ) only = aberrant commitment, not following what is true

## E. Applying the Proper Method of Training

☐ We are growing our children up in _____ three of these areas so that they will grow up to be committed to Christ.

☐ Anytime they have a problem or issue, it is going to fall into one of these three categories. If we train ourselves to look at each situation in this way, we will be able to apply the proper method of *training* .

| | REPLACE: | WITH: |
|---|---|---|
| ☐ **MIND** | | |
| Intellect | *ignorance* | *teaching* |

| | REPLACE: | WITH: |
|---|---|---|
| ☐ **WILL** | | |
| Volition | *rebellion* | *discipline* |

| | REPLACE: | WITH: |
|---|---|---|
| ☐ **EMOTION** | | |
| Affection | *discouragement* | *encouragement* |

---

**Proverbs 13:24**, "He who withholds his rod hates his son,
but he who loves him disciplines him diligently."

**Proverbs 29:15**, "The rod and reproof give wisdom,
but a child who gets his own way brings shame to his mother."

If your child is being rebellious or disobedient, it isn't going to help to speak encouraging words to him. In the same way, it will not help to reason with him or teach him.

- Disobedient, rebellious behavior ___requires___ discipline. It requires ___intervention___ to reset their course. Any other effort will be in _____ because it won't be addressing the problem.

- In the same way, we don't discipline the discouraged child. This child needs to have his heart refocused to ___trust___ in the Lord. Discipline would only further dishearten the child.


## III. *Focusing on Discipline – Committed to Training: The Will*

Most of us already know the right thing to do; we usually need to grow in actually doing it or doing it with the right heart attitude.

- If your child doesn't do what you say the ___first___ time you say it and with a ___good___ attitude, they are disobeying you.

  A practical definition of **"obedience"** for younger children is to do what you are told: "*Right away, all the way, and with a happy heart.*"

- Don't let yourself start ___excusing___ their sin or treating it as either of these other two areas.

  When you know it's an act of the will, don't excuse it. Act on it.

**Example #1:** A mother asks her child to put on his coat and he doesn't respond because he doesn't want to stop what he is doing. The mother excuses the sin by saying something like, "I guess he didn't hear me" (she takes the blame for his disobedience) or "I guess it's not really fair to ask him to come now, he's having so much fun" (she allows the child to become self-absorbed and passively defy her authority) and why wouldn't he? She has just undermined herself and diminished her authority with her own mouth by second-guessing her request of him as not fair.

**Example #2:** A mother is in the checkout line of the grocery store and her child is screaming for a candy bar. The mother excuses the sinful behavior by saying, "Oh, she's tired." This child will have a difficult time learning self-control because her mother excuses her lack of it and will not step in to discipline the situation.

This is difficult in public places but here is the principle to remember: you don't have to go "full circle" in the store. Because you are consistent with this training at home, a word from you or a look will convey that they will be held accountable for this behavior. When you get home, you make the event a priority and be sure to go full circle.

- If they know that they are ____not____ getting out of the accountability for their disobedience,

  they won't be so quick to disobey.

- It doesn't mean that our children won't ever be disobedient but it means they will be growing in the

  ____sure____ understanding that there is always an _____ for their behavior.

- Discipline is for our own good that we might share in His ____holiness____.

- **Proverbs 19:18**
  *Discipline your son ____while____ there is hope, and do not desire his death.*
  *("do not set your heart on his destruction" -NKJV)*

- "Discipline steps ____between____ a child and the ways that lead to death. Withholding

  discipline is a sure way to ____send____ your child down a path of destruction."

  (Tedd Tripp, *Shepherding a Child's Heart*)

We discipline for defiant or rebellious behavior, for an act of their will against our own. Take them through the full circle. There are basically two forms of discipline: rebuke & spanking. The first five years we are setting the foundation in this area of discipline and establishing authority. It makes raising kids so much more enjoyable when we get this part down in the early years of life.

---

Proverbs 13:24, "He who withholds his rod hates his son,
but he who loves him disciplines him diligently."

Proverbs 29:15, "The rod and reproof give wisdom,
but a child who gets his own way brings shame to his mother."

▢ The perspective of society says that children don't ___need___ correction, but rather instruction, because they are viewed as innocent or neutral.

▢ We don't "instruct" or "reason" with a sin nature, we are called by God to "___discipline___" wrong behavior.

▢ **Psalm 58:3**
*The wicked are estranged from the womb; these who speak lies go astray from birth.*

▢ **Proverbs 3:12**
*For whom the LORD loves He reproves, even as a father corrects the son in whom he delights.*

▢ ✗**Proverbs 13:24**
*He who withholds his rod hates his son, but he who loves him disciplines him diligently.*

▢ If your child needs a spanking and you withhold it, God says you hate him, because if you really loved him you would be ___determined___ to spank him.

▢ **Proverbs 29:15**
*The rod and reproof give wisdom, but a child who gets his own way brings shame to his mother.*

▢ Spanking and verbal reproof ___humble___ the heart of a child so that he learns to subject himself to his parent's authority.

▢ "God commanded the use of the rod in discipline and correction of children. He says that there are ___needs___ within your child that require it and you ___must___ use it.

The rod always refers to spanking done in the context of the parent-child relationship.

▢ The spanking is designed to RESCUE the child from his ___foolishness___ out of commitment to him." (*Shepherding a Child's Heart,* pp. 130-132)

## IV. Popular Misconceptions (What Spanking is Not)

☐ 1. *Spanking is NOT a God-given right to vent rage on your children.* Rage is a wicked sin. Our discipline is to be controlled and firm and to go full circle. It ends with a right relationship between the parent and child.

☐ 2. *Spanking is not the right to hit a child.* In fact, it is not hitting at all. It has a specific context with discipline. The parent who bullies a child will embitter the child against him.

☐ 3. *Spanking is not your opportunity to let out all of your frustrations.* If you are overly upset or out of control, you must not spank.

Consider whether a spanking is even justified, or if they are just getting on your nerves. Be sure to be in control if a spanking is required.

☐ 4. *Spanking is not retribution for the child's disobedience.* It is not payment for his sin.

## V. Anatomy of a Spanking Event (What Spanking Is)

☐ 1. *Spank the fleshy part of their seat only.* Never swat, slap, or hit them on the head or on their face. Never spank in anger.

☐ 2. Don't act __shocked__ or they will learn to __hide__ their sin.

☐ 3. Be firm and in __control__. Talk through what happened, carefully listening to their side, but don't let them steer you away from the correction that needs to occur.

☐ 4. *Discuss what the wrong behavior was and what the right behavior is.*

☐ 5. Help them understand __how__ they got to this point—that they chose the wrong way—and deal with any issues of the heart.

☐ 6. *Spank in privacy.* Inform them how many spanks they will get. This way you maintain control.

---

**Proverbs 13:24,** "He who withholds his rod hates his son, but he who loves him disciplines him diligently."

**Proverbs 29:15,** "The rod and reproof give wisdom, but a child who gets his own way brings shame to his mother."

📖  ✗ **2 Corinthians 7:10**

*For the sorrow that is according to the will of God produces a repentance without regret, leading to salvation, but the sorrow of the world produces death.*

This verse distinguishes the "I'm sorry I got caught and have to deal with the consequences," from the "I am grateful for the correction so that I am in proper standing with God." One brings death and one gives life.

📖  7.  *Deal with any forgiveness or restitution that needs to take place between the two of you or anyone else.*

📖  8.  *Hug and kiss them.* Tell them that it is completely  _over_ .

## VI. Conventional Objections to Spanking

📖  1.  **People say,** "I am afraid they won't _love_ me and they won't think I love them."

**God says,** *He who withholds his rod hates his son.* **(Proverbs 13:24a)**

📖  2.  **People say,** "It might cause emotional or bodily _____."

**The Bible says** (because you never discipline in anger), *Do not hold back discipline from the child, although you strike him with the rod, he will not die. You shall strike him with the rod and rescue his soul from Sheol.* **(Proverbs 23:13-14)**

📖  3.  **People say,** "I'm afraid if I spank him I'll be teaching him to use _violence_ to solve his problems."

Spanking is not violence. It is not a way of life. It is a controlled, purposeful event, applied in the context of willful disobedience to redirect the child.

📖  **God says** the opposite in **Proverbs 29:17,** *Correct your son, and he will give you comfort; he will also delight your soul.*

📖  Discipline brought full circle produces children who are at peace with you.

▢ 4. **People say, "It doesn't __work__."**

**Spanking is ineffective usually for one of five reasons:**

▢ • The child challenges the parent because the parent is __inconsistent__.

▢ • The parents give up and do not __persist__ because they don't see the fruit when they think they should.

▢ • There is a breakdown in the __method__. The event isn't brought full-circle—one of the four steps was missing or ineffective.

▢ • The parent is spanking in __anger__. Children have a difficult time yielding their __heart__ to an intimidating or angry parent.

▢ • Parents back down from discipline instead of addressing the child's will. The parent attempts to reason with the child, give them a "time out" or another misdirected remedy.

*no time outs for defiant will*

▢ 5. **People say, "I'm afraid of getting accused of child __abuse__."**

A properly administered spanking is never abusive. Nevertheless, it is a private and not a public matter. Evaluate your method to determine that you are not too harsh. Go full circle.

## VII. Reproof as Discipline (Older Children)

We spank our children when they are young and when they are older, spankings are rare. They may now be at the age to be disciplined by reproof.

▢ The key is still going through all four steps and for them to understand that their __accountability__ for wrongdoing remains consistently strong.

▢ Our goal here is to keep them accountable for the integrity of their __character__.

If we ignore this, and fail to discipline them, we compromise intimacy with them. Don't allow estrangement.

---

**Proverbs 13:24,** "He who withholds his rod hates his son,
but he who loves him disciplines him diligently."

**Proverbs 29:15,** "The rod and reproof give wisdom,
but a child who gets his own way brings shame to his mother."

☐ **Proverbs 20:5**

*A plan in the heart of a man is like deep water, but a man of understanding draws it out.*

We don't give kids a pass on bad attitudes or sassy remarks, or any type of disobedience.

☐ We have to practice talking and ___drawing___ them out when they are younger so that when they are teenagers they will enjoy ___explaining___ to you about what is going on in their lives.

☐ But this takes lots of practice and ___commitment___ on your part. So start young.

As they get older, they can take themselves "full circle" on their own.

☐ If we implement the four steps of discipline we won't need time outs, sending kids to rooms, grounding, or other penalties. Withholding ___privileges___ will have more significant impact if they are relevant to the situation.

☐ We are not teaching children to be "___good___," lest they grow up proud and self-righteous. We are training them to fo<u>cus</u> <u>on</u> Christ who is able to strengthen them to do what is ___right___.

☐ They learn to be convicted of sin and to indict themselves, seek forgiveness, and be restored. This builds ___hope___ in them because they will always know there is a ___remedy___ for sin. *They learn to obey for their sake, not yours*

☐ **Revelation 3:19a**

*Those whom I love, I reprove and discipline . . .*

☐ The principle here is to be committed in our discipline. We will have to do the same thing over and

over and over again, but don't _____ heart.

☐ We practice and practice and it gets a little easier and we keep going and eventually we will see the

fruit in God's timing. Remember that ___We___ are being trained also.

☐ **Be committed to discipline your children:**

☐ Help them see you as a _~~good~~ Source_ of truth,

their biggest ___cheerleader___,

their always available ___confidant___,

their most devoted prayer ___warrior___,

and the quickest to ___~~praise~~ react___ when they need correction.

---

**Proverbs 13:24,** "He who withholds his rod hates his son,
but he who loves him disciplines him diligently."

**Proverbs 29:15,** "The rod and reproof give wisdom,
but a child who gets his own way brings shame to his mother."

# *Homefront Application*

## COMMITTED TO DISCIPLINE
### A godly mother is committed to discipline

1. Do you and your husband agree on how your children are to be disciplined? If not, work on coming to an agreement so that your children will learn to see you as backing up each other in these matters.

   If you are not united in your approach, your children will quickly learn how to manipulate the situation and play you against each other while they walk away free from any accountability.

2. Discuss how an understanding of the mind, will, and emotions affect our choices in training and discipline. As you consider these areas, have you applied discipline for the wrong reasons?

Practice analyzing situations that come up this week. Are they matters that need teaching, encouragement, or correction?

God bless you as you implement these principles, especially if they are new to you. Hang in there. It takes practice, practice, practice to get the results (*Hebrews 12:11*).

3. Remember *Galatians 6:9*, *Let us not lose heart in doing good, for in due time we will reap if we do not grow weary*. There are seasons of planting and watering and pruning before we see the fruit in a child's life. Be encouraged (and encouraging) with small "breakthroughs" and "buds of progress." The harvest comes in time.

## I CHOOSE TO LIVE BY CONVICTIONS.

Signature: _____    Date: _____

# Lesson 12 Outline

## RECOGNIZING & HANDLING MANIPULATION
### A godly mother is aware and ready to respond appropriately

I.   Introduction

II.  Rating Your Child's Manipulative "Skills"

III. The Biblical Response to Manipulation

## This week's Scripture memory verse:

**Proverbs 26:4–5,** Do not answer a fool according to his folly,
or you will also be like him.
Answer a fool as his folly deserves,
that he not be wise in his own eyes.

# *Lesson 12*

## RECOGNIZING & HANDLING MANIPULATION
### A godly mother is aware and ready to respond appropriately

## *1. Introduction*

This lesson on manipulation and disrespect is huge for us as moms. It is is one of the reasons I wrote this study. I really want to encourage you to be "perseverers"—to not give up!

**The definition of manipulation** is "to skillfully manage or control by artful, unfair or insidious means to serve one's own purposes." There is nothing innocent about manipulation. Children know what they are doing.

☐ Even ___babies___ can manipulate their parents.

☐ You thought you gave them a ___simple___ directive and three minutes later everyone is upset. They want to ___win___, but you must win and win ___decisively___.

☐ But, there is hope, always. It does ___not___ have to be a part of how you relate to your child.

☐ **Proverbs 20:11** (NKJV)
*Even a child is known by his deeds, whether what he does is pure and right.*

## 11. Rating Your Child's Manipulative "Skills"

0-Never   1-Very Rarely   2-Seldom   3-Occasionally   4-Often   5-Very Often

Write the first initial of each child in one of the spaces. Keep a column for each child according to the key above and rate their behavior with each of the following:

### 1.  PLAYING ONE PARENT AGAINST THE OTHER

**Sample situation:** Child asks parent, "May I sleep over at Joan's tonight?" Parent says no. WITHOUT the other parent's knowledge, the child asks the other parent the same question. This parent may say, "Sure." The child returns to the first parent with "permission."

**Sounds like this:** "But Dad (or Mom) said I could."

**They are trying to:** find a "loophole" in the system.

**Parents are made to feel:** diminished in their authority or appear uncertain.

**HOW TO END THE MANIPULATION:** Teach them that they cannot ask the other parent if they have already been told "no" by one. If they do, they are in big trouble. If they know this before any situation comes up, it won't even occur to them to try this.

### 2.  COMPARING YOU TO OTHER PARENTS

**Sounds like this:** "But Ryan's parents let him."

**They are trying to:** make you second guess your family standards and convictions.

**Parents are made to feel:** guilty or overbearing.

**HOW TO END THE MANIPULATION:** Reemphasize your family's standards and personal convictions. Help them understand that you and your husband agree and that this is how we do it in the "Smith" family.

Offer explanations using Scripture so they can see that you have purpose in your decisions and convictions.

---

**Proverbs 26:4–5,** Do not answer a fool according to his folly,
or you will also be like him.
Answer a fool as his folly deserves,
that he not be wise in his own eyes.

### 3. MAKING ACCUSATIONS OR CRUEL REMARKS

**Sounds like this:** "I hate you." "I'm never going to talk to you again." "You are so mean."

**They are trying to:** make you doubt yourself.

**Parents are made to feel:** sad and upset.

**HOW TO END THE MANIPULATION:** Look beyond foolish words that our children will say sometimes and think about what is really true about me in that situation.

Don't return evil for evil or insult for insult, but give a blessing instead, "I love you, but you still have to clean your room." They are trying to steer you away from the real issue with inflammatory remarks. Stick to the real issue that needs to be handled.

### 4. DEMANDING JUSTIFICATION

**Sounds like this:** "Why?" or "Why not, that's not fair." "Just tell me why."

**They are trying to:** counter you with a better argument and have the last word. They are not really interested in your reason but only the fact that you are being drawn into a debate so that they may still have a chance to "win" by continuing to challenge you. *They want the last word*

**Parents are made to feel:** exhausted because of constant challenges.

**HOW TO END THE MANIPULATION:** Your instructions are not debatable. They learn that you are fair, so that when you say, "yes," it means yes, and when you say "no," it means no. Their only acceptable answer is, "Okay, mom."

*boredom is a choice if you are a thinking person you should be able to think of something to do*

### 5. WHINING, BEGGING, GRUMBLING, COMPLAINING, (EVEN SCREAMING)

*those are behaviors evil + will be disciplined ← look up*

**Sounds like this:** "Pleeeaaassseee, Mom!"

**They are trying to:** wear you down.

**Parents are made to feel:** overwhelmed and frustrated to the point that they can hardly handle or bear the situation any longer.

**HOW TO END THE MANIPULATION:** This behavior indicates that they do not accept your answer. They are second-guessing and challenging you to change your decision. Tell them "yes means yes" and "no means no" and tell them any of these responses are not acceptable and they will be disciplined if they do it again.

**6. POINTING OUT YOUR WEAKNESSES**

**Sounds like this:** "Why do I have to do it, you don't do it?" Or "Why can't I do it, you do?"

**They are trying to:** make you feel that you are asking too much of them OR that they are "big enough to figure life out for themselves."

**HOW TO END THE MANIPULATION:** Explain again that you are their God-given authority until you release them and as such you will not let them make choices contrary to the Word of God. Show them Scriptures that back up your reasons.

Teach them how you will give them gradual choices when they are responsible in present areas of privilege. Consider what they are saying to you. Is there any habit in your life that needs to be changed? If the child is referring to a one-time bad choice, the teaching here is "choose to sin, choose to suffer."

**7. SAYING THEY WILL DO SOMETHING, THEN NOT DOING IT**

**Sounds like this:** "Sure, Mom, I'll do it."
Later: "I would've done it, but I just didn't have time."

**They are trying to:** appease you for now so they can avoid or postpone the required task.

**HOW TO END THE MANIPULATION:** This is an example of passive rebellion. There are no privileges until the task is done. Talk through with them that what they did was actually passive rebellion and will be disciplined if it happens again.

---

**Proverbs 26:4–5**, Do not answer a fool according to his folly,
or you will also be like him.
Answer a fool as his folly deserves,
that he not be wise in his own eyes.

8.  **FEIGNING (FAKE BEHAVIORS—CRYING, "FEEL SICK," "TOO TIRED," AFRAID)**

**Sounds like this:** "I just can't do it now, I'm too tired."

**They are trying to:** get sympathy to avoid doing something.

**Parents are made to feel:** sympathetic or frustrated.

**HOW TO END THE MANIPULATION:** First determine if the behavior is real or faked. Sometimes it is hard to tell at first, but if the physical complaints are recurring ones, follow them up with a physician's visit. Withhold all privileges until the task is complete. In other words, the first thing to get their attention will be the incomplete task.

9.  **PROCRASTINATION (DAWDLING OR POOR PLANNING)**

**Sounds like this:** "I'm hurrying as fast as I can."

**They are trying to:** make sure there is not enough time because they don't want to go; OR take their time because they are not taking your instruction seriously; OR they want you to step in and help them out.

**HOW TO END THE MANIPULATION:** Explain your guidelines and expectations. Make it a challenge to them. Dawdling is poor planning. We are training our children to manage their time. If they dawdle, it affects other people's schedules. Let them reap the consequences of poor planning. But on occasion, when you know they are just overwhelmed and discouraged, step in and help them. Teach them how to plan and pace projects and "to do what you have to do first."

## 10. MAKING EXCUSES

**Sounds like this:** "Can Lisa do it, I don't have time." or "Mom!! I have way too much to do!!"

**They are trying to:** get someone else to do it, most likely you.

**HOW TO END THE MANIPULATION:** Determine if this is a case of poor planning or laziness. Are they discouraged and overwhelmed and need you to step in and help calm them down or do they just think someone else should do what you have asked them to do? If it is the latter, you redirect them to what you have asked of them.

Go through with them all that they need to accomplish and how what you have asked them to do will fit into that plan. Also decide what won't be happening until the prioritized items are complete.

## 11. PUTTING THEMSELVES DOWN

**Sounds like this:** "I can't do this math, I've never been any good at math."

**They are trying to:** enlist assistance or avert attention for sympathy.

**HOW TO END THE MANIPULATION:** Direct their attention to the task at hand. Explain some math to them until you see that they are catching on. You can tell if they just want you to do it. In those cases, they do it on their own and you can look it over when they are done.

---

Proverbs 26:4–5, Do not answer a fool according to his folly,
or you will also be like him.
Answer a fool as his folly deserves,
that he not be wise in his own eyes.

### 12. IGNORING YOU OR TRYING TO MAKE YOU THINK THAT THEY DIDN'T HEAR YOU

**Sounds like this:** "But, Mom, I didn't hear you!"

**They are trying to:** come up with an "acceptable" excuse or wear you out by having you keep repeating your request.

**HOW TO END THE MANIPULATION:** Make sure they hear you. Speak directly and clearly. And when you're finished, wait for them to say, "Okay, Mom." With little children, get down and talk to them face to face. Make sure they understand you; have them repeat the directions. *make it fun, mission impossible*

Teach them that your voice is an important voice. Children need to learn to be listening for Mom or Dad's voice. Not responding to it is a matter of disobedience.

### 13. TALKING YOU OUT OF DISCIPLINARY ACTION

**Sounds like this:** "Please don't take my phone privileges away; I'll never do it again."

**They are trying to:** avoid discipline.

**HOW TO END THE MANIPULATION:** The discipline stands. Remember to be committed to discipline for their sakes. Also, they are to be trained not to second guess your decisions. Mercy is not given when it is expected or thought to be deserved by the one receiving discipline or correction.

*Be reasonable*

Discussing beforehand any disciplinary action with your husband, before even talking with the child, will have the two of you in agreement over the course of action and prevent you from overreacting or going overboard in revoking privileges.

### TOTALS/EVALUATING YOUR RESULTS:

**0–14:**  Doing well

**15–35:**  Need to work on handling manipulation

**36+:**  Urgently need to work on handling manipulation

### III. The Biblical Response to Manipulation

▢ In handling manipulation, we are continually redirecting the child __back__ to what is true and what is right.

▢ __Each__ time we are to remember:

**Proverbs 26:4**
*Do not answer a fool according to his folly, or you will also be like him.*

**Proverbs 26:5**
*Answer a fool as his folly deserves, that he not be wise in his own eyes.*

▢ The ultimate __biblical__ example of manipulation comes from **Matthew 4**, where Satan attempts to overthrow the authority of Christ in the wilderness.

**Here are some principles to follow:**

▢ His plan is to __usurp__ God's redemptive plan by manipulating Jesus to his __schemes__ and rendering Him powerless to defeat sin.

▢ In this same way, Satan presents us with every possible craftily disguised counterfeit to __trip__ us up and send us down the wide path of destruction.

---

Proverbs 26:4–5, Do not answer a fool according to his folly,
or you will also be like him.
Answer a fool as his folly deserves,
that he not be wise in his own eyes.

- Even after forty days and nights of fasting (in the wilderness), Jesus was _not_ the least bit swayed.

- He _withstood_ the fiery darts of the evil one with _truth_ — the Word of God. He continually brings the _focus_ back and does not chase Satan down his clever _side_ _trails_.

- Jesus _redirects_ the conversation back to truth and _makes_ Satan align with Him. Satan, feeling exposed, slithers to a new approach: probing for a _vulnerable_ spot.

- He tries to present his plan as more logical, _easier_. He makes _false_ claims and gives misinformation. But Jesus does not allow Himself to follow Satan's _train_ of thought or be distracted.

- Satan _gives_ _up_ and runs, knowing he cannot manipulate the Son of God.

- Children must learn that you will not "_cave in_" or be manipulated.

- Otherwise, as they get older they will become _bolder_ and more determined to have their own way. The height of manipulation is _intimidation_. *master manipulator goes to intimidation even if they don't know it*

**Matthew 4:1-11**

*Then Jesus was led up by the Spirit into the wilderness to be tempted by the devil. And after He had fasted forty days and forty nights, He then became hungry. And the tempter came and said to Him, 'If You are the Son of God, command that these stones become bread.' But He answered and said, 'It is written, "MAN SHALL NOT LIVE ON BREAD ALONE, BUT ON EVERY WORD THAT PROCEEDS OUT OF THE MOUTH OF GOD." Then the devil took Him into the holy city and had Him stand on the pinnacle of the temple, and said to Him, 'If You are the Son of God, throw Yourself down; for it is written, "HE WILL COMMAND HIS ANGELS CONCERNING YOU', and 'ON THEIR HANDS THEY WILL BEAR YOU UP, SO THAT YOU WILL NOT STRIKE YOUR FOOT AGAINST A STONE,"' Jesus said to him, 'On the other hand, it is written, "YOU SHALL NOT PUT THE LORD YOUR GOD TO THE TEST."' Again, the devil took Him to a very high mountain and showed Him all the kingdoms of the world and their glory; and he said to Him, 'All these things I will give You, if You fall down and worship me.' Then Jesus said to him, 'Go, Satan! For it is written, "YOU SHALL WORSHIP THE LORD YOUR GOD, AND SERVE HIM ONLY."' Then the devil left Him; and behold, angels came and began to minister to Him.*

☐ **Proverbs 19:19**

*A man of great anger will bear the penalty, for if you rescue him you will only have to do it again.*

☐ When children learn that manipulation will not _deter_ you from the task at hand, and if they are held accountable for the wrong behavior, they will give up on their feeble attempts.

☐ **1 Kings 1:6a** "letting kids off"

*His Father had never crossed him at any time by asking, 'Why have you done so?'*

☐ **Jeremiah 4:22**

*For My people are foolish, they know Me not; they are stupid children and have no understanding. They are shrewd to do evil, but to do good they do not know.*

Discipline
w/ love ologic

---

**Proverbs 26:4–5,** Do not answer a fool according to his folly,
or you will also be like him.
Answer a fool as his folly deserves,
that he not be wise in his own eyes.

# *Homefront Application*

## RECOGNIZING & HANDLING MANIPULATION
### A godly mother is aware and ready to respond appropriately

1. Make an effort this week to be more aware of how you relate to each of your children.

   If you find yourself getting "caught up" in some difficult situations, then take some time later in the day to briefly write out and retrace the dialogue.

   Figure out where the situation broke down and how you should have responded, then throw away your notes.

   You may even retrace the event with your husband and get his input.

2. Your children are accustomed to your responses, also. So when they push your buttons and don't get the expected response, they may try harder.

   Keep praying for grace to respond properly. It takes practice.

   And when we completely blow it, as in lashing out in anger, we need to ask their forgiveness.

## I CHOOSE TO LIVE BY CONVICTIONS.

*Signature:*

# *Lesson 13 Outline*

## DEALING WITH REBELLION: "NEVER GIVE UP"
### A godly mother goes to battle for the heart of her child

*I.*    *The Process*

*II.*    *Principles of Rebellion*

*III.*    *The Contract*

*IV.*    *Emily's Testimony*

*V.*    *Note for Parents of Strong-willed Children*

*VI.*    *Conclusion*

## *This week's Scripture memory verse:*

**1 Samuel 12:23,** "Moreover, as for me, far be it from me
that I should sin against the LORD by ceasing to pray for you;
but I will instruct you in the good and right way."

# *Lesson 13*

## DEALING WITH REBELLION: "NEVER GIVE UP"
### A godly mother goes to battle for the heart of her child

This lesson is dedicated to the mother who says, "I don't think I have my child's heart with me. They're too old to spank and I'm feeling very discouraged. I don't know what to do about it anymore. I don't think anyone understands what I'm going through." If you are feeling that heartbreak, then this lesson is dedicated to you.

## *1. The Process*

☐ Some days you will think that your discipline and instruction did not _accomplish_ anything.

☐ You will wonder if you are doing the right thing. You will _question_ how you handled a situation. And the next time the same situation comes up, you _again_ follow the biblical principles of discipline.

☐ And _still_ you may feel, "it didn't work." But the next time, you do it again, and _eventually_ you will see that your child is beginning to understand, "this is what happens _every_ time I do this."

☐ They will give up and submit to you. It is a _process_, hang in there; _never_ _give_ _up_.

They can't have the *last word*. You have to win decisively over their wills. The anchor of your authority holds with your children and they learn that. You have to set that anchor deep and strong.

## II. Principles of Rebellion

☐ **Principle #1:** We are all ___flawed___ in our parenting, but even if we were flawless in our parenting, we could ___still___ have prodigal children.

☐ God is our biblical example of the complete and ___ultimate___ loving Father, ___yet___ the nation of Israel rebelled against Him. Even on a more personal level, we as individuals ___rebel___ against our Heavenly Father.

*10th grade r up*

☐ It is so helpful to know that God ___understands___ when we go through a child's rebellion because Satan would like nothing better than for us to believe that we are ___poor___ parents and feel ___defeated___.

☐ Instead, because we know God is with us, we can ___endure___ and not give up. We need to be understanding of parents going through this type of crisis and ___testing___ of their faith.

God's Word says we are to be willing to go to battle for them.

☐ **Principle #2:** Children have a ___choice___ to submit their heart to God or choose their ___own___ way.

☐ There is nothing we as parents can do to ___guarantee___ that they will live for God. It is ultimately their own choice.

☐ Still, we are called by God and ___entrusted___ with them to ___train___ them biblically; to direct them toward the ___best___ possible path. Before God we do what He ___calls___ us to do and we never give up.

Our children can make some very bad choices. As parents, we can become more focused on sheltering them rather than letting them bear the consequences of foolish choices.

---

**1 Samuel 12:23,** "Moreover, as for me, far be it from me
that I should sin against the LORD by ceasing to pray for you;
but I will instruct you in the good and right way."

⬜ **Principle #3:** The Lord is not so concerned that things go perfectly in your life; He is much more concerned with how you respond when things go __wrong__, even terribly wrong.

Life on this earth is not going to be perfect and God wants you to trust and obey Him, even when things seem to go impossibly wrong. He wants to build your faith.

Allow God to have His way with your child. This includes testing, trials and consequences if they choose to step out from fearing Him. They are really the Lord's and not ours. He can do whatever is in His will that would please Him and ultimately bring glory to Him. He will mold them into who He wants them to be through these circumstances.

⬜ **Isaiah 55:8-9**

*"For My thoughts are not your thoughts, Nor are your ways My ways," declares the LORD. "For as the heavens are higher than the earth, so are My ways higher than your ways and My thoughts than your thoughts."*

When some of the things we prayed would never happen *do* happen, we feel shaken to the core of our faith. That is when we must rely on the Lord and not on our own understanding.

**Choosing God's Great Blessings of Obedience or the Penalties of Disobedience:**

**Deuteronomy 28 & 30**

**Leviticus 26**

**God's Response to Rebellion:**

⬜ I will __appoint__ over you a sudden terror.

⬜ I will __set__ My face against you. (judgement)

⬜ I will also __break down__ your pride of power.

⬜ I will __let loose__ among you the beasts of the field.

⬜ I will __act__ with hostility against you.

⬜ I will also __bring__ upon you with a sword.

**God's Plan for Restoration:**

☐ If they ___confess___ their iniquity . . .

☐ If their uncircumcised heart becomes ___humbled___ . . .

☐ . . . So that they make ___amends___ . . .

☐ . . . Then I will ___remember___ My covenant . . .

☐ God's way to ___squash___ rebellion is not to wait it out until they "grow up." He comes down ___@ hard___ and if they still defy Him, He comes down harder and harder and harder until they ___realize___ that He does not give up.

We do not terrorize our children in any way at all, but we do understand from this passage how seriously God takes rebellion. These verses in **Romans 1:28-32** provide all the reasons in the world to address rebellion strongly. As parents, we are stepping in between our child and the ways that lead to their destruction.

☐ **Numbers 32:23**
*But if you will not do so, behold, you have sinned against the LORD, and be sure your sin will find you out.*

☐ If we fail to be obedient to what God calls us to do, then we are ___sinning___ against Him.

If you find yourself in that place today, my prayer for you is that you would be encouraged in Christ to never give up. Pray over these key verses.

☐ **Jeremiah 31:16-17**
*Thus says the LORD, 'Restrain your voice from weeping and your eyes from tears; For your work will be rewarded,' declares the LORD, 'And they will return from the land of the enemy. There is hope for your future,' declares the LORD. 'And your children will return to their own territory.'*

**1 Samuel 12:23**, "Moreover, as for me, far be it from me that I should sin against the LORD by ceasing to pray for you; but I will instruct you in the good and right way

13.4

☐ **Principle #4:** We trust in the Lord to bring them _back_ as we do our part.

We continue to _pray_ for them and to instruct them in the good and right way.

☐ **1 Samuel 12:23**

*Moreover, as for me, far be it from me that I should sin against the LORD by ceasing to pray for you; but I will instruct you in the good and right way.*

☐ God tells us that we are to _rebuke_ our children when they rebel. It is our _job._

☐ **1 Samuel 3:12-13**

*In that day I will carry out against Eli all that I have spoken concerning his house, from beginning to end. For I have told him that I am about to judge his house forever for the iniquity which he knew, because his sons brought a curse on themselves and he did not rebuke them.*

☐ It is always for our own _good_ to obey.

**Deuteronomy 6:24-25**

*So the LORD commanded us to observe all these statutes, to fear the LORD our God for our good always and for our survival, as it is today. It will be righteousness for us if we are careful to observe all this commandment before the LORD our God, just as He commanded us.*

**Deuteronomy 7:9-10,**

*Know therefore that the LORD your God, He is God, the faithful God, who keeps His covenant and His lovingkindness to a thousandth generation with those who love Him and keep His commandments; but repays those who hate Him to their faces, to destroy them; He will not delay with him who hates Him, He will repay him to his face.*

**Isaiah 47:10-11**

*You felt secure in your wickedness and said, 'No one sees me,' your wisdom and your knowledge, they have deluded you; for you have said in your heart, 'I am, and there is no one besides me.' But evil will come on you which you will not know how to charm away; and disaster will fall on you for which you cannot atone; and destruction about which you do not know will come on you suddenly.*

☐ God says: If you disobey, I will make life _tough_, and if you still disobey I will make it

tougher and so on and so on until you come to the end of yourself and you _submit_

your whole heart before Me, _repent_, and _obey_.

☐ Carefully watch their choice of _friends_.

## III. The Contract

**Stage 1**:   No Choice

**Stage 2**:   Our Choice

**Stage 3**:   Your Choice with Supervision and within Boundaries

**Stage 4**:   Your Choice with Accountability

## IV. Emily's Testimony

*Design for Discipleship*

## V. Note for Parents of Strong-willed Children

Don't believe that a strong-willed child will automatically be a rebellious teen. Also, don't allow yourself to believe that the Lord gave you a strong-willed child to get back at you or that having a child with these tendencies is going to be a negative for your family.

God purposely creates people of strong will for wonderful and grand purposes if they learn to surrender that will to Him. Strong-willed people are some of the most exciting people in history. If you know you have a strong-willed child, you will be challenged to keep on the alert and remain two steps ahead of them. Still, know that life with them can be a wonderful adventure as they grow into men and women who are sold out to accomplish great things for Christ.

Many people believe that only strong-willed children rebel. But any will, left unchecked, lives in defiance against God. We all live in rebellion against God until we surrender our hearts and lives to Him—regardless of our temperament.

---

**1 Samuel 12:23**, "Moreover, as for me, far be it from me
that I should sin against the LORD by ceasing to pray for you;
but I will instruct you in the good and right way."

## VI. Conclusion

☐ _Relationships_ cannot continue as if nothing is wrong when someone is living in rebellion.

☐ They need to feel the ___pain___ of broken fellowship. Otherwise they will never realize their need to submit to God's authority in their life.

If we believe that it's loving to continually rescue them or spare them from consequences, they will no longer see the need to change.

☐ So if you understand the ___heartbreak___ of enduring either of these two types of family trauma, remember, ___never___ give up. And if you have a friend who is living through this, be ___understanding___.

### Notes:

# *Homefront Application*

## DEALING WITH REBELLION: "NEVER GIVE UP"
### A godly mother goes to battle for the heart of her child

1. For serious ongoing rebellion: Do you have an older child or teen who has chosen to assert their own will against your authority in such a way that it is ongoing and disruptive to the family?

   Remember, this is a situation dealing with the will, not the mind or emotions—though both may enter in somewhat. Defiance of the will calls for discipline. Discuss with your husband the commitment you are going to have to make to turn the situation around. Perhaps a "restoration plan" is needed.

   Be in full agreement with your husband before beginning such an undertaking. It will take a united front for your child to know that you are serious. Don't let your child's rebellion divide you.

   Make sure your child understands everything you have decided upon and why. It is not necessary that they agree. Help them understand the purpose in your actions and God's view of disobedience. Let them know your concern and love for them and that choosing to sin means choosing to suffer consequences. This, too, is a process. Deep rebellion doesn't turn around in a week or even a month. No rebellion turns around without true repentance and humility. So keep strong and in the Word so you will remain focused and resolute for however long it takes.

## DEALING WITH REBELLION: "NEVER GIVE UP"

### A godly mother goes to battle for the heart of her child

2. For occasional challenges: At various ages, many children will "test the anchor" to see if it still holds. They are testing to see if you will respond as you did in the past. It is important that you persevere in bringing them back under your authority each time because it will help prevent an extended rebellious state.

   Be on guard regarding things that can exasperate a child. Check to make sure you are being attentive to them, listening carefully, showing tenderness daily, etc. Be watchful of their hearts. Don't let them stray. We can practice being watchful so that we can prevent a child's heart from getting to a dangerous place, though they are still free to choose.

   Even a child who purposefully defies their parents and goes their own way for an extended period of time will remember the foundation of authority that their parents established. It will go a long way in keeping them "afraid" of straying too far. The most rebellious child still wants limits because they are a demonstration of love, security, and protection. Deep down they want their parents to fight for them and bring them back.

3. For a friend who is enduring this hardship: Be understanding, yet give godly counsel. Don't encourage her to keep bailing out the child or protecting them from the consequences they have earned. Encourage restoration because these are lifelong relationships, but not by rescuing the child so they can continue as usual. They need to learn the pain of walking away from God. Provide Scripture for her; pray with her and encourage her to go to battle if need be, incorporating the guidelines already discussed in the lesson.

## I CHOOSE TO LIVE BY CONVICTIONS.

Signature: _____     Date: _____

# Lesson 14 Outline

## WORDS THAT EDIFY
### A godly mother chooses her words wisely

I. Introduction

II. We Edify Each Other with our Words by:
   A. Using Wholesome Words
   B. Having a Righteous Purpose for Our Words
   C. Stepping in at the Proper Time
   D. Building Up the Child in the Lord
   E. The Blessing that Ensues

## This week's Scripture memory verse:

 **Ephesians 4:29,** "Let no unwholesome word proceed from your mouth, but only such a word as is good for edification according to the need of the moment, so that it will give grace to those who hear."

# Lesson 14

## WORDS THAT EDIFY
### A godly mother chooses her words wisely

1. Introduction

- __Memories__ are a fascinating thing. Children will remember the most random things. Things you may __not__ remember at all.

- You will have great memories in which you can recall every __detail__ and treasure the event. But they will have their __own__ memories and things that were of great __significance__ to them.

- What __words__ will your children remember you for? What __tone__ will your children remember you for?

- When a woman is frustrated, she tends to resort to two devices to gain __control__ in her family relationships:

  In regard to her husband, she may withhold __intimacy__ .

- In regard to her children, she may raise her voice.

  - Though there is a place for a firm voice, these two methods are __counterfeits__ . Don't do them. They will __undermine__ your relationships.

- **Ephesians 4:29**
  *Let no unwholesome word proceed from your mouth, but only such a word as is good for edification according to the need of the moment, so that it will give grace to those who hear.*

- **EDIFICATION** is building up a person in the __Lord__ .

**14.1**

## II. We Edify Each Other with our Words by:

**A.** Using _____wholesome_____ Words

☐ Choosing our words wisely, conveying an attitude of love and understanding.

☐ Edifying words are spoken to _____Strengthen_____ a person in the Lord; to motivate them to _____Persevere_____, to encourage them to become more like Christ.

☐ We do not use words that _____belittle_____ or tear down.

We are not to use sarcastic words or blast our children with angry words. We are not to use profane language or take the Lord's name in vain.

☐ When we stumble in any of these areas, we need to confess it to the Lord and ask our child's _____forgiveness_____.

We need to be mindful of how we speak to our husbands also.

Angry or harsh words are often the words that you will forget or try to forget, but they might be the very thing that your child remembers. If they are forgiven, they are quickly forgotten by our children. Make sure that this isn't a habit, because then it's not easily dealt with.

☐ **Ephesians 5:4**
_And there must be no filthiness and silly talk, or coarse jesting, which are not fitting, but rather giving of thanks._

☐ **Colossians 3:8**
_But now you also, put them all aside: anger, wrath, malice, slander, and abusive speech from your mouth._

☐ **James 3:9-10**
_With it (the tongue) we bless our Lord and Father, and with it we curse men, who have been made in the likeness of God; from the same mouth come both blessing and cursing. My brethren, these things ought not to be this way._

☐ **Proverbs 15:4**
_A soothing tongue is a tree of life, but perversion in it crushes the spirit._

---

**Ephesians 4:29,** "Let no unwholesome word proceed from your mouth,
but only such a word as is good for edification according to the need
of the moment, so that it will give grace to those who hear."

🖵 **Proverbs 12:18**

*There is one who speaks rashly like the thrusts of a sword, but the tongue of the wise brings healing.*

🖵 **Proverbs 15:28**

*The heart of the righteous ponders how to answer, but the mouth of the wicked pours out evil things*

🖵 **Proverbs 16:24**

*Pleasant words are a honeycomb, sweet to the soul and healing to the bones.*

🖵 **Proverbs 25:11** (NKJV)

*A word fitly spoken is like apples of gold in settings of silver.*

🖵 **Proverbs 31:26**

*She opens her mouth with wisdom, and the teaching of kindness is on her tongue.*

## B. Having a Righteous Purpose for Our Words

🖵 These would include ____*admonition*____ and correction.

🖵 **Romans 15:2**

*Each of us is to please his neighbor for his good, to his edification.*

*We look out for others with what we say.*

We should be looking out for another person in the things that we say, for their best interest.

🖵 **1 Corinthians 10:23-24**

*All things are lawful, but not all things are profitable. All things are lawful, but not all things edify. Let no one seek his own good, but that of his neighbor.*

🖵 These people believe that they have every ____*right*____ to do what they are doing, but

that is vastly different from doing what is ____*right*____. What is their motivation? What is their

____*purpose*____? to tear down for their selfish motivation

🖵 **Proverbs 10:19-21**

*Where there are many words, transgression is unavoidable, but he who restrains his lips is wise. The tongue of the righteous is as choice silver, the heart of the wicked is worth little. The lips of the righteous feed many, but fools die for lack of understanding.*

🖵 **Discretion:** Our children need to learn to ____*hold*____ their tongues.

☆ Galatians 2:20

☐ **Proverbs 11:22**

*As a ring of gold in a swine's snout, so is a beautiful woman who lacks discretion.*

☐ **Proverbs 16:28** (NKJV)

*A perverse man sows strife, and a whisperer separates the best of friends.*

☐ **Proverbs 18:8** (NKJV)

*The words of a talebearer are like tasty trifles, and they go down into the inmost body.*

☐ **Proverbs 21:23** (NKJV)

*Whoever guards his mouth and tongue keeps his soul from troubles.*

☐ **Proverbs 23:16**

*And my inmost being will rejoice when your lips speak what is right.*

☐ **Proverbs 29:11** (NKJV)

*A fool vents all his feelings, but a wise man holds them back.*

☐ **Proverbs 18:2**

*A fool does not delight in understanding, but only in revealing his own mind.*

☐ **Proverbs 20:19**

*He who goes about as a slanderer reveals secrets, therefore do not associate with a gossip.*

☐ **Proverbs 26:20**

*For lack of wood the fire goes out, and where there is no whisperer, contention quiets down.*

☐ **Proverbs 29:20**

*Do you see a man who is hasty in his words? There is more hope for a fool than for him.*

☐ **1 Corinthians 11:19**

*For there must also be factions among you, so that those who are approved may become evident among you.*

True
Helpful        think before you speak
Important
Necessary
Kind

---

Ephesians 4:29, "Let no unwholesome word proceed from your mouth,
but only such a word as is good for edification according to the need
of the moment, so that it will give grace to those who hear."

◻ **Jesus's response to false testimony: (the epitome of persecution)**

**Mark 14:55-62**

*Now the chief priests and the whole Council kept trying to obtain testimony against Jesus to put Him to death, and they were not finding any. For many were giving false testimony against Him, but their testimony was not consistent. Some stood up and began to give false testimony against Him, saying, "We heard Him say, 'I will destroy this temple made with hands, and in three days I will build another made without hands.'" Not even in this respect was their testimony consistent. The high priest stood up and came forward and questioned Jesus, saying, 'Do You not answer? What is it that these men are testifying against You?' But He kept silent and did not answer. Again the high priest was questioning Him, and saying to Him, 'Are You the Christ, the Son of the Blessed One?' And Jesus said, 'I am; and you shall see* THE SON OF MAN SITTING AT THE RIGHT HAND OF POWER, and COMING WITH THE CLOUDS OF HEAVEN.'*

*Sometimes when people say awful things to us, about us, about our children, our husbands, our church, etc., we have to let it go. God will stand for you.*

✷ ◻ **Exodus 14:14**

*The LORD will fight for you while you keep silent.*

◻ We need to train our children to ___ rest ___ in the Lord during such times.

◻ We are not called to fight for our ___ reputations ___.

**Acts 5:38-39**

*. . . if this plan or action is of men, it will be overthrown; but if it is of God, you will not be able to overthrow them; or else you may even be found fighting against God.*

◻ Do not be ___ tempted ___ to respond.

**James 1:13-14**

*Let no one say when he is tempted, 'I am being tempted by God'; for God cannot be tempted by evil, and He Himself does not tempt anyone. But each one is tempted when he is carried away and enticed by his own lust.* our lust to make things right or even the score

**1 Corinthians 10:13**

*No temptation has overtaken you but such as is common to man; and God is faithful, who will not allow you to be tempted beyond what you are able, but with the temptation will provide the way of escape also, so that you will be able to endure it.*

☐ We teach our children not to return evil for evil or insult for ___insult___, no matter what another person's ___motive___ is.

They need to learn to rest in it.

**Matthew 5:39** instructs us to *bear up under a deep insult*, which can be really, really hard to do.

Sometimes people hear things and they distort the truth without even realizing it. It becomes twisted and it goes on and on because they're spreading their own perception. Don't speak until you know the full story. And then ask yourself, "Does this even need to be said?" Just because it's true doesn't mean we should repeat it.

Be very careful about the things that you share and the things that you tell. You may not have the full story.

☐ **2 Timothy 2:16-17**
*But avoid worldly and empty chatter, for it will lead to further ungodliness, and their talk will spread like gangrene . . .*

☐ Suffering persecution for your ___faith___:

☐ **Matthew 5:10-12**
*Blessed are those who have been persecuted for the sake of righteousness, for theirs is the kingdom of heaven. Blessed are you when people insult you and persecute you, and falsely say all kinds of evil against you because of Me. Rejoice and be glad, for your reward in heaven is great; for in the same way they persecuted the prophets who were before you."*

C. **Stepping In at the Proper ___time___.**

☐ Say what needs to be said, when it needs to be said, but don't humiliate, shame or correct a child in front of others.

☐ Be ___ready___ when the "need of the moment" calls for you to step in.

The ___timing___ of your words is important.

---

Ephesians 4:29, "Let no unwholesome word proceed from your mouth,
but only such a word as is good for edification according to the need
of the moment, so that it will give grace to those who hear."

▢ **Colossians 4:6**

*Let your speech always be with grace, as though seasoned with salt, so that you will know how you should respond to each person.*

▢ According to the need of the moment also refers to applying the proper __training__ to the situation.

Remember the three categories: mind/will/emotion; teaching/reproof/encouragement. *mind- teach the ignorant | will - Rebuke the defiant | emotion- encourage the faint hearted*

▢ **1 Thessalonians 5:14**

*We urge you, brethren, admonish the unruly, encourage the fainthearted, help the weak, be patient with everyone.* *teach the ignorant | Rebuke the defiant | encourage the faint hearted*

▢ **Isaiah 50:4a**

*The LORD GOD has given Me the tongue of disciples, that I may know how to sustain the weary one with a word.*

**D. Building Up the Child in the __Lord__.**

▢ Your words minister to his __spirit__, not his __flesh__. They encourage him to do the difficult thing, to go beyond the required or the ordinary, to live a life of __excellence__ before the Lord.

▢ Because the Word of God has __power__, His Words are often the __best__ choice of words to help convey what you are teaching.

▢ **2 Timothy 3:14-17**

*You, however, continue in the things you have learned and become convinced of, knowing from whom you have learned them, and that from childhood you have known the sacred writings which are able to give you the wisdom that leads to salvation through faith which is in Christ Jesus. All Scripture is inspired by God and profitable for teaching, for reproof, for correction, for training in righteousness; so that the man of God may be adequate, equipped for every good work.*

▢ **Hebrews 4:12**

*For the word of God is living and active and sharper than any two-edged sword, and piercing as far as the division of soul and spirit, of both joints and marrow, and able to judge the thoughts and intentions of the heart.*

**1 Thessalonians 2:13**

*For this reason we also constantly thank God that when you received the word of God which you heard from us, you accepted it not as the word of men, but for what it really is, the word of God, which also performs its work in you who believe.*

**Proverbs 15:2**

*The tongue of the wise makes knowledge acceptable, but the mouth of fools spouts folly.*

God's words are eternal and powerful. They are great words to use in edifying our children – it will bless them. It will also help them learn how to grow up to be a bold witness because the Word of God empowers us.

**E. The Blessing that _ensues_**

Gracious words _bless_, rather than _blast_, a child. They minister to a child's heart so that he is _grateful_ for the instruction.

Don't miss your _opportunity_ to bless a child. Edification is _not_ false praise or flattery.

It conveys love and appreciation for the child in the Lord.

Sometimes a child's words can minister back to us so deeply. We want our words to minister deeply to our children, but sometimes the opposite will happen. We can live off of edifying words for a long time.

**Proverbs 12:25**

*Anxiety in a man's heart weighs it down, but a good word makes it glad.*

What are the words our children will always _remember_ us saying?

Let's pick them _wisely_.

**Psalm 19:14**

*Let the words of my mouth and the meditation of my heart be acceptable in Your sight, O LORD, my rock and my Redeemer.*

---

Ephesians 4:29, "Let no unwholesome word proceed from your mouth, but only such a word as is good for edification according to the need of the moment, so that it will give grace to those who hear."

# *Homefront Application*

## WORDS THAT EDIFY
### A godly mother chooses her words wisely

1. Be very aware of your words and tone (including volume) this week. Think about the things you are saying. Are your words edifying to your children and husband?

2. Have a private discussion with your husband. Discuss between the two of you how you speak to your children in each of the following three scenarios:

   A.   Instructing your children

   B.   Reproving your children

   C.   Encouraging your children

How do you think each of your children would characterize how you speak to them and how you speak to each other? Would the Lord have you change anything in how you speak to members of your family? Confess sinful patterns and consider how you will determine to replace the old with the new.

Remember to speak the edifying words of *Ephesians 4:29* to each other even in this conversation.

*Let no unwholesome word proceed from your mouth, but only such a word as is good for edification, according to the need of the moment, so that it will give grace to those who hear.*

## I CHOOSE TO LIVE BY CONVICTIONS.

Signature: _____      Date: _____

# Lesson 15 Outline

## GUARDING A CHILD'S MIND
### A godly mother chooses her child's environment wisely

I.  The Battle

II.  Trust in the Truth

III.  No Compromises

IV.  Our Defense

V.  Shoring Up Personal Convictions
  - A.  Materialism
  - B.  Reading Materials
  - C.  Movies
  - D.  Television
  - E.  Music
  - F.  School Assignments
  - G.  Slumber Parties
  - H.  Dating/Courting/Purity

VI.  Principles to Remember

## This week's Scripture memory verse:

**Colossians 2:8**, "See to it that no one takes you captive through philosophy and empty deception, according to the tradition of men, according to the elementary principles of the world, rather than according to Christ."

# *Lesson 15*

## GUARDING A CHILD'S MIND
### A godly mother chooses her child's environment wisely

## I.  The Battle

Today's lesson is about the many things in this world that are competing for your child's thoughts—things that are fiercely battling to push aside the things of God. We cannot afford to be complacent.

- [ ] We are _**battling**_ for the hearts and minds of our children. We are at _**war**_.

Jesus often drew spiritual "lines in the sand" for people. You can see this when you listen to the parables in the Bible. He says, "If you cross this line, we will be at war." So many people are at war and do not even know it.

- [ ] **James 4:4**

  *Adulterers and adulteresses!* (referring to spiritual unfaithfulness) *Do you not know that friendship with the world is enmity with God? Whoever therefore wants to be a friend of the world makes himself an enemy of God.*

- [ ] The plan is to help your children _**own**_ their faith so that when they leave your home they will have their own _**convictions**_ that they will stand on.

Sometimes, their convictions will be challenged. You've taught them your convictions at home and then they go out in the world and their convictions are going to be challenged. They're going to say, "Wait, is this my parents' conviction or is this my own?" It's a testing ground for them.

Sometimes it will make them think twice and ask, "Wait a minute, what do I really believe?" Hopefully, they will go back to the source of truth, to the Word of God, and to their parents.

## *11. Trust in the Truth*

- As they grow up they will continually hear nonsense that they will learn to _filter_ through the Word of God. The Word can _withstand_ any of man's wild philosophies and made-up foolishness.

- **Colossians 2:6-8**
  *Therefore as you have received Christ Jesus the Lord, so walk in Him, having been firmly rooted and now being built up in Him and established in your faith (owning their faith), just as you were instructed, and overflowing with gratitude. See to it that no one takes you captive through philosophy and empty deception, according to the tradition of men, according to the elementary principles of the world, rather than according to Christ.*

- **Ephesians 4:14-15** (referring to maturing in Christ)
  *As a result, we are no longer to be children, tossed here and there by waves and carried about by every wind of doctrine, by the trickery of men, by craftiness in deceitful scheming; but speaking the truth in love, we are to grow up in all aspects into Him who is the head, even Christ.*

- **Romans 12:2**
  *And do not be conformed to this world, but be transformed by the renewing of your mind, so that you may prove what the will of God is, that which is good and acceptable and perfect.*

- **Isaiah 26:3**
  *The steadfast of mind You will keep in perfect peace, because he trusts in You.*
  *You will keep him in perfect peace whose mind is stayed on You, because he trusts in You.* (NKJV)

- **Philippians 4:6-8**
  *Be anxious for nothing, but in everything by prayer and supplication with thanksgiving let your requests be made known to God. And the peace of God, which surpasses all comprehension, will guard your hearts and your minds in Christ Jesus. Finally, brethren, whatever is true, whatever is honorable, whatever is right, whatever is pure, whatever is lovely, whatever is of good repute, if there is any excellence and if anything worthy of praise, dwell on these things.*

  Because of the world we live in, sometimes we realize we are not dwelling on the things that are excellent, true and lovely. We can get bogged down by thinking about things that aren't edifying.

*One truth many beliefs*

---

Colossians 2:8, "See to it that no one takes you captive through philosophy and empty deception, according to the tradition of men, according to the elementary principles of the world, rather than according to Christ."

**Isaiah 54:17**

*No weapon that is formed against you will prosper; and every tongue that accuses you in judgment you will condemn. This is the heritage of the servants of the LORD, and their vindication is from Me,' declares the LORD.*

The Word has power and it ministers to us.

▢ We are not to think that we can be involved with feeding our minds __garbage__ and not be affected by it.

▢ We must have convictions regarding what __enters__ our minds and we need to be developing and applying them even when our children are __small__.

Sometimes people say, "Well, I can watch this stuff on TV because my kids are two and three and when they're older, I'll change. But children know.

▢ **Proverbs 23:7**

*For as he thinks within himself so he is . . .*

**Psalm 119:112**

*I have inclined my heart to perform Your statutes forever, even to the end.*

What was common and acceptable 20 years ago (as far as not letting these things infiltrate American homes) has drastically and dramatically changed.

▢ The morality pendulum has swung so far to the __extreme__ so fast that we haven't even begun to realize all the havoc it will reap.

People are screaming to have their own way and their own choices apart from God. They are completely oblivious to the fact that they have stepped over that line in the sand that Jesus drew. And they are at war. They claim it's nobody else's business and that they are not really hurting anyone. They don't even know that they are at war with God.

▢ But evil unchecked __eventually__ affects everyone.

▢ We must not __deceive__ ourselves into believing that we can harbor evil thoughts without them affecting us, or that they will remain hidden.

Don't be taken captive by philosophy and empty deception. Counterfeit values have infiltrated our society and much of the thinking in our culture.

**Isaiah 13:11**
*Thus I will punish the world for its evil and the wicked for their iniquity; I will also put an end to the arrogance of the proud and abase the haughtiness of the ruthless.*

Evil has become bold and ruthless in the world.

Sometimes evil seems to have more power because it appears to have no ____rules____ for itself.

But it does not have more power.

____God's____ holy and righteous power is infinitely ____more____ powerful. Evil has to have ____permission____.

**Examples:** Job & Peter

It is a big job to guard our children's minds against the evil of the world, but always remember that God is sovereign and Satan is not. It's not even a close comparison. Satan is a creation. He is not the Creator.

We can rise above the wickedness of the world and still see the sovereignty of God through it all. We can have self-controlled lives. We can draw more closely to God and depend on Him.

## III. No Compromises

We cannot let our children's minds be ____broken____ ____into____ and ____plundered____.

I get this visual of a very fancy gift box, wrapped up just as beautiful as you could possibly imagine. That's how evil presents itself, "Here, this is for you." But you open it up and inside there's a deadly snake, just waiting to strike. It seems like it happened suddenly, but it really didn't at all. We've been looking at that box for awhile.

**Proverbs 7:21-27**
*With her many persuasions she entices him; with her flattering lips she seduces him. Suddenly he follows her as an ox goes to the slaughter, or as one in fetters to the discipline of a fool, until an arrow pierces through his liver; as a bird hastens to the snare, so he does not know that it will cost him his life. Now therefore, my sons, listen to me, and pay attention to the words of my mouth. Do not let your heart turn aside to her ways, do not stray into her paths. For many are the victims she has cast down, and numerous are all her slain. Her house is the way to Sheol, descending to the chambers of death.*

---

Colossians 2:8, "See to it that no one takes you captive through philosophy and empty deception, according to the tradition of men, according to the elementary principles of the world, rather than according to Christ."

Evil presents itself as, "This is all right. This is fun. This is good. There is nothing really wrong with this. This won't hurt you."

What things are irresistible enticements to your family members? Do you have any beautiful poison boxes in your lives? How much can you handle that box before the lid falls off? How much can you dabble in something before it bites?

▢ Every downfall begins with ___*small*___ compromises. That is why we build a series of ___*gaurdrails*___ from our personal convictions.

▢ **Luke 16:10**

*He who is faithful in a very <u>little</u> <u>thing</u> is faithful also in much; and he who is unrighteous in a very little thing is unrighteous also in much.*

Little things matter. It's assuring to know that it works both ways.

## IV. Our Defense

▢ **Our biggest defense:** The Holy Spirit in us (Salvation)

Thank God for His gift of the Holy Spirit which we receive at salvation. If we're going to go into battle against all these things in the world, we have to be prepared with the "full armor of God".

▢ **Ephesians 6:10-20**

*Finally, be strong in the Lord and in the strength of His might. Put on the full armor of God, so that you will be able to stand firm against the schemes of the devil. For our struggle is not against flesh and blood, but against the rulers, against the powers, against the world forces of this darkness, against the spiritual forces of wickedness in the heavenly places. Therefore, take up the full armor of God, so that you will be able to resist in the evil day, and having done everything, to stand firm. Stand firm therefore, HAVING GIRDED YOUR LOINS WITH TRUTH, and HAVING PUT ON THE BREASTPLATE OF RIGHTEOUSNESS, and having shod YOUR FEET WITH THE GOSPEL OF PEACE; in addition to all, taking up the shield of faith with which you will be able to extinguish all the flaming arrows of the evil one. And take THE HELMET OF SALVATION, and the sword of the Spirit, which is the word of God. With all prayer and petition pray at all times in the Spirit, and with this in view, be on the alert with all perseverance and petition for all the saints, and pray on my behalf, that utterance may be given to me in the opening of my mouth, to make known with boldness the mystery of the gospel, for which I am an ambassador in chains; that in proclaiming it I may speak boldly, as I ought to speak.*

☐ THE ___*full*___ ARMOR OF GOD

☐ TRUTH

RIGHTEOUSNESS

GOSPEL OF PEACE (Believers know that they are at peace with God)

FAITH

SALVATION (Assurance of Salvation)

☐ Be ___*watchful*___ and ___*persevere*___.

## V. *Shoring Up Personal Convictions*

We need our full armor, especially when we consider these areas that we war against:

## A. Materialism

☐ **Clothing** – What is our attitude about our clothes? What are our kids' attitudes about the clothes that they wear? If you "have to have that thing", it controls you. If it controls you, it should be out. If clothing controls them, then it's more of a heart issue.

No wonder we're not grateful people. We don't need so much *stuff*. We need to be doing things together and enjoy spending time with our kids. Be creative. Have family hobbies.

*If you have to have that thing - then it is controlling you*

*1950's 5 year old had 5 toys*
*Now days they have 250 toys*

*No wonder we are not grateful people because we have too much stuff*

*Be creative*

---

Colossians 2:8, "See to it that no one takes you captive through philosophy and empty deception, according to the tradition of men, according to the elementary principles of the world, rather than according to Christ."

**Ideas:**

_____

_____

_____

**Examples:**

_____

_____

_____

Kids have much more "disposable wealth" than most of their parents.

Book - *Material World: A Global Family Portrait*

▢ All Americans are wealthier than ___90%___ of the world's population.

▢ God does give ___good___ gifts and we are to enjoy them fully. But we are always to recognize where they came from; they come from His hand ___alone___.

▢ So we are to have an attitude of gratitude and a ___thankful___ heart for His provision , no matter how great or how small.

▢ It is all ___His___ and everything we have is from Him. He calls us to be ___content___ and ___grateful___.

Greed and ungratefulness are universal conditions of the heart. They span the entire history of man. No matter how much or how little we have, we will always struggle with these two huge issues of the heart.

□ **Ecclesiastes 5:10**

*He who loves money will not be satisfied with money, nor he who loves abundance with its income. This too is vanity.*

□ **Hebrews 13:5**

*Make sure that your character is free from the love of money, being content with what you have; for He Himself has said, 'I WILL NEVER DESERT YOU, NOR WILL I EVER FORSAKE YOU.'*

No matter how little we have, we always have Christ and in Him we have an abundance.

□ **Colossians 3:2**

*Set your mind on the things above, not on the things that are on earth.*

□ **1 John 2:15**

*Do not love the world, nor the things in the world. If anyone loves the world, the love of the Father is not in him.*

□ God ___provides___ for his children; He always has and always will. It is one of those biblical

principles you can be ___sure___ of.

□ **Psalm 37:25-26**

*I have been young and now I am old, yet I have not seen the righteous forsaken or his descendants begging bread. All day long He is gracious and lends, and his descendants are a blessing.*

□ **Proverbs 30:15a**

*The leech has two daughters, 'Give,' 'Give.'*

**Let's be grateful people:**

• If you have never experienced the danger of battle, the loneliness of imprisonment, the agony of torture, the pangs of starvation, you are ahead of 500 million people in this world.

• If you can attend a church meeting without fear of harassment, arrest, torture, or death, you are more blessed than 3 billion people of the world.

• If you have any money at all in the bank, a little bit of money in your wallet, or some spare change in a dish in your home, you are in the top 8% wealthiest in the world.

• If you have a smile on your face because you are truly grateful, you are in a blessed minority, because everybody should have it, but very, very few do live to embrace it.

---

**Colossians 2:8**, "See to it that no one takes you captive through philosophy and empty deception, according to the tradition of men, according to the elementary principles of the world, rather than according to Christ."

☐ Our children need to learn to put off thinking of what they can __get__ for themselves and put

✗ on thoughts of what they can __give__ or __share__ with another.

## B.  Reading Materials:

☐ **Books/Newspapers/Magazines**

There are so many things our kids can read that are not edifying. What messages are kids getting from the reading materials today?

There's a huge upsurge in the supernatural and mystical themes.  Our children need to know what the Bible says about these things.

With so many kids thinking it's harmless or fun to get involved in horoscopes, astrology, palm reading, witchcraft, satanic worship, etc., be careful!

☐ **Jeremiah 10:2**

**Isaiah 47:12-15**

Don't get wrapped up in playing with the fancy box!

## C.  Movies

☐ **Some websites for you to look up movies and screen for your children:**

www.previewonline.org

www.screenit.com

www.pluggedinonline.com

☐ **Matthew 18:7**

*Woe to the world because of its stumbling blocks! For it is inevitable that stumbling blocks come; but woe to that man through whom the stumbling block comes!*

God is very, very fired up about those who cause young people to stumble. They are in danger of God's judgment.

### D. Television

☐ Is television a controlling factor in your home? What are your convictions regarding television? Do you live with a clear conscience before God in what you allow yourself or your children to see?

### E. Music

☐ What are your convictions regarding music in your home? Often, music is what kids turn to when they are having a problem and it has a huge influence on them.

*#1 music*
*#34 mom (talking w/)*
*#58 dad (talking w/)*

### F. School Assignments

☐

### G. Slumber Parties

☐

### H. Dating / Courting / Purity

☐

---

**Colossians 2:8**, "See to it that no one takes you captive through philosophy and empty deception, according to the tradition of men, according to the elementary principles of the world, rather than according to Christ."

## VI. Principles to Remember

We have something so much stronger than the world. The Word of God and prayer are infinitely more powerful than the evil of the world. Don't think of them as equal.

### 💻 Principle #1:

Guarding a child from everything in this world does not work. Not just because it is impossible to shield a child from every evil, but because the child's heart is inherently inclined towards evil, as our own hearts are. Isolating a child from the world does not solve the problem of a sinful nature. That is why a child must learn to give his mind over to God, to grow in the character quality of self-control.

### 💻 Principle #2:

Teach children to flee from evil and guard their own thought lives. They must learn to handle the huge amounts of garbage that the world displays in front of them that they sometimes cannot escape. They are going to see some garbage, so how are they going to process it?

💻 We cannot protect our children from every evil thing. They must learn not only how to protect themselves from evil, but also how to respond in unexpected situations in such a way as to honor the Lord.

Teach them that they always have a choice. God will never put them in a situation where they have to choose the wrong choice.

💻 **Psalm 101:3** (NKJV)
*I will set nothing wicked before my eyes.*

### 💻 Principle #3:

The Lord wants us out __in__ the world, but not __of__ the world, so that we can be His message to a lost world.

💻 We have to have strong convictions ourselves about each of these things so that when they are brought under scrutiny, they will still stand. If we are wishy-washy, we'll cave.

💻 Even beyond this, our number 1 and number 2 __defenses__ are: The Word and Prayer.

💻 Every verse you __memorize__ will be a __direct__ hit in the battle for your mind and certainly in your child's mind. They need to be loading up on Scripture memory.

☐ The Lord will bring thoughts of His Word to you at very ___*needy*___ times to minister to you.

Don't we want the same for our children?

☐ **Romans 8:5**

*For those who are according to the flesh (sinful nature) set their minds on the things of the flesh, but those who are according to the Spirit, the things of the Spirit.*

*Ephesians 4:13 - nothing is hidden in Christ*

---

Colossians 2:8, "See to it that no one takes you captive through philosophy and empty deception, according to the tradition of men, according to the elementary principles of the world, rather than according to Christ."

# *Homefront Application*

## GUARDING A CHILD'S MIND
### A godly mother chooses her child's environment wisely

1. Discuss with your husband what it means to guard a child's mind. What steps do you agree are necessary within your home to create an environment that honors God and trains a child to guard his own mind?

   We can't keep them shielded entirely from the world but we can definitely purify our homes so that they know there is a distinction between the world and the ways that glorify God.

   Are there things in your home that do not glorify God or that can cause family members to stumble? This includes Mom and Dad.

2. Talk with your husband about some of the ideas that came up in your small group time regarding personal convictions.

   Is there anything your family can glean from the discussion that would assist you in your own personal convictions?

   As you come to agreement in some of these areas, decide how you are going to convey these family standards to the whole family so that they will all understand and have time to ask questions. They will see that you have spent some time coming to your conclusions and that you are "convinced" together that this is what is best for your family.

   Have a great family chat!

## I CHOOSE TO LIVE BY CONVICTIONS.

Signature: _____     Date: _____

# Lesson 16 Outline

## CHARACTER BUILDING
A godly mother trains her children in godly character

I.   Introduction

II.  Growing Beyond Obedience

III. Modeling Love

IV.  Love Acted Out

V.   Teaching Them to Think

VI.  Observing Character Strengths and Weaknesses

VII. Discerning Character Issues

VIII. Going Deeper – Three Levels of Motivation Revisited

IX.  Strengthening Character

## This week's Scripture memory verse:

**1 Corinthians 13:4-7**, "Love is patient, love is kind and is not jealous;
love does not brag and is not arrogant, does not act unbecomingly;
it does not seek its own, is not provoked, does not take into account a wrong suffered,
does not rejoice in unrighteousness, but rejoices with the truth; bears all things,
believes all things, hopes all things, endures all things."

# Lesson 16

## CHARACTER BUILDING
### A godly mother trains her children in godly character

## 1. Introduction

I want to give an overview of what we have done so far this year. So much of what we have been talking about lately is discipline.

Let's think about the entire picture of your family as a big circle. The outside of the circle represents the boundaries you are setting for your children. When they cross over those boundaries, we discipline them. Sometimes we get caught up in thinking that family life is all about the exterior, the border of the circle and discipline. But, in fact, the majority of family life is about the interior of the circle, which is having great relationships with your kids. When we create a loving environment in the home, they don't want to go to the exterior of the circle and cross over that line and enter into a discipline situation.

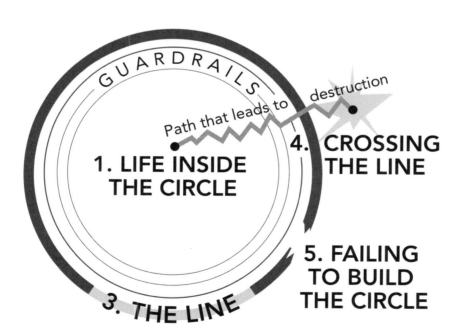

You will find that when you are raising your kids, some days will be hard, because during those first five years, we are setting up that boundary. They will challenge the line and when they get older, they'll challenge it again, but eventually they will see that the line holds.

I want you to understand that we are talking about this inward part of the circle. That's what we are going to concentrate on today, the relationship we are building with our kids.

Your kids will start to think more about the family relationships (their connection with you) and less about challenging you, so I do not want to be overly focused on the outside. Oftentimes, moms focus too much on the inside and that is why we emphasize the exterior of the circle, too. It has to be a proper balance.

*The love of Christ compels me.* (**2 Corinthians 5:14a** NKJV) We are compelled by Christ and through Christ to love our children and build these relationships. They grow to see these exterior borders not as something restrictive, but as loving protection.

## II. Growing Beyond Obedience

- [ ] The first five years we concentrate mainly on establishing __authority__.

- [ ] From ages 5-12 we concentrate on __character__ building. Though it really is a __lifelong__ process, these are the years that we are laying a firm foundation for godly character.

- [ ] This means we are now dealing with wrong __choices__, not defiance.

- [ ] If we are consumed with obedience __only__, we will fail to train them in godly character.

- [ ] We can wrongly address this with more __rules__, but then we are controlling external behavior and not inspiring the __heart__ to be surrendered to God's ways.

- [ ] Too many rules will actually teach a child that the emphasis of obedience is on their __behavior__ rather than their heart.

---

1 Corinthians 13:4-7, "Love is patient, love is kind and is not jealous;
love does not brag and is not arrogant, does not act unbecomingly;
it does not seek its own, is not provoked, does not take into account a wrong suffered,
does not rejoice in unrighteousness, but rejoices with the truth; bears all things,
believes all things, hopes all things, endures all things."

When we think about the exterior part of the circle, the rod and reproof are used for establishing authority—the quick surgical responses to a crisis. The inner part of the circle of character development is the ongoing exercise and diet. We do not always do it exactly right, but we are growing stronger and more disciplined, becoming more like Christ in our character.

If we consistently do our part when our children are young, and they fully grasp living under authority, then living within the circle is a great time with your kids. And if you have the outer part done by the age of five, the grade school years are great fun with your kids!

Of course, now and then they will challenge you and go to the edge of the circle. But you will find they will come in more and more, not so close to the edge. They are growing in godly character, working towards the center. At times, they will test that anchor.

The circle expands with more freedom, privileges and responsibilities, as they mature. It is a part of the training process of growing them up.

One way they may challenge you during these years is by trying to have the last word. There are many ways a child will try to do this—mutter under their breath, make a big sigh, make a face, slam the door, etc. They do not get the last word!

Think about yourself right now and your home. Are you so focused on the externals and the outer part of the circle that you are failing to provide a loving, tender atmosphere in your home? Our foundation is to be firmly set inside the circle.

The middle of the circle is when we get to be glorified like Him. We will never quite make it to the center because we are always growing in godly character.

It has been said that "more things are caught than taught". This is absolutely true! They are learning what we are modeling for them.

I am amazed by how much our children gauge themselves and their emotions by how we are in this circle. Our kids are very perceptive of us.

### III. Modeling Love

☐ What is it we are determined to __model__ consistently before our children?

☐ **1 Corinthians 13:4-7**

☐ Love is patient and __gentle__ with people.

Love is kind and __gracious__ to people.

☐ Love is not jealous or __envious__ of others.

Love is not prideful, haughty, __boastful__ or bragging.

☐ Love does not act unbecomingly, __rudely__ or selfishly.

Love is not irritable, __touchy__ or demanding of its own way.

☐ Love doesn't remember every wrong thing you ever did, it does not take personal offense, it does not harbor bitterness or resentment or hold __grudges__.

☐ Love is devoted to truth; it takes no pleasure in someone else's sin; it is never glad about injustice, but rather __rejoices__ when truth wins out.

☐ Love is __loyal__ despite difficult times of sacrifice.

☐ Love says, "I believe the __best__ about you, I expect your best and I will defend you, endure with you, and protect you in all things."

Our love is love when it is fully acted out. It's more than just how we feel. Love is demonstrated to our children.

☐ **1 Corinthians 13:1**
*If I speak with the tongues of men and of angels, but do not have love, I have become a noisy gong or a clanging cymbal.*

☐ Love not acted out is __empty__.

---

**1 Corinthians 13:4-7**, "Love is patient, love is kind and is not jealous;
love does not brag and is not arrogant, does not act unbecomingly;
it does not seek its own, is not provoked, does not take into account a wrong suffered,
does not rejoice in unrighteousness, but rejoices with the truth; bears all things,
believes all things, hopes all things, endures all things."

**16.4**

## IV. Love Acted Out

Love is long-term. It is a commitment. It goes way beyond how I feel about someone at the moment.

**Romans 5:8**
*But God demonstrates His own love toward us, in that while we were yet sinners, Christ died for us.*

"Waste of Life" – Humble yourselves before each other. Don't live compelled by your emotion. We live because we are compelled by the love of Christ and what He acted out.

"Wishing Life Away" – Live in the moment and be grateful. Have an attitude of gratitude.

**Mark 6:41-44**
*And He took the five loaves and the two fish, and looking up toward heaven, He blessed the food and broke the loaves and He kept giving them to the disciples to set before them; and He divided up the two fish among them all. They all ate and were satisfied, and they picked up twelve full baskets of the broken pieces, and also of the fish. There were five thousand men who ate the loaves.*

We must be on guard against being a wasteful person. God gives us "extra", even in the little things of life. God is so gracious and provides beyond what we really even need.

Every day is a day that God is building them into the person that they are going to be.

They are very impressionable and eager to learn, so we really want to be there for them. We want to be building the inside of this circle and be ready to train them, teach them, care for them, understand them, and listen to them.

Watch your kids and see what they are like. Really enjoy them!

- Appreciate _____ child and take note of them daily.

## V. Teaching Them to Think

- _____ putting in the extra time and care. It always pays off. Don't stop, even when

  you feel _____, because love is commitment demonstrated.

**Examples:**

- "Thinking Time" – Children lie on their beds and think, listen to music, or read a book.

- "Hours" – Children get one hour in the house to do an activity of their choice with you.

## VI. Observing Character Strengths and Weaknesses

God is at work in us. He promises to develop these characteristics in us through His Holy Spirit.

We do not demand complete compliance. Instead, we hold the bar high and are patient with our children to grow in these things.

## VII. Discerning Character Issues

☐ **Galatians 5:22-23**
*But the fruit of the Spirit is love, joy, peace, patience, kindness, goodness, faithfulness, gentleness, self control; against such things there is no law.*

☐ The fruit of the Spirit means that God _____ in us to bear this fruit if we are truly

His children.

☐ The Holy Spirit comforts us, prods us to make right choices, _____ our conscience,

convicts us when we make wrong choices, and helps us grow in godly _____.

## VIII. Going Deeper – Three Levels of Motivation Revisited

☐ **We need to ask ourselves these questions about our children:**

☐ 1. **Self:** think about your child's view of himself. Does he have a proper view of himself in perspective to God? Does he have a heart to please God in his choices or to seek his own way? What personal convictions is he developing?

☐ 2. **Others:** think about how your child relates to others. In the family, parents and siblings; to other adults and authorities; to his friends? What tendencies do you see?

☐ 3. **God:** think about your child's relationship with God. This is not referring to their salvation, but rather their understanding of God, what the child thinks about God. Is the child spiritually sensitive? Is he concerned with glorifying God with his life? Does he live by biblical convictions?

---

**1 Corinthians 13:4-7,** "Love is patient, love is kind and is not jealous;
love does not brag and is not arrogant, does not act unbecomingly;
it does not seek its own, is not provoked, does not take into account a wrong suffered,
does not rejoice in unrighteousness, but rejoices with the truth; bears all things,
believes all things, hopes all things, endures all things."

**16.6**

▢ We don't want our children to live lives of spiritual mediocrity because they never learned to trust God in difficult times, learning instead to _____ for the easy way and compromise character.

▢ In other words, we can let God have His way in their lives to _____ them or we can keep lowering the standards that we require of them until we allow them to live a life that does not require faith or sacrifice or stretching.

▢ Hold your standards high and let them grow into them without demanding immediate and complete compliance. Let them see the standards as what they are working towards.

▢ Ted Tripp says, "A change in behavior that does not stem from a change in heart, is not commendable, it is condemnable, because it is _____."

## IX. Strengthening Character

▢ It takes _____ to observe a child's character and to recognize a

_____.

▢ It takes _____ to devise a plan of action; to set a course, _____ them in it, and gauge their _____ over time.

## ▢ STRENGTH TO WEAKNESS CHARACTER SPECTRUM

| Fruit of the Spirit: | Opposite: |
|---|---|
| Love | selfishness |
| Joy | complaining, bitterness, self-pity |
| Peace | worry, fear, anxiety |
| Patience | impatience, easily angered |
| Kindness | unforgiveness, lack of mercy |
| Goodness | disobedience, impurity, deceit |
| Faithfulness | untrustworthy, unreliable |
| Gentleness | harshness, anger, pride |
| Self-Control | impulsive, laziness |

▢ As you and your husband _____ each of your children, you will discover the areas where they are weakest and where they are strongest.

▢ We don't get to _____ the weak areas and just revel in their strengths.

▢ On the other hand, we don't want to overly focus on negatives—that will exasperate a child into believing that you are all about externals.

▢ As parents we can really help them make progress in every area. Any weakness a child has can be _____ as a great strength in their life.

---

**1 Corinthians 13:4-7,** "Love is patient, love is kind and is not jealous;
love does not brag and is not arrogant, does not act unbecomingly;
it does not seek its own, is not provoked, does not take into account a wrong suffered,
does not rejoice in unrighteousness, but rejoices with the truth; bears all things,
believes all things, hopes all things, endures all things."

**16.8**

## Fruit of the Spirit and other Character Qualities:

☐ **LOVE:** the unconditional decision to put the needs of another above my own

☐ **JOY:** the supernatural delight in the person of God, the people of God, and the purposes of God (Dr. James MacDonald)

☐ **PEACE:** the calm assurance that what God is doing is best (Dr. James MacDonald)

☐ **LONG-SUFFERING:** being able to endure injury inflicted by others

☐ **KINDNESS:** a tender concern for others

☐ **GOODNESS:** manifested moral and spiritual excellence

☐ **FAITHFULNESS:** loyalty and trustworthiness even in extreme difficulty

☐ **GENTLENESS:** strength under control, having a teachable attitude that does not seek retribution or revenge

☐ **SELF-CONTROL:** restraining oneself from passions or appetites

**FAITH:** believing the Word of God and acting upon it, no matter how I feel, knowing that God promises a good result (Dr. Ron Allchin)

**GENEROSITY:** investing in others as much as I can with the time and resources that have been entrusted to me

**ORDERLINESS:** arranging my life and surroundings to achieve the greatest productivity; tidiness

**FORGIVENESS:** a decision, a choice, an act of my will, releasing another from the obligation that resulted when they injured me. It says, " You don't owe me."

**SINCERITY:** being as genuine on the inside as people see me on the outside

**VIRTUE:** conformity to a righteous standard

**DILIGENCE:** using all my energies to accomplish tasks assigned to me

**PUNCTUALITY:** arriving early enough to be in place at the appointed time

**ATTENTIVENESS:** showing the importance of a person by giving full concentration to his words and feelings

**OBEDIENCE:** doing what I am told, doing it right away, and doing it with a good attitude

**TRUTHFULNESS:** earning trust by accurately reporting facts

**GRATEFULNESS:** with a thankful attitude, letting others know by words and actions how they have benefited my life.

**DISCRETION:** cautious reserve in speech and decision-making

**CONTENTMENT:** the ability to enjoy present possessions without desiring new ones

**INITIATIVE:** taking steps to seek after God with a whole heart using the best opportunities to witness or encourage others

**HUMILITY:** recognizing my total inability to accomplish anything apart from God's grace

**MEEKNESS:** strength under control in learning to yield personal rights (Bill Gothard, Biblical Youth Institute)

☐ These character qualities are the _____ God has for us in this lifetime.

☐ They give life meaning and purpose, but most of all they _____ God, (which is why we were created) because they _____ His power to transform us so that we can live above impulsive and selfish desires.

---

**1 Corinthians 13:4-7,** "Love is patient, love is kind and is not jealous;
love does not brag and is not arrogant, does not act unbecomingly;
it does not seek its own, is not provoked, does not take into account a wrong suffered,
does not rejoice in unrighteousness, but rejoices with the truth; bears all things,
believes all things, hopes all things, endures all things."

# *Homefront Application*

## CHARACTER BUILDING
### A godly mother trains her children in godly character

1. This week spend some time with your husband discussing areas of character in your children. Review the list in this lesson. For further reference, see also Appendix 4, "Seven Life Stages of Character Building".

   Specifically identify a couple of strengths and weaknesses of your children (and even of yourself). Be grateful for their strength of character and point that out to them when you see it in action. This exercise will mostly apply to older children, when patterns of strengths and weaknesses are becoming more apparent.

   Do you both agree on what their strengths and weaknesses are? You may not, and that is fine. Over time when you have these discussions again you will begin to see patterns emerging.

   If you both identify a character trait as a weakness, look at its counterpart when it is redirected.

   Pray specifically that the child will grow in this area with your guidance.

   Sometimes older children need to spend time with their parents and have these talks together. These talks are not to be critique sessions. We don't want to label our children with negative traits. Rather, point out examples where they have demonstrated a weakness. Support it with a few examples so that they see that you are being helpful, not condemning. For example, are they procrastinating with school assignments? Tell them that you are concerned by several examples that demonstrate that they need to work on this area. They will see that any weakness redirected can be used to honor God and that we are all growing together in character. It is all a part of the lifelong process of becoming more like Jesus.

   *Philippians 1:6, For I am confident of this very thing, that He who began a good work in you will perfect it until the day of Christ Jesus.*

2. Select a "fun" family activity or individual parent/child activity that you would like to implement into your family routine from the examples shared in class or at your table. Maybe you will develop a new "family tradition" that your children will pass down to their children. Don't think of it as another thing you have to do. Just relax and enjoy each other. That makes for the best family times.

## I CHOOSE TO LIVE BY CONVICTIONS.

Signature: _____    Date: _____

# Lesson 17 Outline

## GROWING IN GODLY DISCIPLINES
### A godly mother disciples her children

I.  Introduction

II.  Owning Our Faith
   A. The Lordship of Christ
   B. Vital Signs of a Believer
   C. Discipling the Older Child and Young Adult

## This week's Scripture memory verse:

**Acts 2:39,** "For the promise is for you and your children and for all who are far off, as many as the Lord our God will call to Himself."

**Proverbs 1:8-9,** "Hear, my son, your father's instruction and do not forsake your mother's teaching; indeed, they are a graceful wreath to your head and ornaments about your neck."

# Lesson 17

## GROWING IN GODLY DISCIPLINES
### A godly mother disciples her children

## 1. Introduction

I chose **Acts 2:39** because it says the promise of heaven and eternal life is available to everyone, not just our generation and past generations, but for our children's children's children. That is an exciting promise of the Lord.

Of course, there are no cut and dried lines. We are all working on character our whole lives, but this is a general breakdown.

☐ The first five years we emphasize authority,

from ages 5-12 we emphasize character building, and

from ages 13-20 we emphasize developing a _____ life or godly habits.

☐ We can train a child in just about anything. But we can't train them in _____.

What are the handful of things you are going to pick and choose for your children?

☐ Potential is ___nothing___ without discipline.

## II. Owning Our Faith

### A. The Lordship of Christ

📖 **1 Corinthians 2:14**

*But a natural man does not accept the things of the Spirit of God, for they are foolishness tohim; and he cannot understand them, because they are spiritually appraised.*

📖 This person is still living with their old nature; he has not accepted the Lord as his Savior.

📖 **1 Corinthians 3:3**

*For you are still fleshly. For since there is jealousy and strife among you, are you not fleshly, and are you not walking like mere men?*

📖 This person is a believer but is living as if he is not. He is not living by conviction. Christ is not

____*Lord*____ of his life, he is. (NKJV—"carnal" in place of fleshly.)

📖 **1 Corinthians 2:15-16**

*But he who is spiritual appraises all things, yet he himself is appraised by no one. For WHO HAS KNOWN THE MIND OF THE LORD, THAT HE WILL INSTRUCT HIM? But we have the mind of Christ.*

📖 This person has come to the point of placing Christ on the throne of his life. Jesus is Lord over

all he does.

📖 **1 John 5:11-12**

*And the testimony is this, that God has given us eternal life and this life is in His Son. He who has the Son has the life; he who does not have the Son of God does not have the life.*

📖 **1 John 5:13**

*These things I have written to you who believe in the name of the Son of God in order that you may KNOW that you have eternal life.*

---

**Acts 2:39,** "For the promise is for you and your children and for all who are far off,
as many as the Lord our God will call to Himself."

**Proverbs 1:8-9,** "Hear, my son, your father's instruction
and do not forsake your mother's teaching; indeed, they are a graceful
wreath to your head and ornaments about your neck."

**B.** _Vital_ _Signs_ **of a Believer:**

☐ **1.** Professes Jesus Christ as _Savior_ : 1 John 2:23; 4:6, 15

☐ **2.** Admits and confesses all known _Sin_ : Acts 24:16  1 John 1:8-10; 2:1

☐ **3.** _Obeys_ God's Word:  1 John 2:3-5; 3:7, 9, 10; 5:2-3

☐ **4.** _Loves_ people, especially the brethren:  1 John 2:9-11; 3:10, 14-15, 17-18

☐ **5.** Does not follow the _World's_ value system:  1 John 2:15-16

☐ **6.** _Endures_ or abides to the end:  1 John 2:19, 24; 3:3, 24; 5:4

☐ **7.** _Grows_ in faith and discernment:  1 John 4:6; 5:19-20


☐ A person may pull away from God for a time, but the longer that amount of time continues, the

more likely that person never truly believed, because true believers are _faithful_

and _fruitful_ .

☐ **John 10:10**

*The thief comes only to steal and kill and destroy; I came that they may have life, and have it abundantly.*

30 Key verses memorize

## C. Discipling the Older Child and Young Adult

▢ Quiet time study:

*5th + 6th grade*

▢ Scripture memory:

▢ Discipleship Bible study:

▢ Accountability partners:

▢ Mission trips or service projects:

---

**Acts 2:39,** "For the promise is for you and your children and for all who are far off, as many as the Lord our God will call to Himself."

**Proverbs 1:8-9,** "Hear, my son, your father's instruction and do not forsake your mother's teaching; indeed, they are a graceful wreath to your head and ornaments about your neck."

**17.4**

☐ Family time:

☐ Memorial verses:

Isaiah 44:3-5
54:13
Acts 2:39
date scripture

☐ Prayer:

☐ Sundays:

☐ Youth group:

☐ Schooling:

We are passing the baton to the next generation of disciples, who must also be disciplemakers if we are to fulfill the Great Commission.

- **Philippians 2:22**

  *But you know of his proven worth, that he served with me in the furtherance of the gospel like a child serving his father.* (Generations serving together)

- **1 Timothy 4:12**

  *Let no one look down on your youthfulness, but rather in speech, conduct, love, faith and purity, show yourself an example of those who believe.*

- **Isaiah 44:3-5**

  *For I will pour out water on the thirsty land and streams on the dry ground; I will pour out My Spirit on your offspring and My blessing on your descendants; And they will spring up among the grass like poplars by streams of water, This one will say, 'I am the Lord's'; And that one will call on the name of Jacob; And another will write on his hand, 'Belonging to the LORD,' and will name Israel's name with honor.*

- **Isaiah 54:13** (NKJV)

  *All your children shall be taught by the LORD, And great shall be the peace of your children.*

- **Acts 2:39**

  *For the promise is for you and your children and for all who are far off, as many as the Lord our God will call to Himself.*

- **Psalm 102:18**

  *This will be written for the generation to come, that a people yet to be created may praise the LORD.*

- We are not just raising children, we are raising spiritual ___generations___.

- We _can_ raise godly children despite difficult circumstances or family ___histories___.

- We can set the spiritual ___tone___ for generations not yet born (**Acts 2:39**). And if need be, it can start with ___me___.

- Rahab was delivered from amidst a ___pagan___ nation when the armies of Israel conquered Jericho. Her faith delivered her and God blessed her ___heritage___ by including her in the lineage of ___Jesus___, the Messiah, fourteen hundred years later.

---

**Acts 2:39,** "For the promise is for you and your children and for all who are far off, as many as the Lord our God will call to Himself."

**Proverbs 1:8-9,** "Hear, my son, your father's instruction and do not forsake your mother's teaching; indeed, they are a graceful wreath to your head and ornaments about your neck."

# Homefront Application

## GROWING IN GODLY DISCIPLINES
### A godly mother disciples her children

1. Do you have a discipleship plan for your children when they reach their teen years? Consider some family goals you might establish in such areas as:

   Bible Study

   Sharing the Gospel

   Scripture Memory

   Missions

   Church Ministry Involvement

   Church Attendance

   Youth Group Commitment

   Add others from your notes that you may wish to discuss with your husband.

2. Consider your child's activities. Some of our children will excel in music or athletics, et cetera and that is fine as long as they are not losing out on the most important training that you want for them. Often the spiritual development of a child gets shelved for less important activities. Be on guard that the child's spiritual growth needs to be a family priority.

Are you committed to their spiritual instruction throughout their childhood? Do your children see you and Dad as committed to ministry or some type of Christian service? Are you doing anything as a family to build unity, teach doctrine, develop convictions? That's a huge list. Think about one or two things that your family could do together to serve the body of Christ at your church and around the world.

3. Do you have a family theme verse? Or perhaps verses for your children, husband, ministry, et cetera?

   Discuss with your husband some of his favorite verses that he claims. Even if your husband is not a believer, you can still have a family verse.

4. Think about some Scripture verses that are especially meaningful to you. What has made them "memorial verses" for you? Enjoy this exercise.

   Mark and date some in your Bible and may God bless you as you remember His faithfulness in your life!

## I CHOOSE TO LIVE BY CONVICTIONS.

Signature: _____

Date: _____

# Lesson 18 Outline

## GROWING IN RELATIONSHIPS, PART ONE

A godly mother mother teaches her children to be loving and forgiving in relationships and wise in choosing friends

I.    Introduction

II.   Requirements of Lifelong Relationships, Part One

## This week's Scripture memory verse:

**1 Peter 3:8-9**, "To sum up, all of you be harmonious, sympathetic, brotherly, kindhearted, and humble in spirit; not returning evil for evil or insult for insult, but giving a blessing instead; for you were called for the very purpose that you might inherit a blessing."

# Lesson 18

## GROWING IN RELATIONSHIPS, PART ONE
### A godly mother mother teaches her children to be loving and forgiving in relationships and wise in choosing friends

## 1. Introduction

There really are no perfect relationships this side of eternity. But the ones that are the best are the ones where biblical principles are applied and conflict is worked through diligently. God sets up a design for us. We WILL have conflicts but the Bible gives us principles for working through these things.

☐ Think about your _____ relationships.

What makes these relationships so _____, so strong?

☐ We all remember delivering our babies. There is a strong _____ that we hope will never diminish. We look into that little face and we pray that we will always be _____.

☐ We have a deep _____ to have strong relationships.

God created us with this deep need.

If we want to have great, lifelong relationships, how are we going to get them?

☐ **Lifelong relationships require three things:**

_____,

_____ and

_____.

## II. *Requirements of Lifelong Relationships, Part One*

☐ **GRACE which includes learning to:**

1. Ask _____ and express genuine _____

☐ **Example:** Sibling rivalry

☐ It's important to _____ _____ _____ that express our feelings of sorrow and

forgiveness when we have offended or hurt another, especially within the family.

This is also true of adults. If one of us struggles with saying the words, "I'm sorry. I was wrong," then it's an issue of pride. Sibling rivalry should be addressed with "full circle without the discipline" because this is not a defiance issue but an issue of immaturity and learning how to relate to each other.

**Steps in resolving sibling rivalry (incorporate the "full circle" in your discussion):**

- The younger sibling tells you what happened while the older one sits quietly.

- The older sibling tells you what happened while the younger sibling sits quietly.

☐ **Proverbs 18:13**
*He who gives an answer before he hears, it is folly and shame to him.*

- We need to listen fully to both sides.

- They learn it's very important to tell the whole truth the first time.

If you build a history of truth-telling with your children, they will have an extremely hard time lying to you, even when they're older. It doesn't mean they won't do it, but you will know it if they do.

When they are older (16 or 17 years old) and you feel like they have said something that was not truthful, you shouldn't jump to the conclusion and call your child a "liar". Sometimes just saying nothing will let the conviction settle into their hearts because you have a history of truth-telling with them. They will struggle immensely with the Holy Spirit who convicts them. Give them some time to come back and tell you the truth.

**1 Corinthians 13:4-7**

---

**1 Peter 3:8-9**, "To sum up, all of you be harmonious, sympathetic, brotherly, kindhearted, and humble in spirit; not returning evil for evil or insult for insult, but giving a blessing instead; for you were called for the very purpose that you might inherit a blessing."

If they are "found out" in a lie, without them coming to you, there are big consequences! Lying is always a capital offense. It becomes more serious now because not only did they lie, but they tried to conceal it over time.

☐ By walking through this process they quickly learned to be _patient_ , _listen_ to the other person, and _____ that I would get to the bottom of the issue and judge fairly.

☐ It was easy for them to trust someone they knew would be _fair_ . Unfortunately, in the real world they have to learn how to _submit_ to unfair rulings. But this is God's plan for growing us up.

☐ 2. _receive_ **forgiveness from another so that the relationship is healed.**

How sad it is if you ask forgiveness of somebody and the other person doesn't receive it. You feel as if this whole thing is not finished and it's not.

**Example:** Sibling rivalry (continued)

☐ After going through the process of understanding the hows and whys of the squabble, they needed to _ask_ each other's forgiveness and _accept_ the other's forgiveness.

☐ Then they both hugged and agreed that it was completely over and went back to playing _together_ . Remember, it is hard to show affection _and_ hold a grudge at the same time, so they had to _hug_ .

Sometimes I would tell them to pretend that I had a giant blackboard and that I was writing down all the offenses of one against the other. "When you hug each other, and ask forgiveness, it's as if we've taken the whole blackboard and we wiped it clean. It's done."

- After they talked through a _____*better*_____ plan of playing together and _____*exchange*_____ forgiveness, the _____*hug*_____ symbolized "wiping the blackboard _____*clean*_____."

- If there were any traces of _____*bitterness*_____ remaining, then the process wasn't over.

  Again, we are working towards <u>peacemaking</u>, not <u>peacekeeping</u>, so we have to address the issues of the heart, not just the external behaviors that they are going through.

- 3. **Grow in** _*long*_ - _*suffering*_**; instead of reacting impulsively we make the** _*intentional*_ **choice to respond in a way that** _____*honors*_____ **the Lord.**

- **Example:** Sibling relationships

- Explain to them that when one of them commits an _____*offense*_____ against the other and the other one _____*reacts*_____ in kind, then they are making a _____ of offenses that will never end because they will learn to keep "one upping" the other.

- They need to learn to _____*be*_____ _____*the*_____ _____*one*_____ to _____*break*_____ the chain of offenses.

- Siblings learn a great deal about _____*coping*_____ with life from each other.

- They will wrestle, tease each other — sometimes mercilessly — intentionally aggravate each other or be competitive, and yet you know they _____*love*_____ each other and there is a line they will not cross. It is the line of _____*cruelty*_____.

- If they have a _____*heart*_____ of malice towards the other, then the situation needs more serious _____*attention*_____.

---

1 Peter 3:8-9, "To sum up, all of you be harmonious, sympathetic, brotherly, kindhearted, and humble in spirit; not returning evil for evil or insult for insult, but giving a blessing instead; for you were called for the very purpose that you might inherit a blessing."

- But because we have ___practiced___ and ___practiced___ this since they were ___little___, they cannot go even a few hours without going to the other ___person___ and making it ___right___.

- We have to ___own___ our part and ___humble___ ourselves to the other person ___regardless___ of their response.

We need to teach them to "own it all and make it right" when we have had a conflict. This is a big, hard lesson to learn, so it is important that we teach our children to humble themselves before each other while they are still young.

Some people do not even realize they have built this chain and it has gone so far because it seems normal to them. They do not realize their need to humble themselves in relation to one other.

**Example:** Parental rivalry

In general, don't let a child's "favoritism" of one parent worry you. Support the other parent. An extreme situation of this is divorce. The children are caught in the middle and the parents are caught with the children picking a favorite parent. Don't allow yourself to get entangled in this.

Children know when you are genuinely for them, if the boundaries you put up are for their best interest. Eventually they will believe that, even if they don't seem like it for a time. Just stay strong in those things. Truth over time wins out. Don't worry if somebody misrepresents you to your children. Your children know the real you.

*Truth over time wins*

- **1 Peter 3:8-9**

  *To sum up, all of you be harmonious, sympathetic, brotherly, kindhearted, and humble in spirit; not returning evil for evil or insult for insult, but giving a blessing instead; for you were called for the very purpose that you might inherit a blessing.*

People do the first half, but they don't do that last part which is to "give a blessing instead". It is hard to say, "I'm going to reverse this chain and build a different chain of godly responses." That is the part so many people miss. Because they miss that, they forfeit the inheritance of the blessing from God. This is the thing that will revolutionize our relationships with people, if we can take it that last step.

▢ **Example:** Playground relationships

As moms, we will hear so many heartbreaking stories about what happened on the playground. Sometimes it is hard to be calm because if your child's heart is broken, your heart will be broken. Sometimes you will be tempted to try to make things right yourself.

▢ They have to learn to _treat_ others _fairly_ without _demanding_ fair treatment themselves.

▢ All these incidents are the very things that the Lord is _allowing_ to grow our sons and daughters into _men_ and _women_ of _character_ .

▢ Kids develop a quick _reputation_ and we want our children to demonstrate _strength_ under control, not out of control, and to learn that they have to _endure_ , not retaliate.

Not retaliating is what diffuses the situation, not returning evil for evil. Bullies are usually products of being bullied. They have learned it somewhere. I am not suggesting that your kids be the brunt of every bad behavior or that they be physically hurt or harmed in any way. But the Lord says we need to learn to bear up under insults and not worry about our reputation. He is honored when we can stand up for good and be a witness for Christ. Just as one child will be known for their bullying, another child becomes known for their kindness.

---

1 Peter 3:8-9, "To sum up, all of you be harmonious, sympathetic, brotherly, kindhearted, and humble in spirit; not returning evil for evil or insult for insult, but giving a blessing instead; for you were called for the very purpose that you might inherit a blessing."

▭ **1 Peter 3:13-17**

*Who is there to harm you if you prove zealous for what is good? . . .*

God is ___*sovereign*___ and fully _____ of your situation. He is watching over

you, desiring that you will respond in a _____ that honors Him.

▭ *". . . But even if you should suffer for the sake of righteousness, you are blessed. AND DO NOT*
*FEAR THEIR INTIMIDATION, AND DO NOT BE TROUBLED but sanctify Christ as Lord in your hearts . . ."*

Remember He is the ___*Lord*___ of all situations

▭ *". . . always being ready to make a defense to everyone who asks you to give an account for the*
*hope that is in you, yet with gentleness and reverence . . ."*

Others will be ___*amazed*___ at how you act and want to ___*understand*___ what makes

you different.

▭ *". . . and keep a good conscience so that in the thing in which you are slandered, those who*
*revile your good behavior in Christ will be put to shame . . ."*

The Lord is just and vengeance belongs to ___*Him*___.

▭ *". . . For it is better, if God should will it so . . ."*

God has a ___*purpos*___ for you to go through this.

▭ *". . . that you suffer for doing what is right rather than doing what is wrong."*

When we suffer for doing wrong, we ___*deserve*___ to suffer, but if we are ___*willing*___

to suffer for doing what is right, God is pleased.

▢ **Proverbs 15:3**

*The eyes of the LORD are in every place, watching the evil and the good.*

Why go through something difficult and not have it count for Christ? Make the right choice and have it count for the Lord.

▢ Kids don't _tend_ to base their relationships on mature qualities/character traits. They will follow the person with the greatest _persuasive_ abilities rather than true leadership abilities.

▢ Learning to _hear_ _up_ in difficult relationships _prepares_ us to handle more difficult adult relationships and also begins a foundational understanding of what a _true_ friend is.

## SACRIFICE which includes:

▢ 1. **Giving to the relationship _past_ the point of comfort or ease**

▢ **Example:** Mother-child relationship

We are attentive to the smallest, little details. We sacrifice sleep, the last piece of pie, "you name it". You would give your very life for your child. We would rather suffer ourselves than see our child suffer.

▢ It is a mother's _heart_ to _give_ sacrificially to her children.

▢ **Example:** Relatives or ministry relationships

▢ If you are in a situation where it is really _____ to serve another, just know that when it gets _____ the point of being fun and easy, it becomes true service as _____ the Lord.

*when it gets hard - is when your sacrificial serving*

---

1 Peter 3:8-9, "To sum up, all of you be harmonious, sympathetic, brotherly, kindhearted, and humble in spirit; not returning evil for evil or insult for insult, but giving a blessing instead; for you were called for the very purpose that you might inherit a blessing."

☐   He Himself will say to __YOU__ someday, "Well done, __My__ good and faithful __Servant__."

Be faithful to what He calls you to do. Be committed and stay strong. The Bible teaches that the greater the sacrifice, the greater the victory, when we do it God's way. **Matthew 10:39** says that he who finds his life must lose it. Sacrificial giving is not commonly taught in our culture.

☐   **2. Giving your best to the relationship to prove that they are __worth__ all the time and effort because your love for __them__ exceeds fulfilling your __own__ desires.**

☐   **Example:** Serving Others

**Isaiah 17** says don't worship the THINGS in life. Give your very best to the Lord. There is no sacrifice in giving up what I don't mind giving up, but when I give up something that is precious, then it's a true sacrifice. So be willing to give sacrificially to those in need.

☐   Give my __best__ because the Lord is __worthy__ of my best. We are to give our best to others if we want __great__ relationships.

☐   **3. Being __willing__ to "suffer loss" for sake of the relationship**

☐   __Loyalty__ and _____ will be challenged by other people and things, but __commitment__ to the relationship keeps us focused on what is of __real__ value and lets us be less concerned with superficial things like image, reputation, or accumulating wealth.

☐   **Example:** Fellowship with believers

☐   Sometimes we have to make __sacrifices__ to be a part of ministry (i.e. finances, time).

☐ There is a _cost_ in following Christ right down to _paying_ for babysitters. When we look at such things as a _sacrifice_ as unto the Lord, even paying the babysitter will be an honor.

Don't hold back. Be generous as unto the Lord.

**Example:** Marriage

☐ Work on setting up guardrails to _protect_ your marriage no matter how other people _view_ them. After all, our personal convictions are a matter of _conscience_.

☐ Guardrails are not a sign of _weakness_. They are a _sign_ of a commitment of _____ to the relationship.

☐ 4. **Making a committed investment of _time_ together (including lots of talking and listening).**

☐ The _counterfeit_ says that "quality time, not quantity of time, is what matters."

☐ Any person who has a deep, _enduring_ relationship knows that _time_ spent together accumulating seemingly small memories adds up to a treasured and lasting _bond_.

☐ **Example:** Marriage

We need to make sacrifices of time to be with our husbands. This is another way we guard our marriages. Make an investment in your marriage.

☐ If we really want to _know_ someone, there is an _investment_ of time.

☐ If we want a _great_ relationship with the _Lord_, five minutes a day won't cut it, not if we want the relationship to be deep.

**1 Peter 3:8-9**, "To sum up, all of you be harmonious, sympathetic, brotherly, kindhearted, and humble in spirit; not returning evil for evil or insult for insult, but giving a blessing instead; for you were called for the very purpose that you might inherit a blessing."

◻ The purpose of our getaways is to _concentrate_ on each other completely.

◻ Be loving and _willing_ to meet his needs for intimacy even when you don't _feel_ like it.

◻ **1 Peter 5:5b-6 says we are to humble ourselves before each other.**

*. . . clothe yourselves with humility toward one another, for GOD IS OPPOSED TO THE PROUD BUT GIVES GRACE TO THE HUMBLE. Therefore humble yourselves under the mighty hand of God, that He may exalt you at the proper time.*

This just flies in the face of everything that the culture tells us. Society says, "Wait a minute, MY needs first. Think about ME and what I need and what I want. " When you hear that, you just can't help but think that that person can't really have a great, deep relationship with another person. There has to be sacrificial giving in a relationship.

◻ God has designed a _plan_ for intimacy in marriage that goes _beyond_ what we could ever _dream_ up. But to get there we have to follow _His_ design.

◻ **1 Corinthians 7:3-5** (NKJV)

*Let the husband render to his wife the affection due her, and likewise also the wife to her husband. The wife does not have authority over her own body, but the husband does. And likewise the husband does not have authority over his own body, but the wife does. Do not deprive one another except with consent for a time, that you may give yourselves to fasting and prayer; and come together again so that Satan does not tempt you because of your lack of self-control.*

If you want to have a marriage that goes beyond the superficial, to the level that you cannot imagine, if you want to have biblical intimacy the way God designed it to be, then you will learn to be sacrificial in your relationship to your husband. The key is always to put the other person's desire above your own. This may sound so wrong to you, but…

◻ It is _pride_ that always _destroys_ intimacy. Pride makes people too _stubborn_ to be vulnerable to another person.

Pride builds that chain that will keep you from unbelievable closeness and intimacy with your husband.

◻ Pride makes us _hold_ something back because we don't _trust_ the other person enough to treat us the way we want to be treated.

**Philippians 2:3-4**

*Do nothing from selfishness or empty conceit, but with humility of mind regard one another as more important than yourselves; do not merely look out for your own personal interests, but also for the interests of others.*

This, of course, works both ways. God would have the man look to meet the needs of the woman and vice versa. I believe that I am responsible for the countenance on my husband's face (for the most part), and he would say the same for me. If our spouse is discouraged about something, we are the best person in the world to encourage them. But this comes from years and years of being vulnerable, sacrificial, and humbling ourselves to each other.

**Proverbs 3:27**

*Do not withhold good from those to whom it is due, when it is in your power to do it.*

We are _____ to withhold ourselves from our husbands. (In any area that is not sinful

or against your conscience.)

Learn to understand the person that you are married to. What are the things that most encourage them? Don't withhold what they need most from you. Be willing to grow in that area for them.

This is one of those things that will _____ your relationship if you will do

it. If we want to have a marriage that grows stronger and stronger as we grow older, then we will

give _____ and _____ to our husbands.

How can I be a more loving person? How can I demonstrate that I'm committed to my husband, that I really love him? How can I place his needs above my own? Is the Lord calling me to be more giving in my relationship? The Bible says, "God loves a cheerful giver"—a person that gives "not out of compulsion", but out of a "cheerful heart".

And as a result we will receive the _opposite_ of what the world would have us expect.

He will be so _drawn_ to you, so devoted and so focused on you, that you will

_Know_ why Satan loves to use this _counterfeit_ to convince husbands

and wives that they need to put themselves first.

---

**1 Peter 3:8-9**, "To sum up, all of you be harmonious, sympathetic,
brotherly, kindhearted, and humble in spirit; not returning evil for evil
or insult for insult, but giving a blessing instead; for you were called for the
very purpose that you might inherit a blessing."

# Homefront Application

## GROWING IN RELATIONSHIPS, PART ONE

A godly mother mother teaches her children to be loving and forgiving in relationships and wise in choosing friends

1. If your children are young, start putting into practice *1 Peter 3:8-9* when dealing with sibling conflicts. Take them full circle, ending with a hug. Helping them say the necessary words of asking and receiving forgiveness will pay off tremendously in years to come!

   Even if you have to formulate the proper sentences for them at first, that is fine. They will learn how to be genuine in their apologies. You are doing their future spouses a huge favor!

2. In regards to playground situations or any difficult childhood relationships, go through *1 Peter 3:13-17* with them. Help them understand God's view of such things. You may want to put a copy of *Proverbs 15:3* in their pocket and tell them you are praying for them to be strong.

3. Reiterate your family dating standards with your children, emphasizing the necessity of being equally yoked with believers.

4. Think about your own relationships—the ones of great importance to you.

   Do you harbor a list of offenses on your own "blackboard"? This list holds you back from having a great relationship with that person.

   Can you recognize what defenses or rationalizations you lean towards to keep from wiping the blackboard clean and moving on? These things tell us a great deal about how we cope in relationships, but is it honoring to the Lord or healthy for you?

   Be determined to not let bitterness or resentment destroy your relationships.

Acts 24:16
Hebrews 12:13-14

## I CHOOSE TO LIVE BY CONVICTIONS.

Signature: _____     Date: _____

# *Lesson 19 Outline*

## GROWING IN RELATIONSHIPS, PART TWO
### A godly mother teaches her children to be accountable in relationships

---

*I.*     *Introduction*

*II.*    *Requirements of Lifelong Relationships, Part Two*

---

## *This week's Scripture memory verse:*

**Titus 2:3-5**, "Older women likewise are to be reverent in their behavior,
not malicious gossips nor enslaved to much wine, teaching what is good,
so that they may encourage the young women to love their husbands, to love their children,
to be sensible, pure, workers at home, kind, being subject to their own husbands,
so that the word of God will not be dishonored."

# Lesson 19

## GROWING IN RELATIONSHIPS, PART TWO
### A godly mother teaches her children to be accountable in relationships

## I. Introduction

▢ **Continuing on from our last lesson, lifelong relationships require three things:**

_____,

_____ and

_____.

- Grace encompasses the ability to humble oneself, to seek and ask forgiveness of another person, and to give a blessing instead.

- Sacrifice is to serve another beyond what is comfortable, easy or convenient.

▢ - The third key to great lifelong relationships is accountability.

## II. Requirements of Lifelong Relationships, Part Two

**ACCOUNTABILITY which includes:**

▢ 1. **Growing in Christ and _____ to the authority of His Word to the point of _____.**

▢ **Example:** Man-to-Man accountability

▢ This area involves a willingness to be _____, _____ and _____.

You let your guard down with this person and what you are really saying is, "I am willing for the Lord to teach me things through you." Do you have that type of relationship with someone? It's a key component of fellowship within the body of Christ and it's a sign of vulnerability. First and foremost, this vulnerability is reserved for our husbands, but do you have an additional person in your life with whom you are vulnerable to that degree? Women are more vulnerable by nature than men. They are more transparent, for the most part. I am using the example of man-to-man accountability simply to emphasize the need that men have for strong accountability partners in their lives.

- Our sons need to grow up and have _____ accountability relationships with other

  _____ men.

- Our husbands need _____ in their lives who keep them accountable.

- **Proverbs 27:17**
  *Iron sharpens iron, so one man sharpens another.*

- **Example:** Young adult relationships

  **Proverbs 18:24b**
  *… but there is a friend who sticks closer than a brother.*

  **Proverbs 27:6a**
  *Faithful are the wounds of a friend…*

  Women tend to be more vulnerable than men and because of that, we can actually get ourselves in trouble in our relationships. We can get too transparent, talk too much, gossip, share too many private things. So, we need to be on guard.

- We need to be _____ in relationships so that we will grow in

  _____ of people.

  **Example:** Marriage

  Let your guard down with your spouse. Let yourself be known to your husband. Being known by that person is what makes us most vulnerable. Sometimes we are afraid of that. But that is God's design—that we be vulnerable to each other in marriage so that we can understand each other and grow together as one.

---

Titus 2:3-5, "Older women likewise are to be reverent in their behavior,
not malicious gossips nor enslaved to much wine, teaching what is good,
so that they may encourage the young women to love their husbands, to love their children,
to be sensible, pure, workers at home, kind, being subject to their own husbands,
so that the word of God will not be dishonored."

## 2. Building relationships according to the _____ model.

- Relationships are to be built like _____, with the base being a strong

  _____ foundation—a relationship with Christ.

- Upon this foundation, relationships are to be based on _____.

  After our confession of faith in Christ, we then develop a bond from common interests and pursuits.

- Over time, an _____ bond develops and we seek out the other person for

  a more exclusive relationship.

- The very pinnacle of the pyramid is reserved for _____ only. It is the

  _____ intimacy between a man and wife. Too many relationships are built in

  _____.

- Once physical intimacy occurs, women especially will often _____ away

  anything to _____ the relationship.

  Physical intimacy is a very strong bond!

- Intimacy was created by God to _____ two people together in a unique and holy

  union so that the two become _____.

- Many teenagers are discovering the _____ this bond has but, unfortunately,

  in an upside-down, opposite way from what God intended for them.

- **Example:** Dating relationships

  **Jeremiah 15:17**
  *I did not sit in the company of revelers ("merrymakers"), nor did I rejoice. I sat alone because
  your hand was upon me for you had filled me with indignation.*

  Your kids will be separated out from other people but don't worry that they are not with the "merrymaker"
  crowd. Let them sit alone. Let them be indignant at what they see. It is okay. The Lord will bring them
  through and provide outstanding relationships for them.

- ☐ In addition to their own convictions, we had _____ standards and convictions regarding dating that were emphasized long _____ those dating years began. We always told them that they could only date _____, no exceptions.

- ☐ If your son or daughter begins a relationship without this biblical conviction soundly established, they may become involved with someone emotionally or even physically and it will be almost impossible to get them to see the _____ about the situation.

- ☐ Bonding with an _____ will cause a great deal of heartache sooner or later as the believing partner begins to rationalize the relationship.

  If you are a believer truly pursuing the things of the Lord, it will eventually be very difficult for you. How did it all start? Because one person rationalized the relationship.

- ☐ Rationalizing and _____ ourselves into believing that we can build _____ lifelong relationships solely on the foundation of "he's a great guy" is the ruin of many relationships.

  If this is the bottom of the pyramid, it's not going to hold up.

- ☐ Sadly, women often become emotionally involved before they have _____ the other person to _____ their convictions.

  We need to teach our children to challenge the character of the other person and see how strong they are in the Lord.

  To make matters worse, parents will rationalize the dating choices of their own children. "Well, they are only sixteen. They're only going to this little event. She really likes him. He's a nice guy." There is no spiritual foundation. That should set off flashing lights!

---

**Titus 2:3-5**, "Older women likewise are to be reverent in their behavior, not malicious gossips nor enslaved to much wine, teaching what is good, so that they may encourage the young women to love their husbands, to love their children, to be sensible, pure, workers at home, kind, being subject to their own husbands, so that the word of God will not be dishonored."

We are to be steadfast in our convictions, not wavering or compromising. You may be the last line of defense against your children's involvement in reckless relationships or rationalizing them. Don't let your kids play your emotional strings to be involved in a relationship that you know in your heart is wrong for them.

Christian women who are emotionally involved in a relationship with an unbelieving man often don't want anybody to challenge their choice. Unfortunately, this is very common. You can just about beg this person to consider their spiritual foundation. They may get very defensive. "Can't you just want this very nice thing for me? I'm finally happy." They are deluded into thinking that they are going to be the exception to God's rule. These are all signs of rationalizing the relationship.

- It is unfortunate that many women would rather have a _____ relationship than _____ relationship.

- It proves our desire to have relationships, but it also reveals that when we do this our _____ and _____ is being placed in men rather than _____.

- We tend to think of being _____ as a weakness, but this lie is one of those counterfeits that Satan uses to _____ intimate relationships.

- He wants us to not be vulnerable with each other; to put up _____, to be stubborn, to hold in feelings, to _____ ourselves or put ourselves first.

- **Biblical Example:** Choosing a spouse—Samson: poor choice: (**Judges 14 and 15**)

Sometimes, a person who is living outside of God's will might think, "I'm the exception. It will work out for me. Or God HAS to work it out for me." This person is clearly rationalizing and being deceived. There is no assurance that it will work out. God may not work it out. Remember, it cost Samson his very life.

**Romans 3:8** says that we should not do evil, that good may come. If God tells us not to be yoked with unbelievers, then we cannot assume that God will work it out. You can still have good relationships but you can't have the depth of relationship that you can have when you both believe in the same things - when your faith is your foundation.

Now parents may ask, "Well, how do I really know what this person is like that my child wants to date? How do I know if he is a believer? How can we know where his heart is?" Besides the obvious things like talking to them, you can go back to Lesson 17 and look for the "Vital Signs of Believers". If they say they are a believer, then they will talk about it. It won't be this deep, dark, hidden secret that doesn't come up in the normal course of conversation. If you have talked with this person for awhile, and they never talk about spiritual things, you have to wonder how important it is to them because one of the vital signs is "confession of faith". Are they interested in your son or daughter's spiritual activities or growth? Another vital sign is that "believers love the fellowship of other believers".

☐ 3. **Placing ourselves** _____ **God-given authorities.**

☐     **Example:** Father-child relationships

☐     Fathers are so _____ when our sons and daughters begin dating. They need

    to have a _____ relationship, especially with daughters, so that our daughters

    learn that Dad won't release her to just _____.

☐     **Biblical Example:** Caleb: High Standards **(Joshua 15:13-19)**

☐ 4. **Learning to** _____ **friends wisely.**

☐     This is where we get into the realm of _____ them to choose friends wisely

    because ultimately they will be choosing a _____ as a life-partner.

    **Stay away from people with these characteristics:**

☐     **2 Timothy 3:1-5**
    *But realize this, that in the last days difficult times will come. For men will be lovers of self,*
    *lovers of money, boastful, arrogant, revilers, disobedient to parents, ungrateful, unholy,*
    *unloving, irreconcilable, malicious gossips, without self-control, brutal, haters of good,*
    *treacherous, reckless, conceited, lovers of pleasure rather than lovers of God, holding to*
    *a form of godliness, although they have denied its power; Avoid such men as these.*

☐     **Proverbs 13:20**
    *He who walks with wise men will be wise, but the companion of fools will suffer harm.*

☐     **Exodus 23:2a,** (NKJV)
    *You shall not follow a crowd to do evil . . .*

☐     **Psalm 119:63**
    *I am a companion of all those who fear You, And of those who keep Your precepts.*

---

**Titus 2:3-5,** "Older women likewise are to be reverent in their behavior,
not malicious gossips nor enslaved to much wine, teaching what is good,
so that they may encourage the young women to love their husbands, to love their children,
to be sensible, pure, workers at home, kind, being subject to their own husbands,
so that the word of God will not be dishonored."

▢ **Proverbs 1:7-16a**

*The fear of the LORD is the beginning of knowledge; fools despise wisdom and instruction. Hear, my son, your father's instruction and do not forsake your mother's teaching; Indeed, they are a graceful wreath to your head and ornaments about your neck. My son, if sinners entice you, do not consent. If they say, 'Come with us, Let us lie in wait for blood, Let us ambush the innocent without cause; Let us swallow them alive like Sheol, Even whole, as those who go down to the pit; We will find all kinds of precious wealth, We will fill our houses with spoil; Throw in your lot with us, We shall all have one purse.' My son, do not walk in the way with them. Keep your feet from their path, for their feet run to evil.*

**Going through this passage again:**

▢ *The fear of the LORD is the beginning of knowledge . . .*

▢ Have a _____ basis to all your friendships. Why?

*Because . . . fools despise wisdom and instruction . . .*

It is for our own _____.

▢ *. . . Hear, my son, your father's instruction and do not forsake your mother's teaching . . .*

▢ _____ are to have a role in helping their children learn to choose friends wisely.

▢ *. . . Indeed, they are a graceful wreath to your head and ornaments about your neck . . .*

▢ Heeding parental guidance brings _____.

▢ *. . . My son, if sinners entice you, do not consent. . .*

▢ _____ be drawn away from your convictions.

▢ *. . . If they say, 'Come with us, Let us lie in wait for blood, Let us ambush the innocent without cause; Let us swallow them alive like Sheol, Even whole, as those who go down to the pit . . .'*

▢ Do not allow yourself to have close _____ with evil. The appropriate

response to temptation is to _____.

**19.7**

▣ The _____ of evildoers is really to ensnare the _____. If we

are not wise we can unwittingly succumb to their _____ before we realize we are in a

_____ _____.

▣ *. . . We will find all kinds of precious wealth, we will fill our houses with spoil; Throw in your lot with us, we shall all have one purse . . .*

▣ The _____ kind of friends will not only try to get you to do things you know you

shouldn't, but will embrace you as _____ if you do.

▣ *. . . My son, do not walk in the way with them. Keep your feet from their path, for their feet run to evil . . .*

▣ Make _____ for your life so that you won't even _____ about going

down the path to evil.

▣ We need to be protective of our sons and daughters and their choices of companions

especially during the _____ teenage years.

▣ We don't allow our children to _____ unbelievers for any reason and certainly not with

the _____ that they will lead the other person to the Lord. That would be building on

the pyramid in the wrong _____.

▣ Parents can and must step in and pull kids away from _____ relationships.

▣ **1 Corinthians 15:33**
*Do not be deceived: 'Bad company corrupts good morals.'*

---

**Titus 2:3-5,** "Older women likewise are to be reverent in their behavior,
not malicious gossips nor enslaved to much wine, teaching what is good,
so that they may encourage the young women to love their husbands, to love their children,
to be sensible, pure, workers at home, kind, being subject to their own husbands,
so that the word of God will not be dishonored."

◻ **5. Resolving conflicts.**

◻ **Example:** Marriage

◻ To have a _____ marriage there will be conflict, but the conflicts must also be

_____ to the satisfaction of both husband and wife.

◻ This goes back to the whole idea of living in _____ and

_____ with one another.

◻ Study and enjoy your _____. Grow in understanding of each other and

agreement with _____ issues.

◻ Don't let _____ keep you from resolving conflict and accepting and giving forgiveness.

◻ Unresolved conflicts have a way of _____ _____ over and over if they

are not settled, if you do not _____. Then bitterness and resentment may

_____ _____.

◻ Be determined to talk through disagreements with some _____ that you

will not cross. _____ let a lot of time pass. For example, _____ name calling,

_____ yelling, _____ sarcasm.

◻ _____ to him, _____ him, and he will do the same for you.

_____ through conflict will strengthen your marriage.

☐ On a very few occasions over the years, I have not been able to come to _____ with my husband. But they were never _____, black and white issues, they were matters of _____ conviction or _____.

☐ In those cases, I _____ to his decision as the _____ in our home.

☐ While we are here on earth, the Lord has provided us with a variety of relationships in which we are to find our greatest _____.

☐ Through our relationship with Christ we _____ have eternal _____ with believers in heaven and strong, _____ relationships in the meantime on earth.

Your family is your constant in this lifetime, so work things out with your family. The body of Christ is your constant for eternity. People are eternal. It is my prayer that this year you've grown in many of these relationships. God bless you and your family.

**Titus 2:3-5**, "Older women likewise are to be reverent in their behavior, not malicious gossips nor enslaved to much wine, teaching what is good, so that they may encourage the young women to love their husbands, to love their children, to be sensible, pure, workers at home, kind, being subject to their own husbands, so that the word of God will not be dishonored."

# Homefront Application

## GROWING IN RELATIONSHIPS, PART TWO
### A godly mother teaches her children to be accountable in relationships

1. Consider your personal accountability. Do you have people in your life who will hold you accountable to the things of God? Think of pursuing relationships where accountability becomes a reality in your life.

2. Reiterate your family dating standards with your children, emphasizing the necessity of being equally yoked with believers. Also emphasize the importance of choosing friends wisely.

Thank you for finishing! You have done well. Keep your notebooks for reference in seasons of parenting to come or when weeds pop up.

May you be greatly encouraged in all that you set your hands to do in cultivating the love of Christ in your home. That has been my motivation for writing these lessons.

Still in the garden,

*Betsy*

## I CHOOSE TO LIVE BY CONVICTIONS.

Signature: _____    Date: _____

# Examples of Biblical Convictions

## I CHOOSE TO LIVE BY BIBLICAL CONVICTIONS

*We reap what we sow.*
Galatians 6:7–8; Romans 14:12; 2 Corinthians 5:10

*Choose to sin, choose to suffer.*
Isaiah 8:9–21; Jeremiah 43 & 44

*Honor your parents.*
Ephesians 6:2; Exodus 20:12

*Do not kill (including unborn children).*
Exodus 20:13; Exodus 23:7

*Do not lie, cheat, steal, deceive.*
Leviticus 19:11; Proverbs 19:5

*Do not become unequally yoked.*
2 Corinthians 6:14–15; Malachi 2:13–16

*Honor God with your full tithe.*
Ezekiel 44:30; Malachi 3:8–10; Nehemiah 13:10–12

*Discipline your children according to the biblical model.*
Hebrews 12:7

*Submit to your husband.*
Ephesians 5:22–24; Colossians 3:18; 1 Peter 3:1

*Be involved in ministry.*
Ephesians 2:10; Ephesians 4:11; Matthew 28:19–20

*Share the gospel.*
2 Corinthians 5:18–20; Ephesians 6:19–20;
2 Timothy 4:2–5; Acts 1:8; 1 Peter 3:15

*Memorize Scripture.*
Isaiah 59:21; Joshua 1:8; Psalm 119:9–11

*Be grateful.*
Ephesians 5:19–20; Colossians 2:6–7;
1 Thessalonians 5:16; 1 Timothy 6:6; Psalm 107:1

*Do not read horoscopes or listen to psychics.*
Jeremiah 10:2–4; Colossians 2:8–10; Isaiah 47;
Deuteronomy 18:9–14; Jeremiah 14:14;
Leviticus 19:26, 31; Leviticus 20:6

*Pray, believing God answers.*
Colossians 4:2; Hebrews 11:6; James 5:16–18

*Train your children to glorify God.*
3 John 4; Isaiah 54:13

*Look out for others.*
Philippians 2:4; Hebrews 3:13; Romans 12:15;
1 Thessalonians 2:8

*Be generous.*
2 Corinthians 9:7; 1 Timothy 6:18; Hebrews 13:16

*Be forgiving.*
Ephesians 4:32; Matthew 18:21–22

*Don't demand your rights.*
1 Peter 3:13–16; 1 Peter 5:5; Romans 13:1–2

*Study God's Word: know how to use it accurately.*
Acts 18:25; 2 Timothy 2:15; Ezra 7:10

*Fellowship with other believers.*
Hebrews 10:24–25; 1 John 1:3

*Suffer for the cause of Christ.*
2 Corinthians 1:5–7; Philippians 1:27–30;
Philippians 3:7–10; 2 Timothy 3:12;
James 1:2; 1 Peter 4:16

*Worship God alone.*
Philippians 2:9–11; Colossians 1:15–18;
Revelations 4:11

*Remember the Sabbath.*
Hebrews 4:9–10; Exodus 31:15

*Choose friends carefully.*
1 Corinthians 15:33–34; James 4:4;
Exodus 23:2; Psalm 119:63

*Do not defile your body.*
Romans 12:1–2; 1 Corinthians 3:16–17

*Don't make a promise and then break it.*
Ecclesiastes 5:5; Matthew 5:37

*Don't be lazy.*
2 Thessalonians 3:10; Proverbs 24:33–34

*Leave vengeance to God.*
Hebrews 10:30–31; 2 Samuel 22:47–48;
Proverbs 24:29

*Become like Christ.*
Ephesians 4:14–15; Ephesians 5:1;
Philippians 2:12–13; 1 John 2:6

*Signature:* _____     *Date:* _____

# *Appendix 2*

| | |
|---|---|
| Emily | MARKS: 𝍸 𝍸 𝍸 |
| Luke | |
| Lee | |
| NOVEMBER | 1 2 3 4 5 6 7 8 9 10 11 12 13 |

**DISCIPLINES OR TASKS:** In this section list "disciplines" you would like to teach your children. Assign a monetary value for each point (for example 10¢ per point) allotting more points for more difficult tasks or areas needing added emphasis. Record each child's points at the end of the day in the section above. Gauge your tasks according to age. Older children may receive more points if their tasks are more demanding. Each month create a new chart with new disciplines and keeping those you still wish to emphasize. This will ensure that the chart remains interesting, challenging and effective. There is an ebb and flow to life and at the end of the month they will be learning that they will reap what they have sown. Don't worry if they lag a month. They will be motivated to work harder the next month. The beauty of the chart is that you will not need to be their constant reminder but that they will learn to monitor themselves (and become disciplined!).

**The chart is most effective for late preschool through sixth grade. Below are some examples:**

- Homework complete by 7:00 (Emily–3) (Luke–1)
  Older children may receive more points if their tasks are more demanding.
- Mom's Task (2)
  Mom's Task meant that if I asked one of them to do a simple task and they quickly and cheerfully responded,
  they could earn bonus points. (For example: "Clear the table" or "Go upstairs and get the baby's shoes, please.")
- Bible and Pen to Church and Youth Group (1)
- Hygiene (1)
- Teach AWANA section to Lee (2)
- All day without TV or Video Games (4)

DEMERITS: |||

14 15 16 17 18 19 20 21 22 23 24 25 26 27 28 29 30

## DEMERITS: Use very few in contrast to opportunities to earn points. (Max 6)

- Every 1/2 hour past bed time (–1)
  Vary them according to what you are really working on.

- Interrupting Phone Call (–1)

## TOTALS: * Mark "pd." on the 1st of the month and then have a new chart ready!

| NAME: | GROSS: | -TITHE: | -DEMERITS: | -SAVINGS: | =NET |
|---|---|---|---|---|---|
| Emily | EX: $4.80 | .50 | .20 | .50 | PD. $3.60 |
| Luke | | | | | |
| Lee | | | | | |

© 2001 Entrusted with a Child's Heart

DEMERITS:

TOTALS:

| NAME: | GROSS: | -TITHE: | -DEMERITS: | -SAVINGS: | =NET |
|-------|--------|---------|------------|-----------|------|
|       |        |         |            |           |      |
|       |        |         |            |           |      |
|       |        |         |            |           |      |

MARKS:

# Appendix 2

| Monday | Tuesday | Wednesday | Thursday | Friday | Saturday |
|---|---|---|---|---|---|
| | | | | | Sunday |

# Appendix 3
# Attitude

"The longer I live, the more I realize the impact of attitude on life.
Attitude, to me, is more important than facts.
It is more important than the past,
than education, than money, than circumstances,
than failures, than successes,
than what other people think or say or do.
It is more important than appearance, giftedness or skill.
It will make or break a company . . . a church . . . a home.

The remarkable thing is we have a choice every day regarding
the attitude we will embrace for that day.
We cannot change our past.
We cannot change the fact that people will act in a certain way.

We cannot change the inevitable.
The only thing we can do is play on the one string we have,
and that is our attitude.
I am convinced that life is 10% what happens to me,
and 90% how I react to it.
And so it is with you.
We are in charge of attitude."

—Anonymous

# Appendix 4
# Seven Stages of Character Building

## Foundation Stage:

*Ages:* Birth to six years old

*Focus:* Discipline

*Character Qualities:*

**Attentiveness (vs unconcern):** showing the worth of a person by giving sincere attention to his words. **Hebrews 2:1**

**Obedience (vs willfulness):** freedom to be creative under the protection of divinely appointed authority. **2 Corinthians 10:5**

**Contentment (vs covetousness):** realizing God has provided everything I need for my present happiness. **1 Timothy 6:8**

**Orderliness (vs disorganization):** preparing myself and my surroundings so that I will achieve the greatest efficiency. **1 Corinthians 14:40**

**Reverence (vs disrespect):** awareness of how God is working through the people and events in my life to produce the character of Christ in me. **Proverbs 23:17–18**

**Forgiveness (vs rejection):** a decision, a choice, an act of my will, releasing another from the obligation that resulted when they injured me. It says, "You don't owe me". **Ephesians 4:32**

**Gratefulness (vs unthankfulness):** making known to God and others the ways they have benefited my life. **1 Corinthians 4:7**

**Faith (vs presumption):** believing the Word of God and acting upon it no matter how I feel, knowing that God promises a good result. **Hebrew 11:1**

**Truthfulness (vs deception):** earning future trust by accurately reporting past facts. **Ephesians 4:25**

**Security (vs anxiety):** structuring my life around what is eternal and cannot be destroyed or taken away. **John 6:27**

**Meekness (vs anger):** yielding my personal rights and expectations to God. **Psalm 62:5**

**Cautiousness (vs impulsiveness):** knowing how important right timing is in accomplishing right actions. **Proverbs 19:2**

## Training Stage:

*Ages:* Six to twelve years old

*Focus:* Teaching Truth

*Character Qualities:*

**Patience (vs restlessness):** accepting a difficult situation from God without giving Him a deadline to remove it. **Romans 5:3–4**

**Determination (vs faintheartedness):** purposing to accomplish God's goal in God's time regardless of the opposition. **2 Timothy 4:7–8**

**Dependability (vs inconsistency):** fulfilling what I agreed to do even if it means unexpected sacrifice. **Psalm 15:4**

**Punctuality (vs tardiness):** showing high esteem for other people and their time. **Ecclesiastes 3:1**

**Discernment (vs judgment):** seeing through a surface problem to root causes. **1 Samuel 16:7**

**Loyalty (vs unfaithfulness):** using adversity to confirm my commitment to those whom God has called me to serve. **John 15:13**

**Compassion (vs indifference):** investing whatever is necessary to heal the hurt of others. **1 John 3:17**

**Alertness (vs unawareness):** the ability to anticipate right responses to that which is taking place around me. **Mark 14:38**

**Responsibility (vs unreliability):** knowing and doing what both God and others are expecting from me. **Romans 14:12**

**Virtue (vs impurity):** the moral excellence and purity of spirit that radiate from my life as I obey God's Word. **2 Peter 1:5**

**Tolerance (vs prejudice):** acceptance of others as unique expressions of specific character qualities in varying degrees of maturity. **Philippians 2:2**

**Fairness (vs partiality):** looking at a decision from the viewpoint of each person involved. **Luke 6:31**

**Joy (vs self–pity):** the supernatural delight in the person of God, the purposes of God and the people of God. **Proverbs 15:13**

Character definitions used by permission from Bill Gothard, Dr. Ron Allchin and Dr. James MacDonald

# Appendix 4
# Seven Stages of Character Building

## Skill Stage

*Ages:* Twelve to twenty years old

*Focus:* Self–control

*Character Qualities:*

**Wisdom (vs natural inclinations):** seeing and responding to life situations from God's frame of reference. **Proverbs 9:10**

**Self–control (vs self–indulgence):** restraining oneself from passions or appetites. **Galatians 5:24–25**

**Discretion (vs impulsivity):** the ability to avoid words, actions, and attitudes which are not honoring to God. **Proverbs 22:3**

**Diligence (vs slothfulness):** seeing each task as a special assignment from the Lord and using all my energies to accomplish the task. **Colossians 3:23**

**Endurance (vs giving up):** the inward strength to withstand stress to accomplish God's best. **Galatians 6:9**

**Deference (vs rudeness):** limiting my freedom in order to not offend the tastes of those God has called me to serve. **Romans 14:21**

**Sincerity (vs hypocrisy):** eagerness to do what is right with transparent motives. **1 Peter 1:22**

**Generosity (vs stinginess):** investing in others as much as I can with the time and resources that have been entrusted to me. **2 Corinthians 9:6**

**Humility (vs pride):** having an attitude that reveals that I recognize that God is sovereign in my life. **James 4:6**

**Enthusiasm (vs apathy):** expressing with my spirit the joy of my soul. **1 Thessalonians 5:16, 19**

**Initiative (vs unresponsiveness):** recognizing and doing what needs to be done before I am asked to do it. **Romans 12:21**

**Love (vs selfishness):** the unconditional decision to put the needs of another above my own. **1 Corinthians 13:3**

**Creativity (vs underachievement):** approaching a need, task, or idea from a new perspective. **Romans 12:2**

**Decisiveness (vs double–mindedness):** the ability to finalize difficult choices based on the will and ways of God. **James 1:5**

**Sensitivity (vs callousness):** exercising my senses so that I can perceive the true spirit and emotion of those around me. **Romans 12:15**

# Appendix 4
# Seven Stages of Character Building

## Apprenticeship Stage

*Ages:* Twenty to thirty years old

*Focus:* Serving

*Character Qualities:*

**Thoroughness (vs incompleteness):** knowing what factors will diminish the effectiveness of my work or words if neglected. **Proverbs 18:15**

**Resourcefulness (vs wastefulness):** wise use of that which others would normally overlook or discard. **Luke 16:10**

**Flexibility (vs resistance):** not setting my affections on ideas or plans which may be changed by others. **Colossians 3:2**

**Availability (vs self–centeredness):** making my own schedule and priorities secondary to the wishes or needs of those I am serving. **Philippians 2:20–21**

**Hospitality (vs exclusion):** cheerfully sharing food, shelter, and spiritual refreshment with those God brings into my life. **Hebrew 13:2**

**Gentleness (vs harshness):** expressing personal care appropriate to another's emotional need. **1 Thessalonians 2:7**

**Boldness (vs fearfulness):** confidence that what I have to say or do will result in lasting benefit. **Acts 4:29**

**Persuasiveness (vs contentiousness):** guiding another's mental roadblocks by way of vital truth. **2 Timothy 2:24**

## Ministry Stage

*Ages:* Thirty to fifty years old

*Focus:* Public Ministry

*Character Qualities:*

Continue to sharpen character qualities

## Counsel Stage

*Ages:* Fifty years old to the end of my life

*Focus:* Counseling and guidance

*Character Qualities:*

Guiding others in character building

## Heritage Stage

Beyond my life–legacy of character traits in others as a result of my life.

# Tips

## PRACTICAL IDEAS FOR BUILDING UNITY AND ORDER IN OUR CHILDREN

### *Some Corning Family Favorites*

1. **Giant paper roll**

   - Birthday door breakthrough
   - Life–size valentines (mail in paper tube)
   - Murals

2. **"Thinking Time"**

   - When they've just outgrown napping; (3–5 years old)
   - A precursor to quiet time
   - No toys, may have music or book, but nothing is best
   - It's just time to meditate or think (and you get a small break)
   - 30–45 minutes long (who knows, they might take a nap)
   - I timed it so I could begin dinner and have the house calmed down for when David arrived home.

3. **Laundry Bins**

   - Laundry in laundry room Sunday night (includes bringing down extra hangers)
   - Pick up bin and ironed clothes on Tuesday after school
   - Color–coded hangers (toss in bin as the item is worn so they don't forget to take the hanger to the laundry area)
   - Learn to do their own laundry senior year of high school

4. **Make a big deal of birthdays; holidays**

   - Decorate the house; sometimes put something special on their bedroom door or a garland of lights in their room at Christmas.
   - Have lots of family traditions: "white elephant bingo", "egg cracking", gingerbread houses, etc.

5. **School files**

   - Store every "worthy" paper, award, picture from each grade in velcro tabbed file (one per year)
   - Each child has their own color file. (Include a paper with teacher's name, likes, dislikes, fads . . .)
   - Art file (only one per child) store all large "worthy" art pieces

6. **Evening Reading**

   - Quiet time of day when the family is together
   - Have quiet times together (reading alone, but in same room)
   - Sit by fire; talk or Mom reads book aloud to whole family

7. **Sundays**

   - No excuses for being late to leave
   - Take Bible and pen
   - Take sermon notes
   - Whole family sits together
   - Afterwards we all have to be at the car in 25 minutes (unless previously excused) or we can't go out to eat
   - Leisurely late lunch together at a restaurant (so Mom doesn't have to cook at all)

## PRACTICAL IDEAS FOR BUILDING UNITY AND ORDER IN OUR CHILDREN

8. **Company**

   - Have lots of company—cousins, missionaries, college students . . .

   - Be open to have them for a weekend or a few weeks. They are a great influence on our kids.

9. **Charts**

   - Designed for teaching "disciplines of daily life," not for chores

   - Paid at end of month; deducting demerits, tithe, savings

   - Alter reward to motivate area lacking in discipline

   - Great through 5th or 6th grade.

10. **Thank–you notes**

    - If someone was kind enough to give a gift or do a service for us, the least we can do is take the small effort to write a note to them.

    - Includes birthday party gifts (Family saying, "it's not yours until you have properly thanked the person"); not allowed to use the gift until the note is written.

11. **Art Projects**

    - Make lots of projects.

    - Always have lots of supplies—old pans, poster board, et cetera so you are prepared when creativity strikes! Let them make messes. Then teach them how to clean up completely. An old muffin tin makes a perfect pan for paints. You can leave it full of watercolors or tempera. They will just dry out and be ready for water next time. They don't even need to be covered. Frame several of your favorite pieces of their artwork and hang them in the house.

12. **Wedding File**

    - When you see a picture of a great wedding cake or the perfect dress, or you go to a great wedding, save the ideas with your daughter in a file. It's fun to talk about how you might picture your daughter's wedding and you need to know now if she's got her heart set on being barefoot!

13. **Making cards**

    - A handmade card is so special. Train your kids to make all your birthday, Mother's Day, Father's Day and Valentine cards. Even teenagers make great cards.

14. **Recipe Rating and Dating**

    - When a child or teen tries a recipe, have them sign the recipe, date it, and rate it, 1–4 stars. It's fun to look back at them.

15. **School Lunch "Break–Away"**

    - If at all possible, arrange for your child to come home for lunch. They get a much more nutritious meal, it "grounds" their day, and gives you a special time together. Have them bring their friends once in awhile (high–schoolers)

16. **"Silent Butler"**

    - Ask them to pick up or put something away one time. If you still see it, then the "silent butler" gets it for a specified amount of time until they earn it back.

# Tips

## PRACTICAL IDEAS FOR BUILDING
## UNITY AND ORDER IN OUR CHILDREN

### 17. "Pans"

- Keep a bin for each child in a centralized location (like in a back entry closet or pantry).

- Color–code them to match their hangers. Place odd items like sweatshirts, library books, mail, etc . . in the bin instead of running them to their bedrooms.

- They check and empty "pans" often, but meanwhile they are out of sight and you don't have to look at the clutter and they're not asking you if you "know where they put that field trip paper."

### 18. Shoe Scoreboard

- When more than the allotted (1 pair of shoes per child) piled up under the entryway bench, a "score" was taken and loudly announced. They would tease the high scorer and quickly come and get their shoes.

### 19. Family Nursery Duty

- Serve on the nursery team as a family. Then no one misses a service and we all get close to the little ones.

### 20. Family Team Sports

- Have a family water fight using catapults and water balloons. Play doubles tennis, go golfing, shag baseballs . . .

- Adapt a sport or game so that every age can play. Example, our favorite—Family Football with 2 year–old Lee as the "secret weapon." Every fifth play or so give the ball to the "secret weapon." He can run anywhere he wants. So the team either gains or loses yards. And Lee would also fall down quickly because that was his favorite part. Everyone cheers, everyone is included.

### 21. Cell phone Use

Regarding phones for children and teens, some things to consider are:

- What age is appropriate for a child to have his own phone?

- What are the potential dangers that accompany this new avenue of communication?

- What limits are necessary? (time, features enabled, etc.)?

- What is the proper etiquette (e.g., no phones at the dinner table!)?

### 22. Media Limits

- Be diligent about protecting your children from harmful content—whether it's on the TV, at the movie theater, in a video game or on the internet.

- Filtering software is a must!

- Don't let technology control your lives and rob your family of precious time together.

### 23. Allow kids to develop their own interests

- You will definitely get some wild hobbies. You may be stretched to start an aquarium for seahorses or find yourself paying money for feathers and "tackle" so your son can tie some "flies."

### 24. Keeping Organized

- Set items by stairs so that whenever you go up or down you won't forget to take them. Also have one spot where you put everything you need to take the next time you leave the house. Then if you are in a hurry when the time comes, you won't forget anything.

### 25. Hugs and Kisses

- Hug and kiss your kids every day so that it becomes second nature to them. Don't let up even during the junior high years. Train them to hug and kiss you, too, every day!

## PRACTICAL IDEAS FOR BUILDING
## UNITY AND ORDER IN OUR CHILDREN

**26. Giant Paper Ball**

- This was one of our favorite party games.

- Wrap lots of candy and prizes with about six rolls of super cheap toilet paper. Don't worry if the paper breaks apart while you are wrapping it; it will. Have the participants stand outside in a large circle and toss the ball to each other until it has completely unwrapped itself and the prizes go flying.

- Then the kids run around and pick up the treats (and the thousand pieces of tissue). This is even great with older children. The ball starts out very large and heavy, so it rolls across the yard and the kids run to get it and toss it as far as they can.

- This game has been such a tradition at our house we have even mailed them as birthday presents. To make it lighter for the mail, wrap in a few dollar bills instead of heavier treats.

**27. Dad's Chair**

- It's a special spot to have a quiet time, read or just think. It's the chair where Dad reads his Bible and watches for you to come home at night.

**28. A Bible Like Dad's**

- When one of the kids completed 30 days in a row of a journaled Quiet Time, they received a big Bible just like their dad's, complete with their name engraved on it.

**29. Quiet Times**

- Mandatory from 7th grade on.

- Help them develop the discipline and their personal style. Example: the girls liked to journal or write their prayers, Luke has a Bible marking system.

- Pencil cases—those of us who use a Bible highlighting or marking system have our own personal set of markers, pens, and highlighters in a case in our Quiet Time spots so we never have to run around and look for what we need.

**30. "Scripture Memorials"**

- Mark meaningful verses with names and dates of friends and relatives for a promise claimed, a prayer, or especially someone's testimony verse, which is the verse that made them first believe the gospel.

**31. "Hours"**

- Have a weekly scheduled "hour" for each child to spend time just with Mom

- Absolutely no interruptions; phone calls

- Has to be at home

- Has to cost nothing (can use stuff around the house)

- Completely child's choice (look out, you might have to play Monopoly)

- Child will never forget this time even if you only do it once—I remember making a Christmas stocking for my baby brother with my mom.

**32. "Height Chart"**

- Mark people's heights on a doorjamb or wall. It's fun to see all the heights together and how people have grown. Include the relatives and even adult friends.

**33. Mission Trips**

- Make it a goal to have each child go on a mission trip before they graduate from high school. It will forever change their perspective on the world and help them develop a love for people.

**34. Service Work**

- Involve kids, especially teens, in service work. Camp counseling, visiting teen centers, homeless shelters, Walk For Life, visiting local jails with the Prison Ministry are all incredible learning experiences.

## PRACTICAL IDEAS FOR BUILDING UNITY AND ORDER IN OUR CHILDREN

### 35. Youth Group

- Attendance required.

- Commitment expected.

- By the last two years of high school they should be "giving back" to their youth group through leadership, initiating conversations with new kids, serving their leaders. The pure "receiving" phase is over.

### 36. Sets of Rules

- For small children, create brief, concise sets of rules so they can easily remember and follow them.

- When the occasion for their use arises, ask them to repeat them. Example: just before you get out of the car you ask, "What are the 5 Store Rules?" And they hopefully answer, "No begging, no whining, no touching the stuff, no laying on the floor and stay right by Mom." The Restaurant Rule—"if anybody can hear what you are saying at any other table, you are too loud."

### 37. "The List" (for grade–school and younger)

- If a child believes that they need something and I agree, the item gets written on "the list." The next time we are in the appropriate store, we'll look for it. If they suddenly see something and they want it, it is usually just an impulse. I tell them it is not on "the list." I do make exceptions on occasion, but as my husband, David, says, "If you didn't know you needed it before you saw it, then you probably don't need it."

### 38. Learning Posters

- Place a teaching poster on the back of their bedroom or bathroom door.

- Change them every couple of months so that the new one will catch their attention and they might accidently learn something while they're getting dressed.

- Great posters can be found at Learning Centers or teacher's stores with a wide variety of subjects.

### 39. Christmas Shopping

- By unanimous agreement among the aunts and uncles, we stopped buying Christmas gifts for relatives except grandparents. What a relief! Instead, we buy them great birthday gifts and the gift budget is spread out over the whole year rather than hitting all at once.

- The day before Christmas we go downtown Chicago as a family. We have a big day of shopping for the kids, eating out, and seeing all the lights. We are able to pick out what they really like. (Face it, teenagers like clothes and if you shop together you can agree on the item before it is purchased and you won't have to return it. Also, if they like, they can get one larger item instead of several smaller items).

### 40. Christmas Packages

- I will have some packages under the tree. I never put a card on them. Instead, I make up a "code" for each child and write it on the box, usually the bottom. The same code never gets repeated. This way the kids have no idea which packages are theirs. They sit together in the living room and use their best deductive reasoning to "crack the code." I may answer yes or no, but the idea is that they don't figure out the code until Christmas Eve or else they start deducing what's in the box!

- Example: one year the code was the first letter of each of their birthstones. Elizabeth's was "A" for Amethyst, Emily was "S" for Sapphire, Luke was "E" for Emerald, and Lee was "R" for Ruby. (Every year I have to come up with tougher codes, as they get smarter at deducing the code!)

### 41. "Excellence Award" (early grade school and younger)

- Slip name in award and display in prominent place when something exemplary occurs. Can be a school thing, but it was usually a display of character at home.

## PRACTICAL IDEAS FOR BUILDING
## UNITY AND ORDER IN OUR CHILDREN

**42. Go through every closet . . .**

- every box, every cupboard, every year, clean and reorganize.

- If we haven't used something since the last time I went through it, and I don't have a very specific reason to keep it, I give it away or take to a closet that gathers "stuff" for the annual neighborhood garage sale.

**43. Have a file or folder for everything.**

- Example: when you are given directions to any particular place, file it so that the next time you go there you will already have directions even if you don't go there again for a couple of years.

**44. Allowances**

- The word "allowances" conveys the idea that it is a provision, not a payment for a task completed.

- We give allowances up to the point of getting that first job (usually by junior year). But they are also expected to clean their bedroom and bathroom according to the "written definitions of a clean bedroom and bathroom" every Friday after school. When the rooms pass inspection, they receive their allowance.

- After they have jobs and no longer receive allowances, they still have to clean their bedroom and bathroom, and they know they won't be doing any social activity until it's done.

- Allowance envelopes—keep proper amount of allowance in a drawer with child's name on it for the whole month. Then you are always ready to pay it when it "suddenly pops up again."

**45. Seat Belts**

- Whoever doesn't have their seat belt on by the time we get out of the driveway owes Dad a quarter.

**46. Seating in the Car**

- Have a specific system for determining who gets to sit where and when. Example: for long day of errands, they switch after every stop.

- When they are older, one rides in front on even days, the other on odd days . . . This is a BIG deal to them and it changes with older kids and more siblings.

**47. The 4 Gold Chores**

- We don't really pay our kids to do chores. We think they should just help out. But there are 4 things I really can't stand doing that I will pay cash to get done. Shop vac both sets of stairs, clean the wood floors (big bucks), shop vac the car, wash the car.

**48. "Penny a Page Club" (through grade school)**

- They earn a penny for every page they read for themselves or to a sibling.

- They get paid at the same time they get paid for the "Chart."

**49. When I see a great gift, I buy it, and keep it in a special cabinet.**

- Then when a sudden need for a baby shower or birthday comes up I may not have to make a special trip.

- The kids know that they can never look in the bin because I store up Christmas gifts there, also.

**50. "Pop Probation"**

- When we had four kids, including 3 teenagers in the household, the pop allotment was continually challenged because I couldn't monitor it. So, every month when I would buy all the pop, water, Gatorades . . .for the entire month, we'd call in the family and take turns labeling cans with our names. Every 6th one said "Guest," for their friends. (We did the same with yogurt). They had to make their cans last for the month and when they were gone they were gone till the next month.

# Appendix 6
# *Scripture Memory at a Glance*

*Lesson 1*  #1 **Psalm 127:1**, "Unless the LORD builds the house, they labor in vain who build it; Unless the LORD guards the city, the watchman keeps awake in vain."

*Lesson 2*  #2 **2 Timothy 3:14**, "You, however, continue in the things you have learned and become convinced of, knowing from whom you have learned them."

*Lesson 3*  #3 **Psalm 85:8**, "I will hear what God the LORD will say; for He will speak peace to His people, to His godly ones; but let them not turn back to folly."

*Lesson 4*  #4 **Deuteronomy 6:6–7**, "These words, which I am commanding you today, shall be on your heart. You shall teach them diligently to your sons and shall talk of them when you sit in your house and when you walk by the way and when you lie down and when you rise up."

*Lesson 5*  #5 **1 Corinthians 14:33**, "For God is not a God of confusion but of peace, as in all the churches of the saints."

*Lesson 6*  #6 **Proverbs 22:6**, "Train up a child in the way he should go, even when he is old he will not depart from it."

*Lesson 7*  #7 **Hebrews 12:11**, "All discipline for the moment seems not to be joyful, but sorrowful; yet to those who have been trained by it, afterwards it yields the peaceful fruit of righteousness."

#8 **Philippians 2:14**, "Do all things without grumbling or disputing."

*Lesson 8*  #9 **Psalm 147:10–11**, "He does not delight in the strength of the horse; He does not take pleasure in the legs of a man. The LORD favors those who fear Him, those who wait for His lovingkindness."

#10 **Lamentations 3:27**, "It is good for a man that he should bear the yoke in his youth."

*Lesson 9*  #11 **Ephesians 6:1–4**, "Children, obey your parents in the Lord, for this is right. HONOR YOUR FATHER AND MOTHER . . . SO THAT IT MAY BE WELL WITH YOU, AND THAT YOU MAY LIVE LONG ON THE EARTH. Fathers do not provoke your children to anger, but bring them up in the discipline and instruction of the Lord."

*Lesson 10*  #12 **Matthew 5:37**, "But let your statement be 'Yes, yes' or 'No, no'; anything beyond these is of evil."

*Lesson 11*  #13 **Proverbs 13:24**, "He who withholds his rod hates his son, But he who loves him disciplines him diligently."

#14 **Proverbs 29:15**, "The rod and reproof give wisdom, but a child who gets his own way brings shame to his mother."

*Lesson 12*  #15 **Proverbs 26:4–5**, "Do not answer a fool according to his folly, or you will also be like him. Answer a fool as his folly deserves, that he not be wise in his own eyes."

*Lesson 13*  #16 **1 Samuel 12:23**, "Moreover, as for me, far be it from me that I should sin against the LORD by ceasing to pray for you; but I will instruct you in the good and right way."

*Lesson 14*  #17 **Ephesians 4:29,** "Let no unwholesome word proceed from your mouth, but only such a word as is good for edification according to the need of the moment, so that it will give grace to those who hear."

*Lesson 15*  #18 **Colossians 2:8,** "See to it that no one takes you captive through philosophy and empty deception, according to the tradition of men, according to the elementary principles of the world, rather than according to Christ."

*Lesson 16*  #19 **1 Corinthians 13:4–7,** "Love is patient, love is kind and is not jealous; love does not brag and is not arrogant, does not act unbecomingly; it does not seek its own, is not provoked, does not take into account a wrong suffered, does not rejoice in unrighteousness, but rejoices with the truth; bears all things, believes all things, hopes all things, endures all things."

*Lesson 17*  #20 **Acts 2:39,** "For the promise is for you and your children and for all who are far off, as many as the Lord our God will call to Himself."

#21 **Proverbs 1:8–9,** "Hear, my son, your father's instruction and do not forsake your mother's teaching; indeed, they are a graceful wreath to your head and ornaments about your neck."

*Lesson 18*  #22 **1 Peter 3:8–9,** "To sum up, all of you be harmonious, sympathetic, brotherly, kindhearted, and humble in spirit; not returning evil for evil or insult for insult, but giving a blessing instead; for you were called for the very purpose that you might inherit a blessing."

*Lesson 19*  #23 **Titus 2:3–5,** "Older women likewise are to be reverent in their behavior, not malicious gossips nor enslaved to much wine, teaching what is good, so that they may encourage the young women to love their husbands, to love their children, to be sensible, pure, workers at home, kind, being subject to their own husbands, so that the word of God will not be dishonored."

*Additional Verses*  **Deuteronomy 30:11–12,14,** "For this commandment which I command you today is not too difficult for you, nor is it out of reach. It is not in heaven, that you should say, 'Who will go up to heaven for us to get it for us and make us hear it, that we may observe it?' . . . But the word is very near you, in your mouth and in your heart, that you may observe it."

**James 3:17,** "But the wisdom from above is first pure, then peaceable, gentle, reasonable, full of mercy and good fruits, unwavering, without hypocrisy."

**Proverbs 20:5,** "A plan in the heart of a man is like deep water, but a man of understanding draws it out."

**Psalm 78:6–7,** "That the generation to come might know, even the children yet to be born, that they may arise and tell them to their children, that they should put their confidence in God and not forget the works of God, but keep His commandments."

# Scripture Memory
## REVIEW AND CHECKLIST

Date the first square when you have memorized the verse. Date the following squares when you review the verse. The more you review, the more you will retain. Each week you will be requested to share the current verse with your small group. Each week during the year your table will review all the verses. Please be committed to the Scripture memory. Beyond the Home Front Applications, it is your only required homework.

**Deuteronomy 32:46–47** (NKJV)

*Set your hearts on all the words which I testify among you today, which you shall command your children to be careful to observe—all the words of this law. For it is not a futile thing for you, because it is your life.*

| Verse | | | | | | | | | | | | | | | | | | | | | | |
|---|---|---|---|---|---|---|---|---|---|---|---|---|---|---|---|---|---|---|---|---|---|---|
| Psalm 127:1 | | | | | | | | | | | | | | | | | | | | | | |
| 2 Timothy 3:14 | | | | | | | | | | | | | | | | | | | | | | |
| Psalm 85:8 | | | | | | | | | | | | | | | | | | | | | | |
| Deuteronomy 6:6–7 | | | | | | | | | | | | | | | | | | | | | | |
| 1 Corinthians 14:33 | | | | | | | | | | | | | | | | | | | | | | |
| Proverbs 22:6 | | | | | | | | | | | | | | | | | | | | | | |
| Hebrews 12:11 | | | | | | | | | | | | | | | | | | | | | | |
| Philippians 2:14 | | | | | | | | | | | | | | | | | | | | | | |
| Psalm 147:10–11 | | | | | | | | | | | | | | | | | | | | | | |
| Lamentations 3:27 | | | | | | | | | | | | | | | | | | | | | | |
| Ephesians 6:1–4 | | | | | | | | | | | | | | | | | | | | | | |
| Matthew 5:37 | | | | | | | | | | | | | | | | | | | | | | |
| Proverbs 13:24 | | | | | | | | | | | | | | | | | | | | | | |
| Proverbs 29:15 | | | | | | | | | | | | | | | | | | | | | | |
| Proverbs 26:4–5 | | | | | | | | | | | | | | | | | | | | | | |
| 1 Samuel 12:23 | | | | | | | | | | | | | | | | | | | | | | |
| Ephesians 4:29 | | | | | | | | | | | | | | | | | | | | | | |
| Colossians 2:8 | | | | | | | | | | | | | | | | | | | | | | |
| 1 Corinthians 13:4–7 | | | | | | | | | | | | | | | | | | | | | | |
| Acts 2:39 | | | | | | | | | | | | | | | | | | | | | | |
| Proverbs 1:8–9 | | | | | | | | | | | | | | | | | | | | | | |
| 1 Peter 3:8–9 | | | | | | | | | | | | | | | | | | | | | | |
| Titus 2:3–5 | | | | | | | | | | | | | | | | | | | | | | |

# Appendix 8
## Answer Key

**Lesson 1**
poor
captive
blind
downtrodden

first
Jesus

Him

day
eternity

will

authority

giving over
entrusted

how
His behalf

gift
forever
uniquely

breath
life

breath
life

breath

chose
glorify

purpose
life

His
stewards

first
physical

second
spirit
physically

---

accept
reject

not
miracle
realize

place
owe
sacrifice

spirit
everlasting
born again

reborn
agree

only
gift
mouths

penalty
new

reborn

cannot
made
afresh
breathes
Holy

before
absolutely

heart

act
Bible
collapse

**Lesson 2**
biblical principles
stand

feel
think
do
NO MATTER WHAT
true

---

need
informed
right
educated

allowing
watching
Him
easy

evil

confused

hearts
feel

change
loving

place
authority

realize
awe
offending

children
grow up
Him

perfect

faith
convinced
best

convictions
foundational

God
believe
do
trust

conviction

Word
bless
strong
testing
continue

---

Jesus

wavering

reap

negotiable

build

loves
disclose

Himself

battle
convictions

examining
so

personal

personalizing
place of

necessary
(Your last name)

understand
personal
okay

obey
glorify

clash
convictions
(Your last name)

convinced
agreed
our

Consider

feeble
united

agreement

grow up with
follow

---

no
challenge
grateful

**Lesson 3**
believe
why

high
foundation

ourselves
train

conscience
moral
right

fairness
justice

aware

created
suppress
deny

look
confused
stumble
make
compromises

discouraged
angry

question
justice

sure
expose
judge

best
fail
dwell

Holy Spirit
sharpens

---

judge
maturity
understanding

Disputable

each

judge

discord

precedence
central

purpose
diverse

flex
responsibly

ease up
authority
guide
influence

choices
watch
authority
influence

saturated

ways
guidance

filter
not
experience
counterfeit

perfect

doing
not doing

decision
distinguish

steadfast
understanding
flexible

# Answer Key

**Lesson 4**

Biblical

smoothly

importance
faith

choice

abandoned

difficult

first

rightful
subject

follow
accountable
sin

strongest

guarded

Be committed to
each other; guard
your marriage.
Show your children
that you love and
respect their dad.
Learn what encour-
ages him most and
do these things
regularly.
Make home his
favorite place
to be.

agreement

understanding

submissive
sensitive

intimidating

offer
respect
leader
provider
protector

counterfeit

close
priority
Talk

moving
Listen

how

different

agreement

challenge

helpmate
bug

contentious
not

Holy Spirit
resting

promptings

Trust
Pray

understanding

husband–wife
Christ–centered

life

outside

eternal
temporal

committing

why
first

chaos
confusion
pulse
beyond

overwhelmed
stressed
anxious

**Lesson 5**

prove

above
Lord

testing
commitment
overwhelming

compromise

Study

tithe

life routine

Serve

Exalt

abiding

stability
daily
crisis

influence
internal
priorities
non–negotiables

pushing
call

driven
selfish
stable
harmonious
blessed
stressed
internal

peaceful
unity

sidetracked

God
lasting

stand up

**Lesson 6**

first

bond
longs

wonder
your

first
sensitivity

outward
hearts

devalued
nurturing
missing out

choose
conspiracy

more
fulfilled

touch
infancy
release

outgrown
need
parental attach-
ment

rage
lack

Society
abortions
38,000,000

300%

train
first
draws
serve Him

submit
all
biblical convictions
rest
calling

release

Parents

unique
soul
image

purpose
glorify
not
God
not
God

exists
keeping
happy
inflated
elevated
self

choices
opportunities
self–centered

allow
satisfy
inviting
home
heart

surrendered
authority
divided
options
decision

not respecting
decisive

kind
reap
self–centered

inherited

their

Willful

instruction
full circle
wrong
right

assured
boundary
cross

exactly
know
consistent
obey

reminded
sin nature

consistent
purpose
controlling

accept
divine nature
training
put off
put on

**Lesson 7**

automatic

happen

eventually

maturity
heart

apart
focus

# Answer Key

earlier
opposite

duty
over
ends
does

releases

watch
ready

convictions
remain
present
not

Demonstrate
outside

financially

exasperate
ready

accountable

generation
obey
grumbling
fear

realize
fully

fearful

good
providence

apostate
gospel
truth

no
saved

reject
terrified

author
originates
existence

source
rightful

think
tell

speech
affront
affront

zero
defiant
ungrateful
every

weed
quickly
overwhelming
effort

Fathers
doubt

sassy
disrespectful
unshakable

0%
everything
100%

unable
watch

choices

guidance

danger
early
long

choices

5

foundation
new

We
expect

starting

example

respecting

sin

significance
direction

*Lesson 8*
arrogant
prideful
lie
created

impressed
lofty
abilities

delights
who He is
fear

arrogant

free thinkers
outside
enslaved

fear
please
bless

truth
live

save
sorrow
bear
good

lovingly

not
elevates
challenges
affect

gracious
merciful
vulnerable
evil

protection

provision

great
glory
praise

abide

decisions

abundant

fellowship

goodness
stores

rescued
near

witnesses

forgiveness
compassion

always
needs

future

released
fears

protection

cherish
relationships

call
answers

favored

health

wisdom

confident

contentment

meaning
life

families

Church

eternal

first
daily

pervert
refusing

suffer
turning

not
apart

all
from

listen

submit
way of life

dread
lack

man
own
misplace
judges

elevate
down

control
dignity

managers
children

disqualifies
ministry

model
guide
own

protection
ways
faithfulness

prayers
protected

challenges
refocus
everyday

"happen"
allowed
dependence

facing
sparing

small
serious

steps
fear

young
pursue
through
other

believers
struggle
discipline

provides
resists
Word

purposes
restore
realign
protect
body
accountable

unguarded
guards

# Answer Key

easy
towers

grow
loving
wise
umbrella

self–controlled

**Lesson 9**
restrain

manage
out of control

commands
biblical

self

others

God

lowest
rewards

pleasing

heart

motivation

full circle

Why
change
replace
glorify

commands

faithfully

event
not

present
focus

rely

rebel

motivation

Honor

treat

reluctantly

same
heart

parents

deserving

above

honors
do
all

presence

harsh
deserve
just

innocent
right

honoring

maintain
commendable

know

angry

counseling

own
defiance

children

reasonable

unwise

blessing
time

anger

complete

orderly

touch

purpose

sinful

unity

build
wrong

know

sin

understanding

do
do

**Lesson 10**
heart
priority

Lord
husband

replace

false
resist

no room

desire

Grace

maturity

quick

reach

unjust

grace
clear

Understanding

approachable
entreated
how

Grace

Acceptance

materialism

Priorities

bitter

man

Self–control

rewalking

dark

wisdom

Admonishment

Orderliness

value
encouragement

sibling

Tenderness

gradually
before

clear
limits

Sound Judgment

hide

Forbearance

Harmony

Admit
not

future

wedge

Forgiveness

Model

Living By
Convictions

edifying

Love

hearing
full circle

Listening

Integrity

Christlikeness

drawn
want

**Lesson 11**
exempt

apply
committed

sound

decisions
choose

will

affection

joy
applying

obey

unstable

all

training

(refers to Chart
on Page 11.5)
IGNORANCE
Teaching
REBELLION
Discipline
DISCOURAGEMENT
Encouragement

requires
intervention
vain

trust

first
good

excusing

not

sure
accounting

holiness

while

between
send

need

"discipline"

determined

humble

needs
must

foolishness

# Answer Key

shocked
hide

control

how

over

love

harm

violence

work

inconsistent

persist

method

anger
heart

abuse

accountability

character

drawing
explaining

commitment

privileges

good
right

hope
remedy

lose

we

source
cheerleader
confidant
warrior
react

## Lesson 12
babies

simple
win
decisively

not

back

Each

biblical

usurp
schemes

trip

not

withstood
truth
focus
side trails

redirects
makes
vulnerable

easier
false
train

gives up

cave in

bolder
intimidation

deter

## Lesson 13
accomplish

question
again

still
eventually
every

process
never give up

flawed
still

ultimate
yet
rebel

understands
poor
defeated

endure
testing

choice
own

guarantee

entrusted
train
best
calls

wrong

appoint

set

break down

let loose

act

bring

confess

humbled

amends

remember

squash
hard
realize

sinning

back
pray

rebuke
job

good

tough
submit
repent
obey

friends

Relationships

pain

heartbreak
never
understanding

## Lesson 14
Memories
not

detail
own
significance

words
tone

control
intimacy

counterfeits
undermine

Lord

Wholesome

strengthen
persevere

belittle

forgiveness

admonition

right
right
purpose

hold

rest

reputations

tempted

insult
motive

faith

Time

ready
timing

training

Lord

spirit
flesh
excellence

power
best

Ensues

bless
blast
grateful

opportunity
not

remember
wisely

## Lesson 15
battling
war

own
convictions

filter
withstand

garbage

enters
small

extreme

eventually

deceive

rules

God's
more
permission

broken into
plundered

small
guardrails

FULL

watchful
persevere

90%

good
alone

thankful

His
content
grateful

provides
sure

get
give
share

in
of

defenses

memorize
direct

needy

**Lesson 16**
authority

character
lifelong

choices

only

rules
heart

behavior

model

gentle
gracious

envious
boastful

rudely
touchy

grudges

rejoices

loyal

best

empty

each

Keep
unappreciated

works

sharpens
character

settle

transform

hypocrisy

time
pattern

commitment
encourage
progress

study

excuse

redirected

best

glorify
prove

**Lesson 17**
disciplined

everything

nothing

Lord

VITAL SIGNS
Savior

sin

Obeys

Loves

world's

Endures

Grows

faithful
fruitful

generations

can
histories

tone
you

pagan
heritage
Jesus

**Lesson 18**
best
special

bond
close

need

grace
sacrifice
accountability

forgiveness
sorrow

say the words

patient
listen
trust

fair
submit

Receive

ask
accept

together
and
hug

better
exchanged
hug
clean

bitterness

long–suffering
intentional
honors

offense
reacts
chain

be the one
break

coping

love
cruelty

heart
attention

practiced
practiced
little
first
right

own
humble
regardless

treat
fairly
demanding

allowing
men
women
character

reputation
strength
endure

sovereign
aware
way

Lord

amazed
understand

Him

Purpose

deserve
willing

tend

persuasive

bear up
prepares
true

past

heart
give

difficult
past
unto

you
My
servant

worth
them
own

best
worthy
great

willing

Loyalty
faithfulness
commitment
real

sacrifices

cost
paying
sacrifice

protect
view
conscience

weakness
demonstration
loyalty

time

counterfeit

enduring
time
bond

know
investment

great
Lord

concentrate

willing
feel

# Appendix 8
## Answer Key

| | | | | | |
|---|---|---|---|---|---|
| plan | submitting | rationalize | vulnerable | motive | pride |
| beyond | vulnerability | keep | block | innocent | |
| dream | | | | pressures | popping up |
| His | led | bond | walls | death trap | agree |
| | taught | one | withhold | | settle in |
| pride | corrected | | | wrong | |
| destroys | | power | under | family | guidelines |
| stubborn | strong | | | | Don't |
| | godly | family | important | guardrails | no |
| hold | | before | strong | think | no |
| trust | men | believers | anyone | | no |
| | | | | emotional | |
| not | vulnerable | truth | choose | | Listen |
| | understanding | | | date | hear |
| revolutionize | | unbeliever | teaching | hopes | Working |
| generously | biblical | | friend | order | |
| sacrificially | | deceiving | | | agreement |
| | pyramids | strong | spiritual | harmful | biblical |
| opposite | spiritual | | | | personal |
| | | challenged | protection | great | preference |
| drawn | friendship | prove | | resolved | |
| know | | | Parents | | defer |
| counterfeit | emotional | poor | | understanding | leader |
| | | no | blessing | agreement | |
| | marriage | | | | fulfillment |
| *Lesson 19* | physical | security | Don't | differences | |
| Grace | reverse | dependence | | biblical | can |
| Sacrifice | | Christ | contact | | fellowship |
| Accountability | | | flee | | enduring |

# Appendix 9
# *Read Through the Bible*
## CHRONOLOGICAL READING SCHEDULE

| Day: | Date: | Text: | Day: | Date: | Text: |
|------|-------|-------|------|-------|-------|
| 1 | Jan.1 | Gen. 1–3 | 23 | Jan. 23 | Job 8–11 |
| 2 | Jan. 2 | Gen. 4:1–6:8 | 24 | Jan. 24 | Job 12–15 |
| 3 | Jan. 3 | Gen. 6:9–9:29 | 25 | Jan. 25 | Job 16–19 |
| 4 | Jan. 4 | Gen. 10–11 | 26 | Jan. 26 | Job 20–22 |
| 5 | Jan. 5 | Gen. 12–14 | 27 | Jan. 27 | Job 23–28 |
| 6 | Jan. 6 | Gen. 15–17 | 28 | Jan. 28 | Job 29–31 |
| 7 | Jan. 7 | Gen. 18–19 | 29 | Jan. 29 | Job 32–34 |
| 8 | Jan. 8 | Gen. 20–22 | 30 | Jan. 30 | Job 35–37 |
| 9 | Jan. 9 | Gen. 23–24 | 31 | Jan. 31 | Job 38–42 |
| 10 | Jan. 10 | Gen. 25–26 | 32 | Feb. 1 | Ex. 1–4 |
| 11 | Jan. 11 | Gen. 27–28 | 33 | Feb. 2 | Ex. 5–8 |
| 12 | Jan. 12 | Gen. 29–30 | 34 | Feb. 3 | Ex. 9–11 |
| 13 | Jan. 13 | Gen. 31–32 | 35 | Feb. 4 | Ex. 12–13 |
| 14 | Jan. 14 | Gen. 33–35 | 36 | Feb. 5 | Ex. 14–15 |
| 15 | Jan. 15 | Gen. 36–37 | 37 | Feb. 6 | Ex. 16–18 |
| 16 | Jan. 16 | Gen. 38–40 | 38 | Feb. 7 | Ex. 19–21 |
| 17 | Jan. 17 | Gen. 41–42 | 39 | Feb. 8 | Ex. 22–24 |
| 18 | Jan. 18 | Gen. 43–45 | 40 | Feb. 9 | Ex. 25–27 |
| 19 | Jan. 19 | Gen. 46–47 | 41 | Feb. 10 | Ex. 28–29 |
| 20 | Jan. 20 | Gen. 48–50 | 42 | Feb. 11 | Ex. 30–31 |
| 21 | Jan. 21 | Job 1–3 | 43 | Feb. 12 | Ex. 32–34 |
| 22 | Jan. 22 | Job 4–7 | 44 | Feb. 13 | Ex. 35–36 |

| Day: | Date: | Text: | Day: | Date: | Text: |
|------|-------|-------|------|-------|-------|
| 45 | Feb. 14 | Ex. 37–38 | 67 | Mar. 8 | Num. 25–26 |
| 46 | Feb. 15 | Ex. 39–40 | 68 | Mar. 9 | Num. 27–29 |
| 47 | Feb. 16 | Lev. 1:1–5:13 | 69 | Mar. 10 | Num. 30–31 |
| 48 | Feb. 17 | Lev. 5:14–7:38 | 70 | Mar. 11 | Num. 32–33 |
| 49 | Feb. 18 | Lev. 8–10 | 71 | Mar. 12 | Num. 34–36 |
| 50 | Feb. 19 | Lev. 11–12 | 72 | Mar. 13 | Deut. 1–2 |
| 51 | Feb. 20 | Lev. 13–14 | 73 | Mar. 14 | Deut. 3–4 |
| 52 | Feb. 21 | Lev. 15–17 | 74 | Mar. 15 | Deut. 5–7 |
| 53 | Feb. 22 | Lev. 18–20 | 75 | Mar. 16 | Deut. 8–10 |
| 54 | Feb. 23 | Lev. 21–23 | 76 | Mar. 17 | Deut. 11–13 |
| 55 | Feb. 24 | Lev. 24–25 | 77 | Mar. 18 | Deut. 14–17 |
| 56 | Feb. 25 | Lev. 26–27 | 78 | Mar. 19 | Deut. 18–21 |
| 57 | Feb. 26 | Num. 1–2 | 79 | Mar. 20 | Deut. 22–25 |
| 58 | Feb. 27 | Num. 3–4 | 80 | Mar. 21 | Deut. 26–28 |
| 59 | Feb. 28 | Num. 5–6 | 81 | Mar. 22 | Deut. 29:1–31:29 |
| 60 | Mar. 1 | Num. 7 | 82 | Mar. 23 | Deut. 31:30–34:12 |
| 61 | Mar. 2 | Num. 8–10 | 83 | Mar. 24 | Josh. 1–4 |
| 62 | Mar. 3 | Num. 11–13 | 84 | Mar. 25 | Josh. 5–8 |
| 63 | Mar. 4 | Num. 14–15 | 85 | Mar. 26 | Josh. 9–11 |
| 64 | Mar. 5 | Num. 16–18 | 86 | Mar. 27 | Josh. 12–14 |
| 65 | Mar. 6 | Num. 19–21 | 87 | Mar. 28 | Josh. 15–17 |
| 66 | Mar. 7 | Num. 22–24 | 88 | Mar. 29 | Josh. 18–19 |

# Appendix 9
# *Read Through the Bible*
## CHRONOLOGICAL READING SCHEDULE

| Day: | Date: | Text: |
|------|-------|-------|
| 89 | Mar. 30 | Josh. 20–22 |
| 90 | Mar. 31 | Josh. 23–Judg. 1 |
| 91 | Apr. 1 | Judg. 2–5 |
| 92 | Apr. 2 | Judg. 6–8 |
| 93 | Apr. 3 | Judg. 9 |
| 94 | Apr. 4 | Judg. 10–12 |
| 95 | Apr. 5 | Judg. 13–16 |
| 96 | Apr. 6 | Judg. 17–19 |
| 97 | Apr. 7 | Judg. 20–21 |
| 98 | Apr. 8 | Ruth |
| 99 | Apr. 9 | 1 Sam. 1–3 |
| 100 | Apr. 10 | 1 Sam. 4–7 |
| 101 | Apr. 11 | 1 Sam. 8–10 |
| 102 | Apr. 12 | 1 Sam. 11–13 |
| 103 | Apr. 13 | 1 Sam. 14–15 |
| 104 | Apr. 14 | 1 Sam. 16–17 |
| 105 | Apr. 15 | 1 Sam. 18–19; Ps. 59 |
| 106 | Apr. 16 | 1 Sam. 20–21; Pss. 56; 34 |
| 107 | Apr. 17 | 1 Sam. 22–23; 1 Chron. 12:8–18; Pss. 52; 54; 63; 142 |
| 108 | Apr. 18 | 1 Sam. 24; Ps. 57; 1 Sam. 25 |
| 109 | Apr. 19 | 1 Sam. 26–29; 1 Chron. 12:1–7, 19–22 |

| Day: | Date: | Text: |
|------|-------|-------|
| 110 | Apr. 20 | 1 Sam. 30–31; 1 Chron. 10; 2 Sam 1 |
| 111 | Apr. 21 | 2 Sam. 2–4 |
| 112 | Apr. 22 | 2 Sam. 5:1–6:11, 1 Chron. 11:1–9; 12:23–40; 13:1–14:17 |
| 113 | Apr. 23 | 2 Sam. 22; Ps. 18 |
| 114 | Apr. 24 | 1 Chron. 15–16; 2 Sam. 6:12–23; Ps. 96 |
| 115 | Apr. 25 | Ps. 105; 2 Sam. 7; 1 Chron. 17 |
| 116 | Apr. 26 | 2 Sam. 8–10; 1 Chron. 18–19; Ps. 60 |
| 117 | Apr. 27 | 2 Sam. 11–12; 1 Chron. 20:1–3; Ps. 51 |
| 118 | Apr. 28 | 2 Sam. 13–14 |
| 119 | Apr. 29 | 2 Sam. 15–17 |
| 120 | Apr. 30 | Ps. 3; 2 Sam. 18–19 |
| 121 | May 1 | 2 Sam. 20–21; 23:8–23; 1 Chron. 20:4–8; 11:10–25 |
| 122 | May 2 | 2 Sam. 23:24–24:25; 1 Chron. 11:26–47; 21:1–30 |
| 123 | May 3 | 1 Chron. 22–24 |
| 124 | May 4 | Ps. 30; 1 Chron. 25–26 |
| 125 | May 5 | 1 Chron. 27–29 |
| 126 | May 6 | Pss. 5–7; 10; 11; 13; 17 |
| 127 | May 7 | Pss. 23; 26; 28; 31; 35 |
| 128 | May 8 | Pss. 41; 43; 46; 55; 61; 62; 64 |

# Read Through the Bible
## CHRONOLOGICAL READING SCHEDULE

| Day: | Date: | Text: |
|------|-------|-------|
| 129 | May 9 | Pss. 69–71; 77 |
| 130 | May 10 | Pss. 83; 86; 88; 91; 95 |
| 131 | May 11 | Pss. 108–109; 120–121; 140; 143–144 |
| 132 | May 12 | Pss. 1; 14–15; 36–37; 39 |
| 133 | May 13 | Pss. 40; 49–50; 73 |
| 134 | May 14 | Pss. 76; 82; 84; 90; 92; 112; 115 |
| 135 | May 15 | Pss. 8–9; 16; 19; 21; 24; 29 |
| 136 | May 16 | Pss. 33; 65–68 |
| 137 | May 17 | Pss. 75; 93–94; 97–100 |
| 138 | May 18 | Pss. 103–104; 113–114; 117 |
| 139 | May 19 | Ps. 119:1–88 |
| 140 | May 20 | Ps. 119:89–176 |
| 141 | May 21 | Pss. 122; 124; 133–136 |
| 142 | May 22 | Pss. 138–139; 145; 148; 150 |
| 143 | May 23 | Pss. 4; 12; 20; 25; 32; 38 |
| 144 | May 24 | Pss. 42; 53; 58; 81; 101; 111; 130–131; 141; 146 |
| 145 | May 25 | Pss. 2; 22; 27 |
| 146 | May 26 | Pss. 45; 47–48; 87; 110 |
| 147 | May 27 | 1 Kings 1:1–2:12; 2 Sam. 23:1–7 |
| 148 | May 28 | 1 Kings 2:13–3:28; 2 Chron. 1:1–13 |

| Day: | Date: | Text: |
|------|-------|-------|
| 149 | May 29 | 1 Kings 5–6; 2 Chron. 2–3 |
| 150 | May 30 | 1 Kings 7; 2 Chron. 4 |
| 151 | May 31 | 1 Kings 8; 2 Chron. 5:1–7:10 |
| 152 | June 1 | 1 Kings 9:1–10:13; 2 Chron. 7:11–9:12 |
| 153 | June 2 | 1 Kings 4; 10:14–29; 2 Chron. 1:14–17; 9:13–28; Ps. 72 |
| 154 | June 3 | Prov. 1–3 |
| 155 | June 4 | Prov. 4–6 |
| 156 | June 5 | Prov. 7–9 |
| 157 | June 6 | Prov. 10–12 |
| 158 | June 7 | Prov. 13–15 |
| 159 | June 8 | Prov. 16–18 |
| 160 | June 9 | Prov. 19–21 |
| 161 | June 10 | Prov. 22–24 |
| 162 | June 11 | Prov. 25–27 |
| 163 | June 12 | Prov. 28–29 |
| 164 | June 13 | Prov. 30–31; Ps. 127 |
| 165 | June 14 | Song of Songs |
| 166 | June 15 | 1 Kings 11:1–40; Eccl. 1–2 |
| 167 | June 16 | Eccl. 3–7 |
| 168 | June 17 | Eccl. 8–12; 1 Kings 11:41–43; 2 Chron. 9:29–31 |
| 169 | June 18 | 1 Kings 12; |

**Appendix 9.4**

# *Read Through the Bible*

## CHRONOLOGICAL READING SCHEDULE

| Day: | Date: | Text: |
|------|-------|-------|
| | | 2 Chron. 10:1–11:17 |
| 170 | June 19 | 1 Kings 13–14; 2 Chron. 11:18–12:16 |
| 171 | June 20 | 1 Kings 15:1–24; 2 Chron. 13–16 |
| 172 | June 21 | 1 Kings 15:25–16:34; 2 Chron. 17; 1 Kings 17 |
| 173 | June 22 | 1 Kings 18–19 |
| 174 | June 23 | 1 Kings 20–21 |
| 175 | June 24 | 1 Kings 22:1–40; 2 Chron. 18 |
| 176 | June 25 | 1 Kings 22:41–53; 2 Kings 1; 2 Chron. 19:1–21:3 |
| 177 | June 26 | 2 Kings 2–4 |
| 178 | June 27 | 2 Kings 5–7 |
| 179 | June 28 | 2 Kings 8–9; 2 Chron. 21:4–22:9 |
| 180 | June 29 | 2 Kings 10–11; 2 Chron. 22:10–23:21 |
| 181 | June 30 | Joel |
| 182 | July 1 | 2 Kings 12–13; 2 Chron. 24 |
| 183 | July 2 | 2 Kings 14; 2 Chron. 25; Jonah |
| 184 | July 3 | Hos. 1–7 |
| 185 | July 4 | Hos. 8–14 |
| 186 | July 5 | 2 Kings 15:1–7; 2 Chron. 26; Amos 1–4 |

| Day: | Date: | Text: |
|------|-------|-------|
| 187 | July 6 | Amos 5–9; 2 Kings 15:8–18 |
| 188 | July 7 | Isa. 1–4 |
| 189 | July 8 | 2 Kings 15:19–38; 2 Chron. 27; Isa. 5–6 |
| 190 | July 9 | Micah |
| 191 | July 10 | 2 Kings 16; 2 Chron 28; Isa. 7–8 |
| 192 | July 11 | Isa. 9–12 |
| 193 | July 12 | Isa. 13–16 |
| 194 | July 13 | Isa. 17–22 |
| 195 | July 14 | Isa. 23–27 |
| 196 | July 15 | Isa. 28–30 |
| 197 | July 16 | Isa. 31–35 |
| 198 | July 17 | 2 Kings 18:1–8; 2 Chron. 29–31 |
| 199 | July 18 | 2 Kings 17;18:9–37; 2 Chron. 32:1–19; Isa. 36 |
| 200 | July 19 | 2 Kings 19; 2 Chron. 32:20–23; Isa. 37 |
| 201 | July 20 | 2 Kings 20; 2 Chron 32:24–33; Isa. 38–39 |
| 202 | July 21 | 2 Kings 21:1–18; 2 Chron. 33:1–20; Isa. 40 |
| 203 | July 22 | Isa. 41–43 |
| 204 | July 23 | Isa. 44–47 |
| 205 | July 24 | Isa. 48–51 |

# Read Through the Bible
## CHRONOLOGICAL READING SCHEDULE

| Day: | Date: | Text: |
|------|-------|-------|
| 206 | July 25 | Isa. 52–57 |
| 207 | July 26 | Isa. 58–62 |
| 208 | July 27 | Isa. 63–66 |
| 209 | July 28 | 2 Kings 21:19–26; 2 Chron. 33:21–34:7; Zephaniah |
| 210 | July 29 | Jer. 1–3 |
| 211 | July 30 | Jer. 4–6 |
| 212 | July 31 | Jer. 7–9 |
| 213 | Aug. 1 | Jer. 10–13 |
| 214 | Aug. 2 | Jer. 14–16 |
| 215 | Aug. 3 | Jer. 17–20 |
| 216 | Aug. 4 | 2 Kings 22:1–23:28; 2 Chron 34:8–35:19 |
| 217 | Aug. 5 | Nahum; 2 Kings 23:29–37; 2 Chron. 35:20–36:5; Jer. 22:10–17 |
| 218 | Aug. 6 | Jer. 26; Habakkuk |
| 219 | Aug. 7 | Jer. 46–47; 2 Kings 24:1–4,7; 2 Chron. 36:6–7; Jer. 25, 35 |
| 220 | Aug. 8 | Jer. 36, 45, 48 |
| 221 | Aug. 9 | Jer. 49:1–33; Dan. 1–2 |
| 222 | Aug. 10 | Jer. 22:18–30; 2 Kings 24:5–20; 2 Chron 36:8–12; Jer. 37:1–2; 52:1–3; 24; 29 |
| 223 | Aug. 11 | Jer. 27–28; 23 |

| Day: | Date: | Text: |
|------|-------|-------|
| 224 | Aug. 12 | Jer. 50–51 |
| 225 | Aug. 13 | Jer. 49:34–39; 34:1–22; Ezek. 1–3 |
| 226 | Aug. 14 | Ezek. 4–7 |
| 227 | Aug. 15 | Ezek. 8–11 |
| 228 | Aug. 16 | Ezek. 12–14 |
| 229 | Aug. 17 | Ezek. 15–17 |
| 230 | Aug. 18 | Ezek. 18–20 |
| 231 | Aug. 19 | Ezek. 21–23 |
| 232 | Aug. 20 | 2 Kings 25:1; 2 Chron. 36:13–16; Jer. 39:1; 52:4; Ezek. 24; Jer. 21:1–22:9; 32:1–44 |
| 233 | Aug. 21 | Jer. 30–31; 33 |
| 234 | Aug. 22 | Ezek. 25; 29:1–16; 30; 31 |
| 235 | Aug. 23 | Ezek. 26–28 |
| 236 | Aug. 24 | Jer. 37:3–39:10; 52:5–30; 2 Kings 25:2–21; 2 Chron. 36:17–21 |
| 237 | Aug. 25 | 2 Kings 25:22; Jer. 39:11–40:6; Lam. 1–3 |
| 238 | Aug. 26 | Lam. 4–5; Obadiah |
| 239 | Aug. 27 | Jer. 40:7–44:30; 2 Kings 25:23–26 |
| 240 | Aug. 28 | Ezek. 33:21–36:38 |
| 241 | Aug. 29 | Ezek. 37–39 |
| 242 | Aug. 30 | Ezek. 32:1–33:20; Dan. 3 |

# Appendix 9
# *Read Through the Bible*
## CHRONOLOGICAL READING SCHEDULE

| Day: | Date: | Text: |
|---|---|---|
| 243 | Aug. 31 | Ezek. 40–42 |
| 244 | Sept. 1 | Ezek. 43–45 |
| 245 | Sept. 2 | Ezek. 46–48 |
| 246 | Sept. 3 | Ezek. 29:17–21; Dan. 4; Jer. 52:31–34; 2 Kings 25:27–30; Ps. 44 |
| 247 | Sept. 4 | Pss. 74; 79–80; 89 |
| 248 | Sept. 5 | Pss. 85; 102; 106; 123; 137 |
| 249 | Sept. 6 | Dan. 7–8; 5 |
| 250 | Sept. 7 | Dan. 9; 6 |
| 251 | Sept. 8 | 2 Chron. 36:22–23; Ezra 1:1–4:5 |
| 252 | Sept. 9 | Dan. 10–12 |
| 253 | Sept. 10 | Ezra 4:6–6:13; Haggai |
| 254 | Sept. 11 | Zech. 1–6 |
| 255 | Sept. 12 | Zech. 7–8; Ezra 6:14–22; Ps. 78 |
| 256 | Sept. 13 | Pss. 107; 116; 118 |
| 257 | Sept. 14 | Pss. 125–126; 128–129; 132; 147; 149 |
| 258 | Sept. 15 | Zech. 9–14 |
| 259 | Sept. 16 | Esther 1–4 |
| 260 | Sept. 17 | Esther 5–10 |
| 261 | Sept. 18 | Ezra 7–8 |
| 262 | Sept. 19 | Ezra 9–10 |

| Day: | Date: | Text: |
|---|---|---|
| 263 | Sept. 20 | Neh. 1–5 |
| 264 | Sept. 21 | Neh. 6–7 |
| 265 | Sept. 22 | Neh. 8–10 |
| 266 | Sept. 23 | Neh. 11–13 |
| 267 | Sept. 24 | Malachi |
| 268 | Sept. 25 | 1 Chron. 1–2 |
| 269 | Sept. 26 | 1 Chron. 3–5 |
| 270 | Sept. 27 | 1 Chron. 6 |
| 271 | Sept. 28 | 1 Chron. 7:1–8:27 |
| 272 | Sept. 29 | 1 Chron. 8:28–9:44 |
| 273 | Sept. 30 | John 1:1–18; Mark 1:1; Luke 1:1–4; 3:23–38; Matt. 1:1–17 |
| 274 | Oct. 1 | Luke 1:5–80 |
| 275 | Oct. 2 | Matt. 1:18–2:23; Luke 2 |
| 276 | Oct. 3 | Matt. 3:1–4:11; Mark 1:2–13; Luke 3:1–23; 4:1–13; John 1:19–34 |
| 277 | Oct. 4 | John 1:35–3:36 |
| 278 | Oct. 5 | John 4; Matt. 4:12–17; Mark 1:14–15; Luke 4:14–30 |
| 279 | Oct. 6 | Mark 1:16–45; Matt. 4:18–25; 8:2–4, 14–17; Luke 4:31–5:16 |
| 280 | Oct. 7 | Matt. 9:1–17; Mark 2:1–22; Luke 5:17–39 |
| 281 | Oct. 8 | John 5; Matt. 12:1–21; Mark 2:23–3:12; Luke 6:1–11 |

# Appendix 9
# *Read Through the Bible*
## CHRONOLOGICAL READING SCHEDULE

| Day: | Date: | Text: |
|------|-------|-------|
| 282 | Oct. 9 | Matt. 5; Mark 3:13–19; Luke 6:12–36 |
| 283 | Oct. 10 | Matt. 6–7; Luke 6:37–49 |
| 284 | Oct. 11 | Luke 7; Matt. 8:1, 5–13; 11:2–30 |
| 285 | Oct. 12 | Matt. 12:22–50; Mark 3:20–35; Luke 8:1–21 |
| 286 | Oct. 13 | Mark 4:1–34; Matt. 13:1–53 |
| 287 | Oct. 14 | Mark 4:35–5:43; Matt. 8:18, 23–24; 9:18–34; Luke 8:22–56 |
| 288 | Oct. 15 | Mark 6:1–30; Matt. 13:54–58; 9:35–11:1; 14:1–12; Luke 9:1–10 |
| 289 | Oct. 16 | Matt. 14:13–36; Mark 6:31–56; Luke 9:11–17; John 6:1–21 |
| 290 | Oct. 17 | John 6:22–7:1; Matt. 15:1–20; Mark 7:1–23 |
| 291 | Oct. 18 | Matt. 15:21–16:20; Mark 7:24–8:30; Luke 9:18–21 |
| 292 | Oct. 19 | Matt. 16:21–17:27; Mark 8:31–9:32; Luke 9:22–45 |
| 293 | Oct. 20 | Matt. 18; 8:19–22; Mark 9:33–50; Luke 9:46–62; John 7:2–10 |
| 294 | Oct. 21 | John 7:11–8:59 |
| 295 | Oct. 22 | Luke 10:1–11:36 |
| 296 | Oct. 23 | Luke 11:37–13:21 |
| 297 | Oct. 24 | John 9–10 |

| Day: | Date: | Text: |
|------|-------|-------|
| 298 | Oct. 25 | Luke 13:22–15:32 |
| 299 | Oct. 26 | Luke 16:1–17:10; John 11:1–54 |
| 300 | Oct. 27 | Luke 17:11–18:17; Matt. 19:1–15; Mark 10:1–16 |
| 301 | Oct. 28 | Matt. 19:16–20:28; Mark 10:17–45; Luke 18:18–34 |
| 302 | Oct. 29 | Matt. 20:29–34; 26:6–13; Mark 10:46–52; 14:3–9; Luke 18:35–19:28; John 11:55–12:11 |
| 303 | Oct. 30 | Matt. 21:1–22; Mark 11:1–26; Luke 19:29–48; John 12:12–50 |
| 304 | Oct. 31 | Matt. 21:23–22:14; Mark 11:27–12:12; Luke 20:1–19 |
| 305 | Nov. 1 | Matt. 22:15–46; Mark 12:13–37; Luke 20:20–44 |
| 306 | Nov. 2 | Matt. 23; Mark 12:38–44; Luke 20:45–21:4 |
| 307 | Nov. 3 | Matt. 24:1–31; Mark 13:1–27; Luke 21:5–27 |
| 308 | Nov. 4 | Matt. 24:32–26:5, 14–16; Mark 13:28–14:2, 10–11; Luke 21:28–22:6 |
| 309 | Nov. 5 | Matt. 26:17–29; Mark 14:12–25; Luke 22:7–38; John 13 |
| 310 | Nov. 6 | John 14–16 |

# *Read Through the Bible*

## CHRONOLOGICAL READING SCHEDULE

| Day: | Date: | Text: |
|---|---|---|
| 311 | Nov. 7 | John 17:1–18:1; Matt. 26:30–46; Mark 14:26–42; Luke 22:39–46 |
| 312 | Nov. 8 | Matt. 26:47–75; Mark 14:43–72; Luke 22:47–65; John 18:2–27 |
| 313 | Nov. 9 | Matt. 27:1–26; Mark 15:1–15; Luke 22:66–23:25; John 18:28–19:16 |
| 314 | Nov. 10 | Matt. 27:27–56; Mark 15:16–41; Luke 23:26–49; John 19:17–30 |
| 315 | Nov. 11 | Matt. 27:57–28:8; Mark 15:42–16:8; Luke 23:50–24:12; John 19:31–20:10 |
| 316 | Nov. 12 | Matt. 28:9–20; 16:9–20; Luke 24:13–53; John 20:11–21:25 |
| 317 | Nov. 13 | Acts 1–2 |
| 318 | Nov. 14 | Acts 3–5 |
| 319 | Nov. 15 | Acts 6:1–8:1 |
| 320 | Nov. 16 | Acts 8:2– 9:43 |
| 321 | Nov. 17 | Acts 10–11 |
| 322 | Nov. 18 | Acts 12–13 |
| 323 | Nov. 19 | Acts 14–15 |
| 324 | Nov. 20 | Gal. 1–3 |

| Day: | Date: | Text: |
|---|---|---|
| 325 | Nov. 21 | Gal. 4–6 |
| 326 | Nov. 22 | James |
| 327 | Nov. 23 | Acts 16:1–18:11 |
| 328 | Nov. 24 | 1 Thessalonians |
| 329 | Nov. 25 | 2 Thessalonians; Acts 18:12–19:22 |
| 330 | Nov. 26 | 1 Cor. 1–4 |
| 331 | Nov. 27 | 1 Cor. 5–8 |
| 332 | Nov. 28 | 1 Cor. 9–11 |
| 333 | Nov. 29 | 1 Cor. 12–14 |
| 334 | Nov. 30 | 1 Cor. 15–16 |
| 335 | Dec. 1 | Acts 19:23–20:1; 2 Cor. 1–4 |
| 336 | Dec. 2 | 2 Cor. 5–9 |
| 337 | Dec. 3 | 2 Cor. 10–13 |
| 338 | Dec. 4 | Rom. 1–3 |
| 339 | Dec. 5 | Rom. 4–6 |
| 340 | Dec. 6 | Rom. 7–8 |
| 341 | Dec. 7 | Rom. 9–11 |
| 342 | Dec. 8 | Rom. 12–15 |
| 343 | Dec. 9 | Rom. 16; Acts 20:2–21:16 |
| 344 | Dec. 10 | Acts 21:17–23:35 |
| 345 | Dec. 11 | Acts 24–26 |
| 346 | Dec. 12 | Acts 27–28 |
| 347 | Dec. 13 | Eph. 1–3 |

# *Read Through the Bible*
## CHRONOLOGICAL READING SCHEDULE

| Day: | Date: | Text: | Day: | Date: | Text: |
|------|-------|-------|------|-------|-------|
| 348 | Dec. 14 | Eph. 4–6 | 357 | Dec. 23 | Heb. 5:11–9:28 |
| 349 | Dec. 15 | Colossians | 358 | Dec. 24 | Heb. 10–11 |
| 350 | Dec. 16 | Philippians | 359 | Dec. 25 | Heb. 12–13; 2 John; 3 John |
| 351 | Dec. 17 | Philemon; 1 Tim. 1–3 | 360 | Dec. 26 | 1 John |
| 352 | Dec. 18 | 1 Tim. 4–6; Titus | 361 | Dec. 27 | Rev. 1–3 |
| 353 | Dec. 19 | 2 Timothy | 362 | Dec. 28 | Rev. 4–9 |
| 354 | Dec. 20 | 1 Peter | 363 | Dec. 29 | Rev. 10–14 |
| 355 | Dec. 21 | Jude; 2 Peter | 364 | Dec. 30 | Rev. 15–18 |
| 356 | Dec. 22 | Heb. 1:1–5:10 | 365 | Dec. 31 | Rev. 19–22 |

# Read Through the Bible Color Chart Sample

Faith/Blessings of Obedience/ Righteous Living

Rebellion/Consequences of Sin/ Biblical Warnings/Fear of Man

Persecution/Spiritual Warfare/Occult

Witnessing/Evangelism/Ministry

Prophecy

Giving/Money

Promises of God/Memorial Verses

Praise/Worship/Prayer

Family/Raising Children

Marriage/Divorce

Relationships/Forgiveness/Fellowship

Attributes of God/Character of God

Read Through the Bible Color Chart

# Appendix 10
# Prayer Journal

| Date: | Name: | Request: | Answered Prayer: |
|-------|-------|----------|------------------|
| 3-3-11 | Lucy | Michael lost his job today | |
| | | | |
| | | | |
| | | | |
| | | | |
| | | | |
| | | | |
| | | | |
| | | | |
| | | | |
| | | | |
| | | | |
| | | | |
| | | | |
| | | | |
| | | | |
| | | | |
| | | | |
| | | | |
| | | | |
| | | | |
| | | | |
| | | | |
| | | | |
| | | | |
| | | | |

# Prayer Journal

| Date: | Name: | Request: | Answered Prayer: |
|-------|-------|----------|------------------|
|       |       |          |                  |
|       |       |          |                  |
|       |       |          |                  |
|       |       |          |                  |
|       |       |          |                  |
|       |       |          |                  |
|       |       |          |                  |
|       |       |          |                  |
|       |       |          |                  |
|       |       |          |                  |
|       |       |          |                  |
|       |       |          |                  |
|       |       |          |                  |
|       |       |          |                  |
|       |       |          |                  |
|       |       |          |                  |
|       |       |          |                  |
|       |       |          |                  |
|       |       |          |                  |
|       |       |          |                  |
|       |       |          |                  |
|       |       |          |                  |
|       |       |          |                  |
|       |       |          |                  |
|       |       |          |                  |
|       |       |          |                  |
|       |       |          |                  |
|       |       |          |                  |
|       |       |          |                  |
|       |       |          |                  |
|       |       |          |                  |
|       |       |          |                  |
|       |       |          |                  |

# Appendix 10
## Prayer Journal

| Date: | Name: | Request: | Answered Prayer: |
|-------|-------|----------|------------------|
|       |       |          |                  |
|       |       |          |                  |
|       |       |          |                  |
|       |       |          |                  |
|       |       |          |                  |
|       |       |          |                  |
|       |       |          |                  |
|       |       |          |                  |
|       |       |          |                  |
|       |       |          |                  |
|       |       |          |                  |
|       |       |          |                  |
|       |       |          |                  |
|       |       |          |                  |
|       |       |          |                  |
|       |       |          |                  |
|       |       |          |                  |
|       |       |          |                  |
|       |       |          |                  |
|       |       |          |                  |
|       |       |          |                  |
|       |       |          |                  |
|       |       |          |                  |
|       |       |          |                  |
|       |       |          |                  |
|       |       |          |                  |
|       |       |          |                  |
|       |       |          |                  |
|       |       |          |                  |
|       |       |          |                  |

# Prayer Journal

| Date: | Name: | Request: | Answered Prayer: |
|-------|-------|----------|------------------|
|       |       |          |                  |
|       |       |          |                  |
|       |       |          |                  |
|       |       |          |                  |
|       |       |          |                  |
|       |       |          |                  |
|       |       |          |                  |
|       |       |          |                  |
|       |       |          |                  |
|       |       |          |                  |
|       |       |          |                  |
|       |       |          |                  |
|       |       |          |                  |
|       |       |          |                  |
|       |       |          |                  |
|       |       |          |                  |
|       |       |          |                  |
|       |       |          |                  |
|       |       |          |                  |
|       |       |          |                  |
|       |       |          |                  |
|       |       |          |                  |
|       |       |          |                  |
|       |       |          |                  |
|       |       |          |                  |
|       |       |          |                  |
|       |       |          |                  |
|       |       |          |                  |
|       |       |          |                  |

# Prayer Journal

| Date: | Name: | Request: | Answered Prayer: |
|-------|-------|----------|------------------|
|       |       |          |                  |
|       |       |          |                  |
|       |       |          |                  |
|       |       |          |                  |
|       |       |          |                  |
|       |       |          |                  |
|       |       |          |                  |
|       |       |          |                  |
|       |       |          |                  |
|       |       |          |                  |
|       |       |          |                  |
|       |       |          |                  |
|       |       |          |                  |
|       |       |          |                  |
|       |       |          |                  |
|       |       |          |                  |
|       |       |          |                  |
|       |       |          |                  |
|       |       |          |                  |
|       |       |          |                  |
|       |       |          |                  |
|       |       |          |                  |
|       |       |          |                  |
|       |       |          |                  |
|       |       |          |                  |
|       |       |          |                  |
|       |       |          |                  |
|       |       |          |                  |
|       |       |          |                  |

# Appendix 10
# Prayer Journal

| Date: | Name: | Request: | Answered Prayer: |
|---|---|---|---|
| | | | |
| | | | |
| | | | |
| | | | |
| | | | |
| | | | |
| | | | |
| | | | |
| | | | |
| | | | |
| | | | |
| | | | |
| | | | |
| | | | |
| | | | |
| | | | |
| | | | |
| | | | |
| | | | |
| | | | |
| | | | |
| | | | |
| | | | |
| | | | |
| | | | |
| | | | |
| | | | |
| | | | |
| | | | |

# Leader's Guide Overview
## WEEKLY SMALL GROUP TIME

### Scripture Memory Time: (5 to 10 minutes)

Each week, go around the table and have every person recite the verse for the current lesson. Use the sheets at the back of your notebooks (Appendix 6) to view all the verses together, especially as the year progresses. Have each woman initial their own checklist sheets weekly (Appendix 7).

In addition to memorizing the current week's verse, you will also be reviewing the verses from previous weeks. Have a system of review established. Be as creative as you like, being certain that all the verses are reviewed each week. One idea is to use the individual verse cards from your Scripture Memory packet. Pull out the cards for the verses that have been memorized up to that point. Shuffle the verses. Go around the table, having each person draw a card and recite the verse from memory. Since they have no idea which card they will pick, they will need to come prepared to recite all verses up to that point. It's a great review system with built in accountability ~ something we all need!

**Please be committed to learning all the verses yourself. As the leader, you set the standard for your group for the duration of the study.**

### Discussion Time: (30 to 45 minutes)

A few questions are provided with each lesson to help guide your discussion. Feel free to use them however you choose. They are meant to be a springboard for discussion but don't feel that every woman has to answer every question. The point is to make sure all the principles and concepts are understood and that they have some ideas for implementing them in their own families.

Please strive to keep these discussions on topic and away from inappropriate sharing or gossip.

### Prayer Time: (10 to 15 minutes)

Each week spend time praying for each family represented at your table. Keep the prayer time relative to the lesson. Occasionally there may be extenuating requests that may not relate to the lesson and that is fine. We want the ladies to grow in love for each other and to be encouragers. It may take a few weeks for them to become comfortable praying together. You may want to distribute index cards to record prayer requests in advance. This way, the ladies in your group can come each week with prepared, concise requests.

**Carefully guard the prayer time so that praying—not the sharing of requests—remains the priority. Encourage your ladies to intercede for each other during the week. Watch together how God responds as the year progresses.**

### Wrap Up Time: (5 to 10 minutes)

Use the final few minutes to wrap up your discussion. Bring clarity, if necessary, to any deeper topics. Give reminders concerning class details or upcoming events. Encourage the ladies for the coming week.

# *Leader's Guide Lesson 1*

## OUR FOUNDATION: FAITH IN JESUS
### A godly mother embraces Jesus as her Savior

Please refer to the Leader's Guide Overview on the previous page for detailed instructions on how to make the most of your small group time.

## *Scripture Memory Time:* **Psalm 127:1**

Go around the table and have each person recite **Psalm 127:1**.

## *Discussion Time:*

1. Do you remember a point in time when you were spiritually born? Are you certain? Why or why not?

2. If you consider yourself to be a Christian, share some ways your decision to follow Christ has impacted your life.

3. Do you have any questions regarding today's lesson?

## *Prayer Time:*

**Main Focus:**

- Pray for the salvation of family members.
- Thank God for His indescribable gift to you.

## *Wrap Up Time:*

# Lesson 2 Leader's Guide
## THE AUTHORITY OF GOD'S WORD
### A godly mother lives by biblical convictions

*Scripture Memory Time:* **2 Timothy 3:14**

Go around the table and have each person recite **2 Timothy 3:14**. Have a few people volunteer to also say **Psalm 127:1** from last week.

*Discussion Time:*

1. Define **biblical convictions**. Define **personal convictions** (we will go into this topic in depth next week). What is the basic difference between the two? How does this distinction affect the raising of your family?

2. Make a small list of biblical convictions (refer to Appendix 1). Consider for yourself: Is your family committed to these things? Are there any areas of biblical principles that you have treated as a matter of personal choice that you now see are not?

*Prayer Time:*

**Main Focus:**

• Pray for wisdom and agreement in establishing family convictions and following God's commands.

*Wrap Up Time:*

# Lesson 3 Leader's Guide

## PERSONAL CONVICTIONS
### A godly mother establishes family convictions

*Scripture Memory Time:* **Psalm 85:8**

Have each person recite **Psalm 85:8.** Go around the table again and alternate reviewing **Psalm 127:1** and **2 Timothy 3:14.**

*Discussion Time:*

1. What is a conscience? What is its purpose? What is discernment? What is its purpose?

2. Read **Romans 14** in its entirety as a group.

3. Why are we not to judge each other's personal convictions?

4. If you wish, share with the group how your discussion of convictions went with your husband. Or if you are a single mom, did you come up with any personal convictions?

5. Select a topic or two and have a brief discussion of some personal convictions or family standards for that area. (**Example:** standards for television, internet, music, movies . . .)

*Prayer Time:*

**Main Focus:**

- Pray for wisdom and guidance in developing personal convictions and family standards.

- Pray for discernment to distinguish between biblical and personal convictions.

- Pray for commitment to biblical convictions, understanding in personal convictions and flexibility in personal preferences.

*Wrap Up Time:*

# Lesson 4 Leader's Guide

## GOD'S PLAN OF ORDER, PART ONE
### A godly mother lives by biblical priorities

### Scripture Memory Time: Deuteronomy 6:6–7

Continue using the Scripture memory sheets from the notebooks. Have each person say the verse from this week's lesson. Go around the table once more and have each lady say one of the previous week's verses; **Psalm 127:1**, then **2 Timothy 3:14**, and then **Psalm 85:8**. Keep the order and start at different places from week to week if the ladies always sit in the same places. This system may seem fussy, but it is very helpful for reviewing and they will greatly benefit from their diligence. Or you may use another system that you find effective.

### Discussion Time:

1. Read **1 Peter 2 & 3** as a small group.

2. Evaluate your priorities. Is there anything that needs to be changed? What is your conviction regarding priorities?

3. Are you "living in agreement" with your husband regarding your convictions in raising your children? Can you talk through an area in which you have difficulty coming to agreement?

### Prayer Time:
**Main Focus:**

- Pray about family priorities and what changes God would have you make.

- Thank God for your husbands, children and parents.

- Pray for strengthened family relationships and dynamics as you live by priorities.

### Wrap Up Time:

# Lesson 5 Leader's Guide

## GOD'S PLAN OF ORDER, PART TWO
### A godly mother is orderly

*Scripture Memory Time:* **1 Corinthians 14:33**

Continue with the Scripture memory system by having each person recite this week's verse and then alternately reviewing the verses from the previous weeks. Refer to the notebook sheets. Remember to say the reference before and after the verse.

*Discussion Time:*

1. Does God have first place in your life? What are some ways that you prove to Him that He does?

2. Would you characterize your home life as more Christ–centered or child–centered?

3. Read and discuss these verses on oneness: **Acts 2:46, 1 Corinthians 2:16, Ephesians 4:22–25 and Ephesians 4:4–6.**

4. We are not asked to submit to harm, coercion or sin (going against your conscience and the moral will of God). Refer to these verses as they pertain to your group: **Acts 4:18–20, Acts 5:28–29 and Titus 1:6.**

5. What is order? Name a way that you are orderly.

*Prayer Time:*

**Main Focus:**

- Thank God for the system of order He has created.

- Pray for Christ–centered homes and Christ–centered lives.

- Confess any ways that you have allowed your life to become disorderly and ask God for strength to make any necessary changes.

*Wrap Up Time:*

# Lesson 6 Leader's Guide

## A MOTHER'S TOUCH
## AND THE NATURE OF A CHILD
### A godly mother understands the significance of her role

### Scripture Memory Time: **Proverbs 22:6**

Continue with the Scripture memory system by having each person recite this week's verse and then alternately reviewing the verses from the previous weeks. Refer to the notebook sheets. Remember to say the reference before and after the verse.

### Discussion Time:

1. What is the main difference between human beings and the rest of God's creation? For what purpose were we created?

2. How does knowing that we have an inherent sin nature affect how we raise our children?

3. Share an example of when your touch made all the difference in your child's life.

### Prayer Time:

**Main Focus:**

- Express to God your gratitude for your family and how He has given you the wondrous and significant role of mother in a child's life.

- Pray for God's wisdom as you raise children knowing that they are born with a sin nature.

### Wrap Up Time:

# Lesson 7 Leader's Guide

## ESTABLISHING AUTHORITY, PART ONE
## THE FEAR OF GOD
### A godly mother establishes authority in her child's life

*Scripture Memory Time:* **Hebrews 12:11, Philippians 2:14**

Continue with the Scripture memory system by having each person recite this week's verse and then alternately reviewing the verses from the previous weeks. Refer to the notebook sheets. Remember to say the reference before and after the verse.

*Discussion Time:*

Look up the following verses and write down what God has to say about those who fear Him. Divide the verses between the ladies at your table so that each will look up 3 or 4. Have them share their insights with the rest of the table. Share any thoughts you wish regarding the fear of God and the significance it has in training your children.

1. Deuteronomy 10:20–21
2. Psalm 15:1–4; Proverbs 16:6; 2 Corinthians 7:1
3. Psalm 25:12
4. Psalm 25:13
5. Psalm 25:14
6. Psalm 31:19
7. Psalm 34:7
8. Psalm 67:7
9. Psalm 103:11–13, 17
10. Psalm 111:5
11. Psalm 112:1–2
12. Psalm 112:5–8
13. Psalm 115:11
14. Psalm 128:1–4
15. Psalm 145:19
16. Psalm 147:11
17. Proverbs 3:7–8
18. Proverbs 9:10
19. Proverbs 14:26
20. Proverbs 15:16; Proverbs 19:23
21. Isaiah 33:6
22. Jeremiah 32:39
23. Acts 10:35
24. 2 Corinthians 5:11

*Prayer Time:*

**Main Focus:**

- Thank God for His many blessings, praying specifically over some of the Scriptures from today's study.
- Confess any doubts you may have allowed to consume your thoughts regarding God's provision for you and replace them with the truth of God's Word.

*Wrap Up Time:*

# Lesson 8 Leader's Guide

## ESTABLISHING AUTHORITY, PART TWO:
## THE REIGN OF CHRIST IN THE HEART OF MAN
### A godly mother trains her children to see God as their lifelong authority

*Scripture Memory Time:* **Psalm 147:10–11, Lamentations 3:27**

Continue with the Scripture memory system by having each person recite this week's verse and then alternately reviewing the verses from the previous weeks. Refer to the notebook sheets. Remember to say the reference before and after the verse.

*Discussion Time:*

1. As a group, read **Jeremiah 5:14–31**. This very vivid passage lists several evils of man in the sight of God. Identify as many as you can. How does God say He will respond to such evils? What attributes of God show through this passage?

2. In stark contrast, recall the blessings of God to those who fear Him.

3. How are "fearing God" and "submitting to authority" interrelated?

*Prayer Time:*

**Main Focus:**

- Thank Him specifically for His personal care and protection.
- Praise God for who He is and His attributes.

*Wrap Up Time:*

# Lesson 9 Leader's Guide

## MANAGING A CHILD
### A godly mother manages her children well

*Scripture Memory Time:* **Ephesians 6:1–4**

Continue with the Scripture memory system by having each person recite this week's verse and then alternately reviewing the verses from the previous weeks. Refer to the notebook sheets. Remember to say the reference before and after the verse.

*Discussion Time:*

**Reminder to Leaders:** Your discussion may take a natural course which is fine as long as it is relevant to the lesson. The following questions are to help stimulate dialogue so don't feel that you have to get through them all.

1. We don't always have everything under control, but for the most part, how are you doing in regards to managing your children? Do you believe you are able to keep control of your household in a God–honoring way? If this is an area of great difficulty, can you identify why control is difficult?

2. Would anyone like to share any examples of how they are doing in regards to honoring people in difficult circumstances (husband, parents, authorities, child–teacher, siblings, et cetera)?

3. What motivations do you and your husband use to ensure your children's obedience? (These will vary according to different ages.) Discuss the three levels of motivation. Share some examples that have been helpful to your family from any of the three levels. Remember, all rewards are not negative, but also consider the extent to which you use each category.

*Prayer Time:*

**Main Focus:**

- Pray for wisdom to implement biblical principles in managing your children.
- Pray for God–honoring relationships by making necessary changes.
- Thank God for the relationships He has provided for you.

*Wrap Up Time:*

# Lesson 10 Leader's Guide

## PUTTING OFF AND PUTTING ON: LEARNING GODLY HABITS

### A godly mother does not exasperate her children

## Scripture Memory Time: Matthew 5:37

Continue with the Scripture memory system by having each person recite this week's verse and then alternately reviewing the verses from the previous weeks. Refer to the notebook sheets. Remember to say the reference before and after the verse.

## Discussion Time:

**Note to Leaders:** This is the most intense week of the year. The lesson will run into some of the small group time. But it will also be introspective and deeply personal to those who are serious about this topic. Please encourage your ladies to pray over this lesson and spend time with their husbands so that they may follow up on "homefront adjustments". The quiz will promote natural family discussion which can be guided by the "quiz result".

## Prayer Time:

### Main Focus:

- Pray over any areas of the lesson that need special attention in your home. (These areas may be very personal and hurtful to think about for some.)
- Pray for strength to replace old patterns with God–honoring ones.

## Wrap Up Time:

# Lesson 11 Leader's Guide

## COMMITTED TO DISCIPLINE
### A godly mother is committed to discipline

*Scripture Memory Time:* **Proverbs 13:24, Proverbs 29:15**

Continue with the Scripture memory system by having each person recite this week's verse and then alternately reviewing the verses from the previous weeks. Refer to the notebook sheets. Remember to say the reference before and after the verse.

*Discussion Time:*

1. Follow up on the previous lesson regarding exasperating our children. Are there any questions or loose ends that your ladies would like to address?

2. Regarding today's lesson, discuss the significance of understanding the correlation between the mind, will and emotions in choosing an approach to discipline.

3. What two main classifications of attitudes or actions require discipline in the form of spanking for young children and rebuke for older children? (Defiance and disobedience)

4. Discuss any misconceptions you may have had in how the Bible instructs us to discipline our children. Are there any changes you will be making?

*Prayer Time:*

**Main Focus:**

- Pray for wisdom to discipline your children in the ways of the Lord.

- Pray for consistency in the discipline of your children and that you and your husband would be in agreement regarding their discipline.

*Wrap Up Time:*

# Lesson 12 Leader's Guide

## RECOGNIZING & HANDLING MANIPULATION
### A godly mother is aware and ready to respond appropriately

*Scripture Memory Time:* **Proverbs 26:4–5**

Continue with the Scripture memory system by having each person recite this week's verse and then alternately reviewing the verses from the previous weeks. Refer to the notebook sheets. Remember to say the reference before and after the verse.

*Discussion Time:*

1.  Are there any questions regarding the material of the last few weeks?

2.  Did any of the particular areas of manipulation stand out to you that are causing strife in dealing with your children? Did you notice how different children may use different tactics? What will you do or not do to keep from getting on the "merry–go–round".

*Prayer Time:*

**Main Focus:**

*   Pray specifically about how we answer our children; that we would learn to not answer to foolishness, but answer as the situation deserves.

*   Pray for grace to "step back" from the temptation to be drawn into foolish banter and to remain clear–thinking, kind and firm.

*Wrap Up Time:*

# *Lesson 13 Leader's Guide*

## DEALING WITH REBELLION: "NEVER GIVE UP"
### A godly mother goes to battle for the heart of her child

## *Scripture Memory Time:* 1 Samuel 12:23

Continue with the Scripture memory system by having each person recite this week's verse and then alternately reviewing the verses from the previous weeks. Refer to the notebook sheets. Remember to say the reference before and after the verse.

## *Discussion Time:*

1. Why is rebellion so offensive to God? How does He respond to it in the Old Testament? Though we now live under grace, God's heart toward rebellion remains the same. As a result, how should we respond in this present age?

2. How can we encourage each other if one of us is enduring this trial? What counsel is necessary to the parent who has a rebellious teen living at home? How would the counsel differ for the young adult no longer living at home? What is the constant in both situations? (Never give up; keep praying for repentance and restoration).

3. When is broken fellowship necessary in a family and why?

## *Prayer Time:*

**Main Focus:**

- Pray for understanding and wisdom regarding rebellion within your own family, and also for other families going through such a trial.

- Spend time praying for specific children who are living in ongoing rebellion. Pray for their parents, whose hearts are breaking; that they would be encouraged and strengthened to do what God calls them to do.

- Pray that your parenting would be establishing anchors that will hold as your children grow.

## *Wrap Up Time:*

# Lesson 14 Leader's Guide

## WORDS THAT EDIFY
### A godly mother chooses her words wisely

**Scripture Memory Time:** Ephesians 4:29

Continue with the Scripture memory system by having each person recite this week's verse and then alternately reviewing the verses from the previous weeks. Refer to the notebook sheets. Remember to say the reference before and after the verse.

## Discussion Time:

1. Look over the lesson. What Scriptures stood out to you concerning the words we use? In what way?

2. What are edifying words? How do we edify each other with words?

3. Can you share a time when you were blessed by your child's or your husband's words? They may not even realize how significant those words are to you.

4. Would you be willing to relate an incident where you or a family member were persecuted for taking a stand for Christ? It is very difficult to bear, but are you able to understand how God is honored when we rest in Him and let Him be our defender?

## Prayer Time:

**Main Focus:**

- Pray about the words and tone we use.
- Pray about how we speak to our husbands and children.

## Wrap Up Time:

# Lesson 15 Leader's Guide

## GUARDING A CHILD'S MIND
### A godly mother chooses her child's environment wisely

### Scripture Memory Time: **Colossians 2:8**

Continue with the Scripture memory system by having each person recite this week's verse and then alternately reviewing the verses from the previous weeks. Refer to the notebook sheets. Remember to say the reference before and after the verse.

### Discussion Time:

Hopefully, over the past few months, we have all been discussing and formulating personal convictions and standards for our families. We can use our small group time to great advantage if we share some of the convictions with each other. Each lady may select a topic below to share her thoughts. Hearing what others are doing may help you and your husband come to agreement on some of these issues. Remember, we don't have to have the same personal convictions as another family.

- Television
- Movies
- Computer/Internet
- Video games
- Reading
- Slumber parties and overnights
- Music
- Dating/Courting

### Prayer Time:

**Main Focus:**

- Pray for your children to grow in discernment to process all the things that enter their minds.
- Pray about the establishment of guardrails in their lives that they would be developing their own convictions and self–control regarding the things they see and do.

### Wrap Up Time:

# Lesson 16 Leader's Guide

## CHARACTER BUILDING
### A godly mother trains her children in godly character

*Scripture Memory Time:* **1 Corinthians 13:4–7**

This week's verse is long so we won't do review this week. Have the ladies pair up for time's sake.

*Discussion Time:*

1. Share a fun activity that you do with your children that shows them that they are special to you and worth your time and attention. Use this time to brainstorm for creative ideas.

2. How is character building different from establishing authority?

3. Why is character building not about rules that control external behavior?

*Prayer Time:*

**Main Focus:**

- Pray for the character development in your children. Since you know their strengths and weaknesses, pray for the areas of needed growth and thank God for their strengths and areas of character that they exhibit.

*Wrap Up Time:*

# Lesson 17 Leader's Guide

## GROWING IN GODLY DISCIPLINES
### A godly mother disciples her children

*Scripture Memory Time:* **Acts 2:39, Proverbs 1:8–9**

Continue with the Scripture memory system by having each person recite this week's verse and then alternately reviewing the verses from the previous weeks. Refer to the notebook sheets. Remember to say the reference before and after the verse.

*Discussion Time:*

1. What are some of the "vital signs" of a believer from **1 John**? Read one of the verses to support your answer.

2. Do you sense the Lord's leading for your family to have more involvement in missions, Christian service or discipleship training? Do you see any obstacles to your being able to carry out this leading? Why or why not? Discuss how these obstacles could be handled. Don't think about doing everything. Pick something and the Lord will keep unfolding new opportunities for your children as they grow in their own desire to serve the Lord.

*Prayer Time:*

**Main Focus:**

- Pray for opportunities for spiritual growth in your children.

- Pray for their commitments to spiritual activities (youth group attendance, et cetera).

*Wrap Up Time:*

# Lesson 18 Leader's Guide

## GROWING IN RELATIONSHIPS, PART ONE
A godly mother mother teaches her children to be loving and forgiving in relationships and wise in choosing friends

### Scripture Memory Time: 1 Peter 3:8–9

Continue with the Scripture memory system by having each person recite this week's verse and then alternately reviewing the verses from the previous weeks. Refer to the notebook sheets. Remember to say the reference before and after the verse.

### Discussion Time:

1. What are the three basic components to strong, enduring relationships?

2. In which of these areas are you the strongest? How has your strength in this area allowed you to preserve and fortify your relationships? On the other hand, are there any marked areas of weakness that are preventing one of your relationships from being what the Lord wants it to be?

### Prayer Time:

**Main Focus:**

- Pray for any of your relationships that God is leading you to focus on. Be sensitive to areas needing change.

- Pray for each other even if you are unable to express your relational hurts in depth.

- Pray for the many relationships that your children will have, especially friendships and future spouses.

### Wrap Up Time:

# Lesson 19 Leader's Guide

## GROWING IN RELATIONSHIPS, PART TWO
### A godly mother teaches her children to be accountable in relationships

### Scripture Memory Time: Titus 2:3–5

Continue with the Scripture memory system by having each person recite this week's verse and then alternately reviewing the verses from the previous weeks. Refer to notebook sheets. Remember to say the reference before and after the verse. Encourage the ladies to review their verses from time to time.

### Discussion Time:

Conclude any discussions from the previous week as we finish this lesson.

### Prayer Time:

**Main Focus:**

- Pray for the women you have met this year and that you will continue training your children biblically.

- Thank God for what He has taught you this year and how your children have benefited as you look back and see the progress made.

### Wrap Up Time:

Thank the ladies for coming and finishing well.

# Appendix 12
## Table Directory

| Name: | Address/Email: | Phone: | Birthday: | Husband's Name: | Children: |
|-------|----------------|--------|-----------|-----------------|-----------|
|       |                |        |           |                 |           |
|       |                |        |           |                 |           |
|       |                |        |           |                 |           |
|       |                |        |           |                 |           |
|       |                |        |           |                 |           |
|       |                |        |           |                 |           |
|       |                |        |           |                 |           |
|       |                |        |           |                 |           |
|       |                |        |           |                 |           |

# Index

# Index

# ENTRUSTED  MINISTRIES

*Entrusted Ministries* is a 501(c)3 not-for-profit ministry
dedicated to building the body of Christ through sound biblical teaching.
The ministry of *Entrusted with a Child's Heart* works to support and protect
the integrity and survival of the family.

If you have been impacted by this study and would like to bless others,
please consider a gift of any amount to:

Entrusted Ministries
1000 N. Randall Road
Elgin, IL 60124
630-883-0862

www.entrustedministries.com

Your tax-deductible gift will help meet the urgent needs of today's families
and strengthen the Church worldwide.

Thank you for your partnership in advancing this ministry.